PENGUIN BOOKS

HOW HARD CAN IT BE?

Jeremy Clarkson began his writing career on the *Rotherham Advertiser*. Since then he has written for the *Sun*, the *Sunday Times*, the *Rochdale Observer*, the *Wolverhampton Express & Star*, all of the Associated Kent Newspapers and *Lincolnshire Life*. Today he is the tallest person working in British television.

By the same author

Motorworld
Jeremy Clarkson's Hot 100
Jeremy Clarkson's Planet Dagenham
Born to be Riled
Clarkson on Cars
The World According to Clarkson
I Know You Got Soul
And Another Thing
Don't Stop Me Now
For Crying Out Loud!
Driven to Distraction

How Hard Can It Be?

The World According to Clarkson
Volume Four

JEREMY CLARKSON

PENGUIN BOOKS

PENGUIN BOOKS

Published by the Penguin Group
Penguin Books Ltd, 80 Strand, London WC2R 0RL, England
Penguin Group (USA) Inc., 375 Hudson Street, New York, New York 10014, USA
Penguin Group (Canada), 90 Eglinton Avenue East, Suite 700, Toronto, Ontario, Canada M4P 2Y3
(a division of Pearson Penguin Canada Inc.)
Penguin Ireland, 25 St Stephen's Green, Dublin 2, Ireland (a division of Penguin Books Ltd)
Penguin Group (Australia), 250 Camberwell Road,
Camberwell, Victoria 3124, Australia (a division of Pearson Australia Group Pty Ltd)
Penguin Books India Pvt Ltd, 11 Community Centre,
Panchsheel Park, New Delhi – 110 017, India
Penguin Group (NZ), 67 Apollo Drive, Rosedale, Auckland 0632, New Zealand
(a division of Pearson New Zealand Ltd)
Penguin Books (South Africa) (Pty) Ltd, 24 Sturdee Avenue,
Rosebank, Johannesburg 2196, South Africa

Penguin Books Ltd, Registered Offices: 80 Strand, London WC2R 0RL, England

www.penguin.com

First published by Michael Joseph 2010
Published in Penguin Books 2011
011

Copyright © Jeremy Clarkson, 2010
All rights reserved

The moral right of the author has been asserted

Printed in England by Clays Ltd, St Ives plc

ISBN: 978-0-141-04876-5

www.greenpenguin.co.uk

ALWAYS LEARNING   **PEARSON**

To my children

Contents

Clear off, nitwit – I'll rebuild this hospital

Hello and a very happy new year to you all, especially if you are reading this on Rugby railway station wondering why all the tracks are still in the ground waiting to be turned from iron ore into something on which a train one day might run. Or conversely, you might be at Birmingham International pondering the vexing question of why the whole thing had to be shut down for two hours because of what the emergency services called a 'small fire' in a nearby cafe.

Well, I am afraid the answer is simple. In the olden days, all that stood between the bosses and the work being done was the trade union movement. And the unions could be silenced most of the time with a corned-beef sandwich and a vague promise of some jam tomorrow for the workforce.

Not any more. Now, when you want to get something done, the union boys are the least of your worries. Because you must also ensure that no Muslims or gingers are upset in any way by what you're planning, that no creatures, even if they are rubbish ones like snails or foxes, will be dislodged, that you won't make any unnecessary carbon dioxides, that all those involved will wear orange clothes, hard hats and boots made from box-girder bridges, that they are all as sober as a Sunday-best Swede and that, should a small fire break out within 200 miles, provisions are in place to send everyone home for at least a year.

That's before you go to the government, which gives you £2.50 to replace every railway line in the country because all the rest of the money it gets each year is being spent on arresting Pete Doherty and holding public inquiries into how it lost the medical records, banking details, driving records and previous convictions of everyone in the world. These public inquiries can be convened only once all concerned are aware that they can't kill a fox or upset a red-headed person and that if there's a fire nearby they must sail immediately to a point midway across the Atlantic and sit there until it, and every other fire in the world, has been put out. And an investigation then has to be held to find out what caused it and who's responsible and how that person should be punished. Unless they are ginger, in which case they will get a free tinfoil coat, a bit of soup and some counselling.

Plainly, all this has to stop. We must go back to the closing days of the nineteenth century when, without any heavy lifting gear or automation, 177 miles of broad-gauge railway line from London to Bristol and beyond was converted to narrow gauge in just one weekend. Actually, we don't even need to go back that far. The M1 was not there one morning and the next it was. Then there was Spaghetti Junction. The 30-acre site was crisscrossed with two railway lines, three canals and two rivers but despite this they had to build a network of slipways that would link eighteen different roads. And they got the whole thing done in thirty months. Which is about as long as it takes these days to build a garden shed, if you do it by the book.

I believe that the time has come to stop the nonsense and last week we were gifted the perfect opportunity. As I'm sure you heard, the Royal Marsden hospital in Chelsea, west London, was severely damaged by a fire and even a partial loss of its facilities is rather more than an inconvenience. A damaged railway line causes people to be late for work. A damaged hospital, which sees 40,000 patients a year and sits at the centre of an already overstretched National Health Service,

may well cause people to die. Gordon Brown visited the
scene and said that the evacuation of the hospital at the time
of the blaze had seen Britain at its best. And that he would
do everything in his power to get the place up and running
again.

Stirring words and now let's go for some stirring action.
People are already saying that it will take 'months', which is
government speak for 'years', to remove the ruined roof and
replace it with a new one. But why can we not aim to do it in
'weeks'?

Let's go back to the days when governments – and rail
companies for that matter – knew that they existed to serve
us and that we weren't just a nuisance who are told to stay at
home if we're not involved and wrapped up in fluorescent
clothes if we are.

Let's go back to the days when speed was not a dirty word.
In 1994 the Santa Monica freeway in California was destroyed
by an earthquake. You may remember the scenes of total
devastation: crumpled bridges, huge slabs of concrete, twisted
steel and rubble. It was a nightmare, but they had traffic running on it again in just eighty-four days.

Let's aim for the same sort of target with the Marsden.
Let's tear up the rulebook about carbon dioxide and hard
hats and no reversing without a banksman. Let's get the
builders in there tomorrow, or now, and let's allow them
to smoke so they don't have to pop outside every fifteen
minutes.

To achieve this, a vast army of busybodies and nitwits will
need to be kept at bay as they strut about with their clipboards and their concerns that mice may be nesting in the
embers and that they must be taken, in a helicopter, to the
countryside and freed humanely before work can start.

Dealing with them is possible, providing the man in charge

has a side parting, a small moustache and a fondness for telling everyone who gets in his way to eff off. It's a job that I would like very much.

Sunday 6 January 2008

This has been my perfect week

A couple of weeks ago, plans for a wonderful new coal-fired power station in Kent were given the green light and I was very pleased. This will reduce our dependency on Vladimir's gas and Osama's oil and, as a bonus, new technology being developed to burn the coal more efficiently will be exported to China and exchanged for plastic novelty items to make our lives a little brighter.

It's all just too excellent for words, but of course galloping into the limelight came a small army of communists and hippies who were waving their arms around and saying that coal was the fuel of Satan and that, when the new power station opened, small people like Richard Hammond would immediately be drowned by a rampaging tidal swell. They argued with much gusto that if Britain was to stand any chance of meeting Mr Prescott's Kyoto climate-change targets then we must build power stations that produced no carbon emissions at all.

You'd imagine then that last week, when Gordon Brown announced plans for a herd of new nuclear power stations, they'd have been delighted. Quiet power made by witchcraft, and no emissions at all. It's enough, you might imagine, to make Jonathon Porritt priapic with pleasure.

But no. It turns out the eco-mentalists don't like nuclear power either for lots of reasons, all of them stupid. They worry about what would happen if a reactor blew up. Which is a bit like worrying about living in a house in case a giant meteorite lands on it. They claim that people who go within

5 miles of a reactor die of leukaemia instantly. (They don't.) They wonder where the plants will be built. (Wales?) And they ask what we will do with the waste. Simple. Put it in the *Rainbow Warrior*.

The fact of the matter is this. The decision to go nuclear has exposed the whole environmental cause for what it is: not a well-intentioned drive for clean power but a spiteful, mean-spirited drive for less power. Because less power hits richer countries and richer people the hardest.

I've argued time and again that the old trade unionists and CND lesbians didn't go away. They just morphed into environmentalists. The red's become green but the goals remain the same. And there's no better way of achieving those goals than turning the lights out and therefore winding the clock back to the Stone Age. Only when we're all eating leaves under a hammer and sickle will they be happy.

I'm serious. All the harebrained schemes for renewable energy are popular among Britain's beardies only because they don't work. I heard one of them on the radio last week explaining that if he were allowed to build 58,000 islands in the Caribbean he could use steam coming off the sea to make enough power for everyone. Yeah, right. And then you have their constant claims that the tide can be used to make electricity. Really? If that's so, why am I not writing this on a computer powered by the Severn Bore? Sure, this summer work will begin on a tidal plant off the coast of Wales. Eight turbines, each 78 ft long and 50 ft tall, will harness the moon's gravitational pull, and if all goes well it won't even provide enough electricity to run Chipping Norton. You'd be better off burning tenners.

So what about wind turbines? Nope. They don't work either. Quite apart from their unmatched ability to mince baby ospreys and keep everyone within 15 miles awake with their mournful humming, they don't provide enough juice to power a Rampant Rabbit. Denmark has built 6,000 wind turbines and it's said that together they can produce enough electricity to meet 19 per cent of the country's (frankly minuscule) needs. But since they came on line not a single one of Denmark's normal power stations has been decommissioned. They are all running at full capacity because, while the wind turbines are theoretically capable of meeting nearly a fifth of the country's demands, they produce nothing at all when the wind drops. And since nobody can predict when that might be, the normal power stations have to be kept on line all the time. It's been a disaster, which brings us back to nuclear power: the only solution if you want to maintain our standard of living and cut carbon emissions.

Not only is the energy clean but there are other advantages too. The new power plants will be privately run, which means you can buy shares in them and you won't lose a penny. Because when things are going well you'll get a dividend, and when they're not going well you won't care because you'll be covered in sulphurous sores and blood will be spurting from where your eyes used to be. Better still, to make sure things don't go badly a vast army of health and safety officers will be employed to ensure the concrete is thick enough and visiting schoolchildren are not allowed to press any of the buttons. This means the high-vis Nazis will have no time left to stop policemen climbing ladders.

What's more, because so many countries are going nuclear, Iran for instance, there is bound to be a global shortage of sufficiently well-qualified atomic engineers. This means wages will rise, and that will cause schoolchildren to stop aiming for stardom in *Heat* magazine or a 2:1 in media studies and start concentrating a bit more in physics and maths.

Best of all, though, when all of our power is being generated by neutrons quietly crashing into one another, Greenpeace will have to leave us alone and go back to unpicking dolphins from Chinamen's fishing nets.

Sunday 13 January 2008

It seems it ain't art if it ain't ethnic – Opinion

Here in Chipping Norton, there is a picture-perfect little theatre. It's exactly the same as a London theatre, with a balcony and a bar, only it's much, much smaller. You really do feel, as you perch on your primary-school chair, gazing on the Punch and Judy stage, that you are locked in a Cotswold-stone dolls' house. It's an enchanting place and everyone round these parts is very proud of it. So consequently everyone is very cross that the Arts Council recently announced it would no longer be supplying £40,000 a year to help fund it.

And Chipping Norton is not alone. Even though the Arts Council has just received a £50m income boost from the government, it has sent letters to 194 mostly provincial playhouses, galleries and so on, saying they no longer fit with its 'agenda'.

'Hmmm,' I wondered, 'and what might this agenda be?' So I checked, and it seems that to get funding these days what you've got to be is black or mad or preferably both. For instance, the Arts Council has recognized that there are very few people from ethnic minorities in senior positions in the arts, but instead of thinking: 'Aha. This shows that very few black or Asian people are interested, so let's concentrate on the white middle classes,' it has now become involved with several schemes to get inner-city kids out of their big training shoes and into an Othello suit.

There's more. The Arts Council has never offered to translate my books into Urdu. Or Jilly Cooper's. But it 'remains committed' to spending a fortune supporting ethnic-minority writers. Indeed, it claims to have six priorities in place at the moment. And of course 'celebrating diversity' is one of them. Not at all surprisingly, 'celebrating Mrs Thatcher' isn't one of the others.

The council spends nearly half a billion pounds a year and, so far as I can tell, in 2007 most of that was given to Benjamin Zephaniah and others in exchange for some ditties about how awful the slave trade was and how everyone in Britain ought to commit suicide.

But wait. What's this? It seems there was some money left over to send a bunch of kids from Calderdale to the Yorkshire Sculpture Park, which is a field full of what look like big bronze sheep droppings. It's not my cup of tea but no matter – the droppings were sculpted by Henry Moore, so that sounds fine. Sadly no. Because afterwards the kids were taught about rap music and how to graffiti a wall. That has absolutely nothing to do with the arts at all. It'd be like teaching kung fu at a flower-arranging class.

Here on the Chipping Norton arts scene things are rather different. Plans for 2008 include a play about space travel, devised by Niki McCretton, who I'm afraid is white. Then there's a tribute to Abba, who were a very popular Swedish pop group featuring no disabled Bangladeshis, and a talk by Arabella Weir, who is the daughter of a notable diplomat. There are films too. But none, so far as I can see, is *Brick Lane* or that tosh from Al Gore. And then of course there's the Christmas pantomime. Much loved by Douglas Hurd, who never misses it, and 7,000 children, all called Henry and Araminta, it's a professional show featuring traditional storylines at this Christian time of year.

You can see immediately why none of this fits in with the Arts Council's 'agenda'. And I'm afraid the concert planned for next Saturday doesn't work either. Yes, the pianist, Helene

Tysman, is foreign, which is good, but I'm afraid she's only French. And that's hopeless because they had an empire too, the bastards.

What the management should be doing to maintain its grip on the Arts Council's funding is hosting a celebration of haiku poetry, in silence, by the Al Gore polar-bear workers' collective. Of course nobody would come, but hey – serving the needs of the area? Since when did that ever matter?

It does, and that's why I'd like to conclude with some words of encouragement for the management of Chipping Norton theatre and the other organizations around the country that don't fit in with the Arts Council's taste. It is extremely likely that you will be better off without the council's forty grand a year. Because tied up in this rather small chalice is a ton of poisonous red tape demarcating what you can do, what you can say and how many ramps have to be fitted at each urinal. You can wave goodbye to all that BBC-regional-news-tick-the-ethnic-boxes nonsense when you replace the lunatics at the Arts Council with a set of different benefactors.

I know this because just last week I spent some time with some chap from a notable charity. Each year, it needs £4m to stay afloat, and none comes from the government.

'Trust me,' he said. 'We don't want even 4p of their money. It's always more trouble than it's worth.'

Or you can look at the Millennium Dome. When it was run by the government the dome was full of faith zones and Cherie Blair, celebrating diversity. And it was a disaster. Now it's in private hands it's full of Led Zeppelin and recently became recognized as the most popular concert venue in the world.

Sunday 20 January 2008

First, fairy cakes – then welding, kids – Opinion

Since it came to power, the Labour government has introduced 2,685 pieces of legislation every year. And each has been either ill-conceived, draconian, bonkers, bitter, dangerous, counter-productive, childish, wrong, thoughtless, selfish, or designed primarily to make life a bit more miserable for everyone except six people in the BBC, fourteen on the *Guardian* and Al Gore.

Still, with such a torrent of new rules and regulations pouring on to the statute books every day, it was statistically inevitable that one day they'd accidentally do something sensible. And last week that day arrived. They decided that everyone who's capable of reaching the takeaway shop without being shot in the face is eating far too much Trex and that the way to get them eating Fairtrade lettuce and organic tofu instead is to make cooking a part of the school curriculum for children aged eleven–fourteen.

Immediately head teachers came up with all sorts of objections. They didn't have the space for normal lessons so where would they find the room for cookery classes? Had they considered, perhaps, using the school's kitchen?

Then the health and safety nutters woke up. 'Aha,' they said, 'PE has to be taken by someone with a degree in sports paramedicry and similarly qualified people would be necessary for cooking classes or children would be going home with knives sticking out of their eyes and pans of boiling water on their heads.'

Oh puh-lease. I spent five years in the chemistry lab playing with sulphuric acid and I'm fine. Sure, Jenkins minor got a bit disfigured one day but his hideous face is hardly a reason to refuse to teach anyone science.

No. Teaching cookery is a great idea. It's all so 1956. A class full of kids in aprons, baking bread, talking like the Queen and then pausing on their way home to scrump a few apples for tomorrow's crumble. Yum. Yum. Rhubarb will become the new crack. And the only thing those new school-gate metal detectors will find is Fotherington's cheese grater.

However, once cooking classes are under way, I think it would be a good idea to overhaul the entire curriculum. I've argued since I was a boy that school, in its present form, is almost completely useless. The dim kids work and work and work until their little hormones are fried and then emerge after five years, suicidal, mad and with an A-level in media studies. The bright kids, meanwhile, lounge around all day, knowing that a CV will never be checked so, when asked how many A-levels they have, they can lie and say 264.

All school does is put you off things that might, in later life, be interesting.

Having been forced into chapel every Sunday for five years, I vowed I would never set foot in a church until the day I died. And not even then. I've said in my will that I want my funeral service to be held in a burger van. What's more, by being made to read William Shakespeare at the age of fourteen, I developed a lifelong aversion to the Bard and his silly witterings. And I still can't eat meat pie. I look back now at those wasted hours in maths lessons, learning about algebra and matrices and sines, and I think, what was the point? It's the same story with linear air tracks and oxbow lakes and civil-war battles. They're all as pointless as a blunt stick.

This is why I fervently believe school should be rather more than a factory-numbering system, churning out kids with a C or a D or an A*. It should be a place where you learn how to be an adult. And cooking is a start.

Polish is a good idea too. Why teach us French when we all know that they can understand what we're on about perfectly well if we poke them in the chest often enough? Far better to be able to say, in a Warsaw burr, 'My boiler is broken. Can you come and mend it?'

Or better still, why not teach everyone how to mend their own boiler instead. Seriously. Why not have plumbing lessons? Because basic welding, I promise, will stand you in better stead as an adult than being able to conjugate Julius Caesar's table.

Do you know something? I distinctly remember being put on to the school minibus when I was fourteen and driven, on vomity roads, to the Peak District simply so that I could see a millstone grit outcrop. Why? Who thought that would be in any way relevant to anything I might one day do for a living? Couldn't they have spent the time instead teaching me to change the spark plugs on a car, or how to remove a low-voltage bulb without burning my fingers, or how to carve a leg of lamb, or how to play poker, or how to cut hair?

Or, and this brings me on to the most important point of all, they could have opened my eyes to the joys and importance of reading a newspaper. I really do mean this. My children can tell you about Portia's gentle rain and when to use the imperative but they don't have the first clue about what's going on in Kenya or why Hillary Clinton is a loony. No teacher sits them down and discusses what we used to call current affairs. This is madness. If we can find forty-five minutes in the school timetable to teach the children how to make food out of tofu and lentils, then surely we could also find a similar period for them to discuss the issues of the day. This way they would be less round and, er, more rounded. If you see what I mean.

Sunday 27 January 2008

Oi, state birdbrains – leave our land alone

Two years ago, a pub and restaurant tycoon called Michael Cannon bought a massive 3,000-acre Co. Durham grouse moor from the family of the Queen Mother. And last week his management company appeared in court, accused of ruining it. Government agents said the moor – a site of special scientific interest – had been crisscrossed with new roads, car parks, turning circles and drainage ditches. In total 4,433 square metres of important upland habitat for merlins, moorhens, short-eared owls, snipe, curlews and redshanks had been buried under 11,300 tons of almost certainly unsustainable, non-organic aggregate.

Cannon's company put its hands up to three breaches of the Wildlife and Countryside Act. But for these misjudgements and 'wounding' the countryside the judge fined it £50,000 and ordered it to pay £237,000 in costs. So there we are. Score: one for the moorhens, and none for the jumped-up, parvenu, bird-murdering vandal bastard.

Unfortunately, however, this case isn't quite as clear-cut as you might imagine. You see, Cannon is painted as a ghastly man who was caught in the nick of time, just before he carpeted the entire estate in inch-thick shagpile and fitted it with dimmer switches. In fact, having paid £4m for the moor, he invested a further £3m on improving the quality of the heather, which he describes as being more important than the rainforest. He employed more keepers, worked with the Royal Society for the Protection of Birds and built a small number of gravel tracks so vehicles could reach peatier parts of the estate without sinking.

The government agents talk about 4,433 square metres being buried under aggregate. This sounds like a huge amount, but in fact it's just over 1 acre. A small sacrifice when it does so much to improve the 2,999 others. The fact is that since Cannon took over, the number of rare black grouse on his land has jumped from four to 150. And last year on the estate the bag was 16,054 birds, the biggest number since 1872.

And there's your problem. Government agents have absolutely no clue what they are talking about. They simply noted the site was of special scientific interest, observed that tracks had been made and drainage ditches installed and, using their tiny bri-nylon minds along with a bottomless pit of government money, reckoned that this was a crime against the moorhen.

These are the people who ran about screaming when I was on television recently driving up a mountain in Scotland. 'You've ruined it,' they yelled, perhaps not realizing that a three-ton car cannot possibly dent a 20-trillion-ton lump of solid granite. 'But you've squashed the heather,' they whimpered. Yes, but if you knew anything at all about the countryside, you'd know that heather is burnt every so often to encourage new growth, which provides food for birdlife using the old woody heather as cover.

I face a similar set of problems in the Isle of Man, where I have a small piece of land. It's listed as a site of special scientific interest, which means I must harvest the crops from the inside of the field outwards and use sheep to keep the grass down. I am willing to do this. I am also willing to avoid fertilizer, which means my turnips look like conkers and my barley is the colour of a U-boat.

But then I am told I must also allow people to go out there with their dogs, which chase the sheep into the sea and leave so much shit around the place that it scares away the birds I'm trying to attract with my DDT-free crops and escape-route harvesting techniques. That's the trouble with environmentalists. Their love of wildlife is almost always outweighed by their hatred of the rich. They think that anyone with a Range Rover and a few quid in the bank must have earned that money by pumping polonium into the ozone layer and beating tramps to death with baby ospreys for sexual kicks. They therefore assume that he or she will view the countryside as nothing more than a site for a factory that can pick up the baton dropped by the people at Bhopal.

The most worrying thing about the Cannon case, though, leaving aside the large fine and costs, is the system that allows blinkered busybodies to poke about in someone else's garden. They are using legislation brought in to prevent fly-tipping, badger-baiting and the theft of rare birds' eggs – which is laudable – to prosecute someone for damaging their own property. Technically this means they could come round to my house and prosecute my children for damaging the grade I & II-listed kitchen door. And you know what? Now I've fessed up they probably will.

But will they arrest someone for paving over their front lawn or replacing the front hedge with a horrid wall made from upended crazy paving? No? Why not? This Jewsonization of the suburbs causes flooding and is largely responsible for the demise of the songbird. That and the stupid cat.

Natural England, the government agency that brought the prosecution against Cannon, would do well to remember that the only reason it exists is to preserve the beauty of the countryside. And the only reason it's so beautiful is that it's been looked after for thousands of years by wealthy landowners. If it wants to keep the land green and pleasant it would be better off tearing up its Fairtrade mission statement that talks of social inclusion and the evils of bullying, and going after those people who fill every rural lay-by with thousands of old mattresses.

Sunday 3 February 2008

Give it up, Hamza – you're too ugly

Soweto was my generation's Baghdad. Every night, we saw pictures of it on the news, scenes of burly policemen cruising the streets in Chevrolets, shooting children for fun. Of mobs setting fire to buses and blocking the roads with burning tyres.

Now, though, just twenty years later, it's a bit like Surrey. There are well-kept lawns and lots of four-wheel-drive cars. There's a shopping centre and a forest of cranes building a stadium for the upcoming World Cup. Sure, there's Winnie Mandela's mansion, which sits like a bulletproofed blister in the middle of it all, and the 'Education is good for you' graffiti doesn't quite ring true. But I spent a day there last week and at no point did anyone put a tyre round my neck and set fire to it. I even had a jolly nice lunch under a jolly nice bougainvillea bush.

So what was it that brought about this transformation? Was it the legion of pop stars who sang about the iniquities of apartheid? Or was it the sanctions? Or could it be that pressure groups back then concentrated on real problems rather than the environment?

You do wonder, don't you? If the firebrands and the beardies would stop worrying about polar bears, could a similar transformation be achieved in Darfur and Zimbabwe and the mayoral office of London?

I'm afraid not. The main reason the war against apartheid was won is that Nelson Mandela looks good on a T-shirt.

I mean it. Look at all the successful freedom fighters and

you'll note they all had one thing in common: a chiselled, romantic figurehead. Che Guevara, for instance, worked well as a screen print, and as a result the rebels still hold power in Cuba. And because Yasser Arafat looked like he'd just stepped out of that bar in *Star Wars*, Palestine is still a prison rather than a country. Why do you suppose Northern Ireland is still part of the United Kingdom? Simple. The IRA was never going to win, because with Martin McGuinness and Gerry Adams they were represented on the world stage by a ginger and a minger. The Basques have a similar problem. I met Eta's political leader a couple of years ago and he was about as charismatic as a root vegetable. Potty Pol had a great name but because his face didn't work on a badge his efforts in Cambodia were always going to come to naught. And it's the same story with Shining Path, the Tamil Tigers and Nazi Germany, for that matter. If Hitler had looked like Jim Morrison who knows what shape the world might be in today?

This of course brings me neatly to the question of Muslim extremists. They are waging a preposterous campaign, trying to make all women in the world wear their headscarves back to front. And there's no doubt that if their international leader was Abu Hamza they wouldn't get anywhere.

One eye is good. Admiral Nelson pulled that off well and so does Gordon Brown. It makes you look sinister and interesting. Then there's the hook for a hand. That's inspirational. The stuff of Bond baddie legend. But I'm sorry, the rest is hopeless; especially that patchy and spartan face fungus, as threadbare as an aristocrat's carpet.

Unfortunately, however, Hamza is not the global figurehead. That role belongs to Osama Bin Laden, and let's cut to the chase on this, shall we? The man's a looker. Teaming those gentle and kind eyes with an ever-present AK-47 keeps us guessing. He even manages to look good in a dress and that beard. Wow. It could so easily have come across as pantomime stupid, and yet you just want to run your hands through it. You imagine it's as soft as silk. In short the man is cool. Cold, actually, because he's almost certainly dead, buried under tons of daisy-cut Afghan rock. And yet, despite this small drawback, the Americans will never be able to beat him unless they wake up, smell the coffee and elect Johnny Depp.

Mrs Clinton really won't do. Quite apart from the fact that she seems to be a strange mix of naked ambition and lunacy, she cannot hope for victory against the forces of evil and savagery with a name like Hillary. Think of all the songs that have been written about girls. Gloria, Emily, Clair, Peggy Sue, Laura, Mary, Nikita. It's hard to think of any name that isn't in a song. Except one. And don't you think that says something? That in all of human history, no one has ever been moved enough by someone called Hillary to write a song about them.

Names matter as much as looks. Boadicea was not called Joan, and as a result was able to whip up a sufficient frenzy among her followers that she defeated the Roman army and laid waste to Colchester. Joan of Arc, on the other hand, was called Joan and got burnt at the stake. It's not for nothing that God chose to call his only son Jesus rather than Roy or Nigel.

I'm being sensible here. Che Guevara realized that he needed the whole package to succeed – not just a beret and a wistful look – so he dropped the name his parents had given him: Ernesto. And Temujin only really got going after he rebranded himself as Genghis Khan.

There is some good news from all of this though. One day Robert Mugabe will be sunk by his silly moustache, Kim

Jong-il will be defeated by his own wardrobe and Jonathon Porritt will fail because even if he were called Clint Thrust he sports the one thing that is guaranteed to end anyone's quest for global domination: a combover.

Sunday 10 February 2008

Skiing through the pain barrier

For your next holiday, why don't you take all your money and put it on the fire? Then stand in a fridge for a week, beating your children with a baseball bat until their arms and legs break. And then, after you've eaten some melted cheese, dislocate your shoulder. If all of this appeals then you are probably one of the 1.3m British people who go on a skiing holiday at this time of year.

Skiing, for those of you who've never tried it, is an extremely expensive way of combining acute discomfort, butt-clenching embarrassment, mind-numbing fear and a light dusting of hypothermia. Plus there's a better than evens chance that at least one member of your family will come home in a wheelchair. The first thing you must understand is the ski boot. It is specifically designed to be as heavy as possible and to ensure that if you fall over – and you will, all the time – your leg will break at its most painful point: just above the ankle. The only way to prevent this happening is to cushion the fall with your face.

These holidays are called winter 'breaks' because at some point you will end up in a doctor's surgery that looks like a Baghdad market after a nail-bomb attack. Once, after I'd broken my thumb for the second year in succession, I sat in the waiting room with a chap who had a ski pole sticking out of his eye. And opposite was a pretty young girl whose left foot was on back to front.

Of course you might think it is possible to avoid such

injuries by going very slowly. Unfortunately this is not possible because to counter the surprisingly powerful effects of gravity you need to dig the edges of your skis into the slope with such force that after a very short time your thigh muscles actually catch fire. When the smell of burning flesh becomes too overpowering you let go, and suddenly you are travelling at 700 mph. Then, equally suddenly, you will be breathing gas and air while the doctor sharpens his hacksaw.

This year, on my skiing holiday, the air ambulance was lifting five newly formed paraplegics off the mountain every day.

Falling over, however, is not the greatest danger. Far worse is being hit by a teenager with baggy trousers on a snowboard. Snowboarding is like skiing, except you have absolutely no control over your direction of travel, mostly because you will have had a lot of marijuana at lunch time.

It's certainly better than eating the food. The food at ski resorts is cooked by people whose only qualification for the job is that they are called Arabella. Once, I was served salt soup. Mostly, though, it's bread, which you dip in melted cheese. And because you are expected to melt the cheese yourself, the Arabella has more time to have sexual intercourse with her surly French ski-instructor boyfriend.

I am a very good skier . . . in my mind. However, video evidence suggests that I'm rubbish. I look like a bus driver in a primary-coloured anorak, sitting on an imaginary lavatory. Also I can only turn right. So to mask my embarrassment, and the pain in my thighs, I ski only when very drunk. I can recommend this wholeheartedly.

However, what you must never do is ski while under the influence of Billy Idol. No, really. I can absolutely guarantee that within five seconds of putting an iPod in your ears one of your bones will shoot out of your skin.

Of course you might imagine that there are other things to do on a winter holiday apart from skiing. 'Fraid not. On a normal summer break you can sunbathe, swim, snorkel, jet ski and, if you like the *Guardian*, go to look at museums. But on a skiing holiday what you do is get up at dawn, eat some salt soup and queue for hours to get on something that makes a Tube train look deserted. Then queue for some more hours because your place keeps being taken by burly Russians who have daggers tattooed on their foreheads. Then you ski until it goes dark.

You have probably heard about après-ski activities. In your mind, you see nightclubs and pretty girls and drinking fiery cocktails till dawn. Well, I'm sorry, but what actually happens is that you get back to your hotel or chalet, climb into a relaxing bath to try to jump-start your burnt-out muscles and fall fast asleep.

This is a good thing because in addition to the cost of the holiday and the flights and the ski rental and the lessons and the ski pass that lets you use the mountain, you will have been utterly bankrupted by your wardrobe. This year the cheapest pair of padded trousers we could find for my thirteen-year-old daughter were £250. And it's not as if she can wear them anywhere else.

Finally there's the weather. If it's poor you will freeze and crash into things because you can't see where you're going. If it's good – and over half-term it was very, very good – you will need sunglasses. And that means you will come home after a week with a face like a barn owl.

The thing is, though, that when the sun shines and you are whizzing along, drunk out of your mind, under a perfect blue dome with your happy, giggling children on a deserted, freshly pisted slope, and you're about to have lunch in a restaurant with a view that is unparalleled anywhere on earth, none of the misery matters. Because there is no feeling quite like it. It's called perfect happiness.

Sunday 24 February 2008

Bleep off, you're driving me mad

I have just bought a dishwasher. And now I am thinking of smashing it into small pieces because when it's finished washing the pots and pans it makes a beeping noise. And if I don't empty it immediately it beeps again. And then again.

How stupid is that? It means you're sitting by the fire, nodding off in front of the television, when you hear the electronic summons and, because you know it will go on until the end of time, you haul yourself out of your chair, pad into the kitchen, open the door and discover, as jets of superheated steam gush into your face, that the beeping was not, in fact, coming from the dishwasher at all.

So now you're standing there, looking like Niki Lauda, wondering what on earth had been making the infernal noise. It could be anything, because these days everything beeps. Mobile phones beep when they are dying. Microwaves beep when your food is ready. Freezers beep when they get too warm. Cars beep if you don't put your seatbelt on. Captains beep before they make an in-flight announcement. Airport golf buggies beep when they move. Children's toys beep when they don't. Lorries beep when they reverse. Parking meters beep when you put money into them. Phones beep when there's a message. Shop doors beep when you open them. Actors beep when they swear before the watershed. There's even a beep in the Radio 2 traffic jingle.

So you creep about the house, with your melted face, hoping that you'll be near the source of the noise when it strikes again. Then, suddenly, you think: 'Jesus. It's a smoke alarm warning us that its battery is dead and that unless I do something about it – right now – everyone will be burnt to a crisp.'

Quickly you get a stepladder and replace the battery and just as the cover snaps shut you hear the beep again. This time, of course, you know it really is the dishwasher. So you open the door and it steam-strips the bits of your face that weren't burnt off the first time. Because actually the noise was coming from the freezer, which has got a bit too warm.

Now I should warn you at this point that I'm not about to embark on a tub thumping tirade about silly technology. Rather, it will be an impassioned plea from an insomniac who's stumbling towards the mid-point of middle age for people to stop making an unnecessary racket. We are constantly being told that light pollution is ruining life for astronomers, that patio heaters are killing polar bears and that your carrier bags will one day choke a turtle. But I don't give a fig about aquatic tortoises or astronomy. All I want is a bit of peace and quiet.

Some things make lovely noises. Playful children, car tyres on gravel, sheep and the Doobie Brothers, for instance. My particular favourite is the mournful throb of a distant light aircraft. Or the fizz of ice cubes being dropped into a freshly made gin and tonic. But mostly I spend my life being bombarded by sounds that screech into my head like polystyrene fingers on a 6-acre blackboard. Motorcycles, crows, other people's strimmers, 'amusing' ringtones, Birmingham accents, Radio 1, dogs, diesel engines, Ken Livingstone, 'Mind the gap', James May's bottom, unnecessary announcements in shopping centres. And then there's the worst noise in the world; a noise that's worse than morris dancing and even that child's toy called Bop It.

I'm talking, of course, about *The Archers*.

I've always said that when I divorce my wife it'll be because we are incompatible at airports. She likes to be there two weeks before the flight leaves. I think two minutes is plenty. But in fact we are much more incompatible at 7 p.m. every night when she turns on the radio and fills the house with the pointless sounds of Ambridge. Should Mike divide the house for Roy and Hayley? I really couldn't give a monkey's. Just turn it off.

There isn't even any respite at work. My office at the BBC is next to the lifts, which spend all day telling everyone within 5 miles what floor they're on. I know this helps blind people but why have the announcement read out by Brian Blessed in his full pantomime baddie mode? Why not use whispering Bob Harris instead? Or play it at a pitch that's audible only to guide dogs?

I appreciate that some things have to make a noise. Heathrow airport, for example. And the Heckler & Koch sub-machinegun. But most things do not and I urge people to think about that when designing products and services. Did you know, for instance, that Microsoft employed Brian Eno to write the four-note welcome chime when you turned on a Windows 95 computer? Why? I know when the sodding thing comes on because when I push the buttons on the keyboard, words appear on the screen. I do not need an audible alert. Nor do I need a car to chirp when I lock it. Oh, and publicans. If you have a jukebox on the premises, here's an idea. Why not allow customers to buy three minutes of silence?

I also have an idea for people who run supermarkets. We managed for many years before you started saying, 'Cashier number four, please,' over and over again. And I'm fairly certain that we could manage again if you stopped.

Normally, I would turn to the Church for help in these difficult and noisy times, but I fear no backing will be forthcoming. Partly because the Archbishop of Canterbury is too busy chopping the hands off shoplifters, but mainly because, with its nonsensical and infernal bell-ringing, it is the worst offender.

Sunday 2 March 2008

Oi, shoppers – that's my petrol

If I were to see someone indulging in antisocial behaviour, such as cycling on the pavement or urinating in a public place, I would roll my eyes and quietly tut. If it were something more serious, such as riding a horse through a supermarket or throwing a baby dog into a ravine, I might even say something.

Strangely, however, when I spot someone dropping litter, I am overcome with a sometimes uncontrollable need to perform experiments on his head involving petrol and scorpions. Prison? No chance. That's for rapists and robbers. Litter louts should be peeled and rolled in a barrel full of salt and snakes.

That's why last week I was delighted when a newspaper called the *Daily Mail* began a campaign to rid Britain of the carrier bag. Gordon Brown was delighted too as he's fast running out of other things to ban. 'Oooh, goody,' he didn't say, but you could see he meant it. 'I hadn't thought of that. Yes. Carrier bags. I'll install a network of cameras throughout the land and anyone caught using one will be fined a million pounds.'

The trouble is that while I support any move to rid the world of carrier bags – and shopping in general for that matter – I cannot think of an alternative. If you have been to the supermarket for your weekly groceries, how else are you supposed to carry them home? Especially if you've gone there on a sustainable bus.

Brown paper is one suggestion but it really works only in

places such as Arizona. Here, where there is rain, it quickly becomes soggy – and then it has the tensile strength of fog. The Women's Institute suggests that bags could be made from hemp or wheat so that they would degrade. But while it might be possible for a little old lady to knit a bag from natural fibres while listening to *The Archers*, I think she might struggle to produce 60m a day.

Some people say supermarkets should charge for bags to encourage people to reuse the one they were given last week. But the figure being bandied about is just 5p, and that, unless you're a refugee or a coastguard, doesn't seem much of a financial hurdle: £5,000 would cause us to think twice; 5p won't. And besides, a charge presupposes that you have gone on a planned shopping trip. Not that you were just passing and suddenly thought: 'God. I wish I had last week's bag with me because I don't half fancy some Smarties.'

I fear, therefore, that we are stuck with the bag, but this does not mean we should give up on our struggle to deprive the stupid and the fat of things they can drop on the street because they are too gormless to go and find a bin. And my suggestion is, we look hard at packaging. Three years ago there was much brouhaha about this – and of course the government made lots of threats and noises. Such was the outcry, in fact, that most of the big food producers and supermarket chains promised to clean up their act.

I should have thought this would be a simple thing to do. A cauliflower, for instance, does not need its own Michael Jackson-style oxygen tent. It will not run off if placed on a shelf naked. Nor will it be embarrassed. Can it possibly take three years to work this out?

Evidently yes, because in my local supermarket everything except the spring onions still comes in a packet of some sort. No, really. Those manky-looking weeds that silly women eat at breakfast time instead of food are served under Cellophane. Apples come in polythene on a polystyrene tray. And you should see the Easter eggs. Jesus. Two hundred tons of petrochemicals diverted from where they belong – in the tank of my car – to puff up a chocolate egg so small that it wouldn't stretch the birthing muscles of a wren.

In just one night at my flat in London – that's one dinner for one person – I generate enough waste to fill a hole the size of Worksop. And it makes me seethe, not because of the carbon emissions from the planes bringing it here – I couldn't give a stuff about that. No. It's the fact that while I will parcel it all up and put it in the right part of the right bin on the right day for the right binmen to take to the right landfill site, thousands will simply drop it in the street.

And have you bought a toy recently? Every single one comes in a steel-hard plastic mould that blunts all your scissors and severs all your fingers. Seriously, you could store Britain's nuclear arsenal in the packaging used by toy companies and it would be completely safe. And then you have those plastic tie strips used to secure the product to the box. By the time you're past those the child is twenty-eight years old.

So, what's to be done? Well, amazingly you are legally allowed to remove all the packaging in the shop and leave it on the counter. But this will infuriate those stuck behind you in the queue. Or you could refuse to buy anything that has been packaged, but I fear that pretty soon you'd be naked and starving.

So how's this for a plan? Companies should be fined if any of their branded litter is found on the street. This would soon encourage them to remove all unnecessary packaging. And if they found that impossible, they'd have to ensure their products were sold only to people intelligent enough to dispose of the waste properly.

I'm pretty certain that if this scheme were introduced we'd have the makers of milk chocolate Bounty, Flora margarine and Kentucky Fried Chicken out of business inside a week.

Sunday 9 March 2008

Join me in a saucy oath to Britain

A big and important lord has suggested that British school-children should swear an oath of citizenship, perhaps in the hope that they'd put down their machineguns, stop stamping on old ladies and all become beefeaters.

Unfortunately, if such an oath is to be introduced, some-one's going to have to decide on the wording. This means the government will have to set up an 'inclusive' committee that represents all of Britain's 'communities'. And can you even begin to imagine what that'd come up with?

'I apologize for my country's shameful involvement in the slave trade. I vow to be homosexual whenever possible and to burn anyone driving a Range Rover. Long live Al Gore and death to the infidel.'

In these difficult times, it's tricky to do better. In America, schoolchildren stand to attention every morning and say: 'I pledge allegiance to the flag of the United States of America, and to the republic for which it stands, one nation under God, indivisible, with liberty and burgers for all.'

Sadly, that sort of thing wouldn't work here because the flag's seen by Channel 4 News as racist and God's a hot potato. What's more, we'd have to substitute 'the Queen' for 'the republic' and I'm afraid that's a big no-no because, we're told, she has little resonance if you're a Lithuanian living in a tent in East Anglia.

This might make you seethe. Perhaps you go all prickly-haired and teary-eyed when they start singing 'Land of Hope and Glory' at the Proms, in which case you might say: 'Look.

It's jolly easy to say what defines us as a nation. The *Daily Telegraph* letters page. Frank Whittle. And all those bronze men with feathery hats in Trafalgar Square.'

Hmm. Fine. But before you force every single child in the land to swear allegiance every morning to Major-General Sir Henry Havelock, you need to be aware that, if your skin is brown, Sir Henry probably killed your great-grandad.

This brings us on to the biggest problem of them all. In America, it doesn't matter whether you are a topiarist or a hedge-fund manager, a petrol-pump attendant in Arizona or a retired Jewish lady in Miami; everyone is united by the American Way. The country is seen as a place where you can get on, where you will be rewarded for hard work, ambition and drive. There is no sense of that here. In his first budget, Alistair Darling announced that if you're too stupid and lazy to get off your fat arse and do any work, you will be given free loft insulation; and that, if you are honest, and industrious, you will be financially raped.

There's more. I listened last week to a debate on the *Jeremy Vine Show* in which callers suggested that the McCanns – whose daughter, remember, is missing – got so much press coverage only because they were middle-class. This was such awful, heartless twaddle, I was nearly sick with rage.

It's not just a class divide either. What common bond can be found between a Pakistani shopkeeper in Bradford and the people you see building Huf houses on *Grand Designs*? What unites a Filipino chambermaid in Abergavenny with Prince Andrew? Unless something can be found, the oath will remain an unrealized dream.

Perhaps it's a good idea to view Britain from the outside. How do foreigners see us? Well, as drunken football hooligans mostly, and I don't think that'd work. Having children swear an allegiance to Millwall every morning is a nonstarter.

A bestselling American book called *The Geography of Bliss* suggests that British people are unified by a general grumpiness. Eric Weiner, the author, says we don't just enjoy misery; we get off on it. 'For the British, happiness is a transatlantic import. And by transatlantic, they mean American. And by American, they mean silly, infantile drivel. Britain is a great place for grumps and most Brits, I suspect, derive a perverse pleasure from their grumpiness.' I don't disagree. But I can't see us promising every morning in school assembly to remember that, while the weather might be nice now, it'll almost certainly be drizzling and cold tomorrow. Unless, of course, we all catch cancer and die in the night.

So what one thing cuts through the political correctness and leaves nobody feeling alienated in their own country? Something that unifies us all, something that's recognizably British and universally seen as harmless, but also wholesome and good? You might imagine the answer is David Attenborough. But, sadly, people die. We need something that will be with us for ever.

The only thing I can think of is HP Sauce. The label features the Palace of Westminster. It contains no meat, which will keep Paul McCartney happy. It can be used to enliven a Melton Mowbray pork pie, and bring a sheen to coins of the realm. And, best of all, it absolutely defines the British. The French have their frogs' legs. The Japanese have their whales. We have our brown sauce. We are the only people on earth who eat it.

Yes, I know it's made in Holland these days by an American company, but so what? Finally, I have the oath. 'I pledge allegiance to the sauce of the United Kingdom of Great Britain, and to the nation for which it stands, one sauce, in two distinct flavours, with nourishment and joy for all.'

Or we could drop the whole scheme and try to remember we've gone for a thousand years without an oath so why the bloody hell do we need one now?

Sunday 16 March 2008

Ruck off, you nancy Aussies

You can never rely on the French. All they had to do was go to Cardiff last weekend with a bit of fire in their bellies and they'd have denied Wales the Six Nations Grand Slam. But no. They turned up instead with cheese in their bellies and mooched about for eighty minutes, seemingly not at all bothered that we've got to spend the next twelve months listening to the sheepsters droning on about their natural superiority and brilliance.

Or worse. Give them a Grand Slam and the next thing you know, all our holiday cottages are on fire.

There are, of course, other reasons I hoped the French would win. I'd rather live in France than Wales; I'd rather eat a snail than a daffodil; I'd certainly rather drink French fizzy wine; and I'd much rather sleep with Carole Bouquet than Charlotte Church. However, as the match unfurled I found myself supporting the Welsh. Even though they seemed to have only three players – Jones, Jenkins and Williams – they were just so damn enthusiastic. And there was no doubt their excellent performance was lifting the spirits of the supporters. This made me feel warm and gooey because, like all civilized beings, I truly enjoy seeing a downtrodden people being given a crumb of something that makes them happy.

I was in Wales last week and it was pretty depressing. The place has more speed cameras and more roadworks per square inch than any other nation on earth. It also has more pebble-dashed housing and more rain too. The only cheer is that children there are given free toothbrushes on the NHS, but this doesn't seem quite enough, somehow, to make up for the shortfalls. That's why I'm delighted to see them walk off with a nice cup. Well done, all of you. You beat the civilized world, fair and square. And now, having got that out of the way, we need your help . . .

The problem is that far, far away, in a sinister place called Australia, there is dirty work afoot. They are trying to change the laws of rugby so that it becomes less about mud, fighting and severe spinal injuries and more like ballet. In other words, more like the delicate nancy-boy running game that they play. This must be stopped.

In football there are seventeen laws – or eighteen if you count the unwritten stipulation that you must be a wet fart to play it in the first place – whereas in rugby there are twenty-two laws. And that's before you get to the subclauses and subdivisions that conspire to make the whole thing more complicated than the assembly instructions for a space shuttle. I know a great many rugby fans who claim to know what's going on out there, but that's just the beer talking. The fact is that no one does. And yet despite this the game works.

We saw examples of the two extremes in Wales's game against France last weekend. In a scrum towards the end of the match, the Welsh forwards simply steamrollered the Frenchies clean off the ball. It was an exquisite demonstration of power. And then, moments later, some ugly little ginger burst out of nowhere and ran the length of the pitch in an exquisite demonstration of speed. You will find this mix in no other game on earth except, I think, American football. But it's hard to be sure because every time anything happens they cut to an advertisement for Budweiser.

The Australians now say that handling should be allowed in a ruck, that there need not be an even number of players from both teams in the lineouts and that rolling mauls can be dragged down. No, don't worry. I don't know what any of it means either. They are already playing games over there in which quick lineout balls need not be thrown straight, and all players except the scrum-half have to be 5 metres behind the rear foot. It's all mumbo jumbo – and how they can understand this when they can't even get to grips with the basics of eating indoors and call an afternoon an 'arvo' is beyond me.

But what I do understand is that, all of the law changes, and there are about 6,000 of them, are designed specifically to take the scrum out of the game. This is important in places such as Sydney. Get that lot into a bending-over position with a bunch of other hunks and you'd never pull them apart. What's more, when you have spent upwards of A$700 on a haircut and colouring, the last thing you need is to spend eighty minutes with your new highlights rammed up a Welshman's muddy bottom. Well now, look, Bruce. If you want to mince about on a pitch, falling over every time anyone goes near your Botox, give up with the Aussie laws nonsense and play the same wetty-footy that's seen in the rest of the world. If on the other hand you want to play a man's game, quit your whingeing – that's our job – and get stuck in. Changing the laws because you're no good in a scrum would be like us saying that the winner of a cricket match should be the team best at saying 'The rain in Spain'.

Happily, despite some support from New Zealand, the Aussies are unlikely to garner much sympathy from their other southern-hemisphere colleagues, South Africa, who did rather well out of the current laws in the last World Cup.

But to make the Barbie Boys give up, we must ensure there's a united front up here in the developed half of the world. That means Jean Claude, Iueeaneuauun, Mick, Leonardo and

William Wallace coming together, united as one, and reminding our Australian friends that if it weren't for Nigel they'd still be scorpions and snakes.

Sunday 23 March 2008

Time to save the world again, lads

You may imagine as you sit back this morning all toasty-warm, thanks to your underfloor heating, and sip on a cup of freshly ground coffee that you want for nothing; that everything that can be invented is already in the shops, on sale for £4.99.

You have a telephone that can send pictures to your sister in Australia.

You have a thing for removing the stubborn lid from a jar of pickled onions. You have pills for when you have a headache and pills to keep you unpregnant when you don't.

Certainly, if I were a modern-day Caractacus Potts and I were sitting in my shed wondering what to come up with next, I'd be suicidal with despair. And a bit murderous every time I thought of that bastard Trevor Baylis, with his bloody wind-up radio.

Maybe I would eventually hit upon the idea of turning someone's foreskin into a spare pair of eyelids, but guess what? Someone's already come up with that as a method for helping burns victims.

When we have reached a point at which a human ear can be grown on a mouse's back, and we have built so many bridges that we are reduced to connecting the tiny Humberside villages of Barton and Hessle just to give the construction companies something to do, it's easy to sit back and relax. In fact, though, we are about to enter an age when engineers, designers and men in sheds everywhere will be needed more than ever before. Because one day soon the oil and gas will run out – and the only alternatives being suggested right now are coming from people who smoke way too much cannabis. Like the tide, man. And, you know, the wind is totally, like, sustainable.

If we want to keep the world warm, lit and moving, this is genuinely alarming. Especially, as I discovered last week, when 351,000 engineers are qualifying every year in China, and India is churning out a further 112,000. Meanwhile Britain is producing just 25,000. And most of those have names like something from the bottom of a Scrabble bag and a ticket on the next plane to South Korea.

You may wonder why this is relevant. I mean, if there is going to be a replacement for oil, who cares what country is responsible? Certainly it's hard to imagine people sitting around in Budapest saying that unless Hungary gets off its arse the world will die. So why should we be worried in Britain? Why don't we let Mr Ng or Mr Patel get on with the work while we get back to what we're best at these days? Hiding our kids under the bed, mostly, and stabbing one another in pubs.

Hmmm. This is all well and good, but unfortunately Mr Ng and Mr Patel couldn't invent a brown paper bag even if you gave them 300 years and a million billion pounds. Oh sure, I've heard the stories about how ancient China had rockets and went to the moon 5,000 years ago, but I'll let you into a little secret. It's all a big bag of rubbish. They haven't even discovered the chair yet so I doubt very much they're even halfway to particle-collector shields in space.

Then there's India, which I can't take seriously until its air force has some planes with fewer than three wings. Yes, they have nuclear missiles – but could they actually hit Islamabad with them? 'I very much doubt it,' said an Indian professor chum of mine recently. 'I'm not even certain we could hit Pakistan.'

The fact of the matter is this: while the Germans can claim to have come up with the car, the Italians with electricity and the French with flight, everything else that has ever mattered in the whole of human history has come from a man in a shed in Britain. Everything. The internet, penicillin, the mechanical computer, the electronic computer, steam power, the seed drill, the seismograph, the umbrella, Viagra, polyester, the lawnmower, the fax machine, depth charges, scuba suits, the spinning jenny . . . I could go on, so I will. Radar, the television, the telephone, the hovercraft, the jet engine, the sewing machine, the periodic table . . . It doesn't matter what field you're talking about – from submarine warfare to erectile dysfunction. The world always turns to Britain when some fresh thought is needed. And with only 25,000 engineers coming out of our universities every year, I fear the world may be doomed.

Of course, you may imagine that the giant economy that is America will ride in on a horse and save the day, but don't hold your breath. They got through the sound barrier only thanks to us; they stole the computer from under our noses; and they got into space only thanks to the Germans, who knew about rockets only because our Spitfires had made mincemeat of their Messerschmitts. The Americans? Pah. Left to their own devices, I doubt they could build a pencil.

Sir James Dyson, who makes purple vacuum cleaners of such immense power that they can suck up rugs, mice and even medium-sized children, is so worried about the situation that he's opening a new academy, which will be called the Dyson School of Design and Innovation.

Backed by Rolls-Royce, Airbus and the Williams Formula

One team, it will be open to 2,500 fourteen–eighteen-year-olds in 2010. I'm thinking of enrolling my kids now, because – hell – even if they fail to come up with an alternative to oil and their time at the academy comes to naught, they can always make a fortune in life. As plumbers.

Sunday 13 April 2008

Potato heads are talking rot on food

A sinister government agency called Wrap (We Rape and Pillage) has spent vast lumps of our money to determine that, in Britain alone, we throw away 5.1m potatoes every day. Apparently this is so morally reprehensible that we should all commit suicide. Hmm. So we have one part of the government telling us that if we continue to eat too much we will become fat and everyone will explode. And now we have another part telling us that we have to finish everything on our plates because it's wrong to throw food away.

Is it, though? Of course, eco-mentalists argue that rotting food gives off methane gas – a global-warming agent twenty-three times more powerful than carbon dioxide. So a potato, casually discarded because you had too many biscuits with your afternoon tea, will cause every polar bear to suffer an agonizing death, crying for its mother and thrashing about in boiling seas. Yes, an unused maris piper will kill the planet more quickly than a Chinese power station.

Funny that, because when I suggested recently that cow farts were creating more global warming than a flock of Range Rovers, environmentalists were quick to point out that methane breaks down so quickly it isn't really an issue. Now, apparently, it is. Except, of course, it isn't – because if you leave a potato in the ground it will rot. If you dig it up then throw it away the council will put it in a landfill site. Where it will rot. And if you eat it, it will come out of your bottom, go to a sewage works and end up in the ground. Where it will rot.

In other words the only way you can prevent a spud from turning into a huge poisonous cloud of suffocating gas is to call the US air force and ask it to carpet bomb the potato-growing flatlands of Lincolnshire with Agent Orange. Who knows? Maybe this is why the government recently announced a proposal to abandon Norfolk to the sea. As payback for the county's farmers, whose produce is primarily responsible for the sea's tempestuousness in the first place.

Of course if we ignore the environmentalists – and we should – an army of Fairtrade lobbyists then ride into the argument, claiming that all the food we don't eat could be shipped to, oh, I don't know – Biafra. I give them the same argument that I gave to my mother at meal times forty years ago. 'How? In an envelope?'

In some ways, however, I'd quite like to see unwanted food being loaded on to ships by Fairtrade enthusiasts. It would set them against the ecoists, who'd argue that the journey would kill some polar bears. There'd be fighting on the docks. It'd be a hippie bloodbath.

Frankly everyone seems to have forgotten one simple thing. If I choose to buy a bag of potatoes, and then I choose not to eat them for some reason, that is my lookout. It is my money that I'm wasting, not George Monbiot's. And similarly it's no good pointing a finger at supermarkets, saying that they throw perfectly good food in the bin every day. Yes, though that's because they are forced to put 'best before' dates on everything to avoid being prosecuted by the government for giving some fat kid a bit of wind. I agree. They should be made to keep every vegetable until it starts to look like a Doctor Who special effect. But then what should they do? Many Africans are desperate, but not so desperate that they'll eat food which has mutated into an enormous bogey. So it goes into the ground. Where – guess what? It'll rot.

The best solution then is to worry about something more important – but sadly we are ruled by a government that will never pass up the opportunity for a bit more interference. If it could have an agent in every house, at every meal time, ready to prosecute parents for using too much salt and not making Johnny eat up his greens – trust me on this – it would.

Unfortunately, however, the civil service is too busy counting discarded potatoes for that – so instead our glorious leaders have decided to make the whole process of waste disposal so bloody complicated that you would rather eat everything on your plate, and consequently explode, than go to all the bother of remembering which bin to use. Round where I live we have green boxes for newspapers, plain white paper and green bottles. But not bottle tops. They have to go in the blue box, along with the shampoo, the junk mail and the paper that isn't quite white. And it gets worse because there's also a garden-waste bag into which you may put hedge clippings, but not food waste. What you're supposed to do if you've eaten half your hedge, which technically makes the other half food waste, I don't know. Happily, though, the council will provide a 'field officer' – called Standartenfuhrer Schmidt, probably – who'll call round with advice and leaflets, which when you've finished reading them should go in the blue bin. Or is it the green one? Honestly, you need to be Mr Memory Man to stand a chance.

What I do to get round this problem is to feed all our waste – even the junk mail, the hypodermic needles and the peelings from the potatoes – to our chickens. It's brilliant. The eggs they produce have actually started to come out in old HP Sauce bottles, which is handy. And I don't have to tip the hens at Christmas.

If you have no chickens, don't despair. You can either wait

for the government's exciting Compost Awareness Week, which starts on 4 May. Or you can live entirely on bars of Cadbury's Fruit & Nut chocolate. Because no one in recorded history has ever thrown one away.

Sunday 20 April 2008

I'd rather hire a dog than a prostitute

Ever since the invention of the saloon bar know-all, we've been told that when it comes to things that float, fly or fornicate, it's better to rent than buy. Rubbish. If you have the money to buy a boat and choose instead to spend it on a pension plan, then you have a plebeian heart and a beige soul. The whole point of disposable income is that you have fun with it. And I'm sorry but you cannot catch 6 ft of air off the coast of St Tropez on a Pep. Whereas you can on a Fairline Targa 52.

The argument for private planes is even more vivid. Of course you can charter one. And of course this makes financial sense. I'm sorry, though; if you have a private plane – provided it's a luxuriously appointed wood'n'leather jet, not one of those sit-up-and-beg propellered vans – you will have dramatically more sex than if you have a slice of the Norwich Union.

And that brings me on to fornication. Anyone who thinks it's better to pay a prostitute than get married and have it on tap is so riddled with venereal disease that he's not thinking straight.

If you don't believe me, take a look at Henry VIII. He caught something nasty from a hooker, went mad and took England out of the Catholic church. This forced a bunch of Bible-bashers to set up shop in America, which consequently became an English-speaking country. And as a result of that, we have to support them in their various military escapades around the globe. Our soldiers, then, are getting blown up in

Helmand simply because Henry fancied some out-of-wedlock rumpy-pumpy with Miss Syphilis 1510.

I don't think you should rent anything. If it's a house, you'll fall out with the owners, because you won't clean it to their level of expectation and they won't mend stuff quite as quickly as you want. If it's a car – who knows what kind of madman was in it last week? Me, probably. So the brakes will almost certainly disintegrate the first time you need them and then you'll be killed. And if it's a holiday cottage, you will be disappointed. This is because no one has ever walked into a seaside villa and thought, wow, this is much better than I was expecting. All rented properties are moderately worse than the pictures in the brochure suggest. This is a fact.

And on top of all this, nothing says you've failed in life quite so neatly as a Hertz key ring or a need to spend your evening bouncing up and down on six stone of Estonian skin and bone.

That said, however, I was drawn last week to the news that Londoners can now rent a dog. The idea is very simple. You pay an American company called Flexpetz an annual fee of £3,350, and for that you get four 'doggy days' a month. It's not cheap, but the firm will give you a lead, and the advantages are huge . . . My house is carpeted with dogs. They are everywhere; and apart from the labrador that ate slug pellets and is now a drooling vegetable, I love them all very much indeed. Which means I shall be extremely tearful when one of them dies. That's the beauty of rent-a-dog. You get those furry chops to stroke and the big brown eyes and the gentle farting noises as it lies by the fire. Then, when it pegs out, you just hose it into the gutter, call Flexpetz and get another.

It gets better. At present my yard is peppered with about forty dog eggs every day. Disgusting. However, you can pick up a rental dog in the morning, after it's been to the lavatory, and then give it back as soon as its legs start to cross. And, of course, you never need worry about leaving a rental dog in the car while you're at work. Or which kennels to use when you're on holiday. Or what to do when it goes bald and starts to smell.

What's more, if you split with your other half, you no longer have to saw the dog in two and then argue about who gets the interesting end. Or worry because your former husband insists on the back.

You can even tailor the dog to meet your requirements. So for my trips to the Isle of Man, where there are many ramblers, I'd get an enormous bull mastiff leopard German Nazi killer dog. And then in London I'd have a yorkie – the only thing in the world guaranteed to get you more sex than a Gulfstream V jet.

You needn't even be put off by Flexpetz's insistence that you feed its animals on holistic food. This sounds like expensive nonsense for weak blonde ladies who lunch. In fact it means food in its natural state. A recently killed rabbit – or rambler – is therefore fine.

Of course, some people say it is cruel to rent out pets in this way. An RSPCA spokesman said last week that 'most dogs need the security of a proper routine with one owner, and without this they could become stressed and unhappy'. He's wrong. My dogs love me because I tickle their tummies. If a burglar did that, they'd love him just as much – more, if he gave them a ham sandwich as well. Dogs love whoever happens to feed them, so you can be assured that if you feed your rent-a-dog it will love you too.

So there we are. If it floats, flies or fornicates, you are better off buying; but if it barks, reach for the rental agreement.

Sunday 27 April 2008

Pricking science's silly sausages

There are food riots in Haiti and Bangladesh. In Kenya hunger has driven half the population to set fire to the other half. In Bolivia they are fighting over vegetables. And even in Italy people took to the streets to complain about the price of pasta. So you might imagine that all of the world's scientists are currently in their bunkers, desperately trying to figure out why the world is running out of food all of a sudden and, more importantly, what can be done. For sure, they had a stab a while back at genetically modifying wheat so that it would grow – with no water, sunlight or soil – into a pre-packed, pre-sliced loaf. Sadly, though, the whole thing had to be abandoned when some anti-GM food activists turned up in white boiler suits and rolled all over the experiment.

And now, it seems, the world's boffins have got more important things on their enormous minds. Last week, for instance, as the fires in Haiti burnt, a group of eggheads at Yale University announced that, after some exhaustive research, they'd proved women who eat chocolate five times a week are 40 per cent less likely to get pre-eclampsia than those who indulge only once a week.

Meanwhile, in Britain, scientists at Manchester and Newcastle universities announced that if you eat two tomatoes a day you are less likely to get sunburnt when on holiday this year. And that you will have a lovely complexion well into old age.

What's more, on the very same day that the Americans were making their announcement about chocolate and the

Brits about tomatoes, leading scientists in Germany published a report that says if you have a dog in your house your children are less likely to develop hay fever. I promise I am not making any of this up.

And then we learnt that a popular osteoporosis drug will break your heart, that hair dye will give you cancer and that those pots of friendly bacteria, which look like jars of sperm, will stop your kids getting eczema.

Furthermore – and I'm still only giving you the scientific news from Tuesday – we heard that women who take HRT will have a stroke; that smokers get depressed more easily; that Range Rovers cause global warming; and that if you take pills for high blood pressure you will become stick-thin and, I don't know, fall through grates in the street or be taken away by a stork.

I thought we'd reached a new pit of scientific balderdash when they announced last month that anyone who eats one sausage a day, or three rashers of bacon, increases their chances of getting bowel cancer by a fifth. But no. Scientists in California decided to go one better and announced last Monday, wait for it, that if you send your children to a playgroup you cut their chances of catching leukaemia by 30 per cent.

Honestly, if you believed everything these scientists say you'd never dare get up, go outside or dip your celery into even the smallest pinch of salt. You'd be terrified that a tomato might turn you into Joan Collins. You wouldn't smoke or drink or go near a pylon in case you caught ebola. In fact you'd spend your entire life in a playgroup classroom, fearful that at any minute the door would be broken down by a swarm of cancerous sausages.

Happily, of course, we pay not the slightest bit of attention because we think we know exactly what's going on here.

We reckon, for instance, that if a scientist says a playgroup will cure the common cold he's being funded by a company that owns playgroups. And similarly we suspect that when a scientist stands up and says you have to eat tomatoes, his clothes, hairstyle and house may well have been paid for by someone with a greenhouse.

And then there's the sausages business. Do they really expect us to believe that a scientist woke up one morning and thought, I know, I'm going to see if a pork chipolata does anything nasty to my bowels. All of which brings me on to a bunch of boffins in Australia who are warning people not to flush their tropical fish down the lavatory. I know several people who keep such fish in England and none has ever felt the need to put his often very expensive collection in the khazi. Apparently, though, that's what they do in Oz; and now one particular breed, called the platys, has made it to the ocean, where it's causing havoc.

It was bred to live in an aquarium because it suffers from what I call Hammond syndrome – an inferiority complex resulting from the fact that it's about 6 ft short of being a shark. It is also tough and bright. Not only is it capable of dealing with the complexities of a U-bend, but it can also swim through several miles of Australian faeces just so it can get into the Pacific, where it is now decimating fish stocks, eating frogs and generally running around shouting: 'You're going home in a f****** ambulance.'

Are you bothered? Neither am I, really, but I am wondering. Why did a scientist get up one day, stretch and then say: 'Hmm, I wonder if any aquarium fish have escaped into the wild today?' And if he didn't, did anyone pay him to find out? And why? Who benefits from all the newspaper coverage? Is it the Spanish, I wonder? Are they about to claim the world is running out of food because the sea is running out of fish? And that this has nothing to do with their giant aquatic vacuum cleaners that charge about the oceans, sucking everything smaller than a pea into their holds, and is entirely the fault of Bruce and Sheila who put their platys down the Armitage Shanks one morning.

Sunday 4 May 2008

Feed them, or they'll slash all the seats

Last weekend, as I spiralled round an endless succession of identical ring roads in the Midlands, looking for somewhere to have lunch, I realized with a heavy heart that the global food shortage had reached Britain. Quite simply, there was nowhere serving anything that a human being might reasonably want to put into its mouth.

I had in my mind a white painted pub, perhaps by a restored lock. I imagined pretty gardens, some brightly painted canal boats, a pint of frothing ale and a hearty ploughman's with lashings of Branston and some crunchy pickled onions.

There were many brown signs with knives and forks on them, pointing down sun-drenched country lanes. Each one, though, led to a conference hotel that was invariably teeming with men in idiotic Oakley sunglasses, looking at flip charts. Or theme pubs with gardens full of purple dinosaurs with steps up the back.

My satellite navigation system was no help either. I asked it to list all the restaurants within 10 miles of the M6 and, after a silicon shrug, it came up with a cafe called something like the Wife Beater. And that was about it.

Most of the restaurants we happened upon were garish, neon-buffed, American add-ons to retail parks. Why? Who wants to make a day out of shopping? 'We'll buy a terrible sofa in the sales, and then before we go to get something that makes an unnecessary noise when we're gardening (which these days is pretty much everything), we'll have a slap-up lunch at the Harvester.'

Here's something you might like to chew on. They always ask in these places if you've ever eaten at a Harvester before. And I bet no one has ever said yes. I have, which is why I found it so easy to drive right on by in search of my increasingly elusive canal-side pub. Eventually, though, the tummy-rumbling became too much, and so in Coventry – which bills itself as a city of peace and reconciliation but is in fact a city ruined by the bloody Germans – we ended up in something called TGI Friday's.

A pretty girl, who was about eight, asked us to have a seat in an anteroom while our table was prepared; and here I noticed something odd. Why, in places where the menu features pictures of the food they're serving, are all the seats in the waiting area slashed? Do people who buy noisy fence-paint sprayers have an inability to sit down for more than thirty seconds without thinking: 'I know. I'll take out my Stanley knife now and cut this chair into ribbons'? Perhaps this is why DFS does so well. Its customers cannot watch *Traffic Cops Action Kill* on Sky 457+1 without tearing their settees into small pieces with knives.

I have similar thoughts whenever I visit the lavatories at large public events. How do they all miss the bowl by such an enormous margin? Are they doing it deliberately or is it a congenital fault with their bomb-aiming equipment? In which case, what on earth must their bathrooms look like at home?

After a short wait, during which time I never felt inclined to throw any of the chairs through a window, we were shown to our table – where I remembered Clarkson's first law of eating in the provinces: 'The chef is from Coventry. He was not trained in Paris.' This means I always select something that can't be mucked up. Celery, usually.

On this occasion, however, I went for a burger, which,

according to the manager, could not be served 'rare' because meat, unless cooked properly, would kill us all. Of course, this isn't true if you buy decent meat from a decent butcher or if you are a dog, but no matter. My nuked beef arrived between two pieces of what, I suppose, you could describe as bread. But only if you were mad. Let me put it this way: if I threw it at you in a food fight, I feel fairly sure that it would take your head clean off.

Plainly, then, this is a place you go to not because you are hungry or because you want to treat your family to a tasty meal. No. You go there to get heavier. As lunches go, it was right up there with an experience I had at a restaurant in Saigon. The menu said, 'Rather burnt rice land slug' and I ordered it because it sounded intriguing, but sadly it wasn't. It turned out to be as described – a rather burnt slug.

I can understand why the Vietnamese serve burnt slugs. I can understand why a chicken I was once given in Mali was skin and bone separated by nothing but warmed air. And I know why in Havana I was once given a spaghetti bolognese that came whole. Like a Frisbee. Here in Britain there is no excuse for eating rubbish. We are bombarded with cookery programmes – and every Christmas the shelves in WH Smith groan under the weight of all the recipe books. Most people could name half a dozen footballers and maybe a handful of royals, but if you asked someone to list all the famous chefs in Britain we'd be here till Doomsday. They're all so famous that we know them now by their Christian names: Gordon, Delia, Jamie, Marco, Heston, Gary, One Fat, the Hairy and so on and so on.

So why is it impossible to eat properly in Britain unless either you are in the middle of London or you are prepared to book six months in advance for a plate of vertical leaves drizzled with something odd? Why can't someone open a restaurant in the provinces that serves bread, cheese, Branston pickle and some onions? Good, honest food for people who know how to use a lavatory and won't slash all the seats.

Sunday 11 May 2008

A vicious Japanese loo ruined my ah so

Superficially Japan is the most foreign, odd and complicated place this side of Jupiter's third moon. Yet, strangely, every time I go there it's like I'm being reunited with a long-lost twin brother.

Think about it. It's an overcrowded island nation that in recent history has enjoyed great power. What's more, the Japanese have a fondness for good manners, bureaucracy and – when the chips are down – great cruelty. They drive on the correct side of the road. They have a royal family. And because they have built a society over thousands of years, they can tell where someone went to school, where they live and what their dreams and hopes are for the future simply by watching them hold a chopstick. In the same way, we know everything about a person if we discover they have a set of serviette rings.

There's more. We used to laugh when Clive James showed us those Japanese game shows in which contestants were made to eat slugs and go to work with their underpants full of stick insects. 'How weird,' we thought. But then, just a few years later, Tara Palmer-Tomkinson was sitting up to her neck in a vat of maggots.

I've been terrified recently that we in Britain have been sliding towards the American system, with our malls and our enormous bottoms. I'd much rather we had continued to walk in step with the Japanese, who are now so civilized that they have a system on the roads where the bus driver lets the car go first and you are allowed to smoke pretty much everywhere. As I enjoyed a cigarette and a beer with a group of friends in a Tokyo bar last week I thought how much more wonderful Britain would be if we adopted a similar policy.

Perhaps because of this relaxed attitude, Japanese people can expect to live longer than anyone else on Earth. Like the French and the Icelanders, who also smoke a lot and eat well, they have a good chance of reaching 100. It's only slaves to the American way who drop dead in a gym, aged six.

There is, however, one aspect of Japanese life that is neither similar to the system we have in Britain nor something we should covet: going to the lavatory. This is a fairly standard procedure over much of the globe. Except in Germany, where you are invited to inspect your stools with a lollipop stick before flushing them away. Unfortunately, though, the Japanese have examined the simple water closet and decided that it could be improved with some electronics. The result, I'm afraid, is a disaster.

It's why the Japanese economy is now in such a mess: all their top people and scientists are stuck in their bathrooms, unable to wipe their bottoms.

First of all the seat is warmed – and there is no way for the round-eye to know this, which means I had to sit there imagining the heat had come from the lorry driver who'd been the last person to use the motorway service-station cubicle. This is unnerving. Soon I became convinced that it was possible to catch encephalitis from the latent heat of a Japanese lorry driver's bottom.

Wanting to get out of there as quickly as possible, I turned and discovered to my horror that the loo roll had been replaced with what can only be described as the Starship Enterprise's dashboard. And it was all in Japanese. The first button I pushed, with a trembly finger, made the seat get even warmer. Realizing that unless I acted quickly I'd be cooked, I stabbed at another button – which made a gout of liquid nitrogen shoot up my bottom. So hurriedly, and in great pain, I turned a hopeful-looking knob that simply redirected the fountain into my scrotum. In a state of some distress I pushed a slider control all the way down and immediately got a pretty good idea of what it might be like accidentally to impale yourself on the fuel rod from a nuclear power station. I was now in real trouble.

And I didn't understand why. Who would want to steam-clean their nether regions? Who wants a lavatory seat that can reach the same temperature as a barbecue? And, conversely, who gets up in the morning and thinks: 'I know, I'll stop off at the Brue Boar services this morning and deep-freeze my testicles'?

Which brings me on to the next question. Why is it necessary to have directional control for the fountain of fire and ice? I can understand why a lady might need – and even enjoy – such a feature. But for chaps it's jolly painful.

And then there's the problem with the flush. The first button I pressed filled the cubicle with karaoke tunes. The second started the tap in the corner. It wasn't till I got to the sub-menu in the eighth quadrant that I was treated to the sound of water being sucked away.

Unfortunately it was just the recording of a flush being played through the WC's speaker system. Am I missing something here? I can think of no reason anyone might want to convince people in neighbouring cubicles that they are flushing the bog when in fact they are not. And why would you want to play this sound at a volume that could kill bats? Because, trust me, you can.

Finally I leant over the unit to see if there was a conventional handle, and somehow while doing this I made a jet of water squirt into my crotch. Which meant I eventually emerged from the cubicle looking as though I hadn't bothered to lower my trousers. Everyone in the restaurant laughed at my misfortune. And once again I felt very much at home.

Sunday 25 May 2008

Argh! I've fallen into a speed trap

On many occasions, the organizers of the Hay-on-Wye literary festival, which is held in a field near Wales every year, have invited me to go along and give a talk. And on an equal number of occasions, I've said no. There's a good reason for this. You might imagine that Hay is a lovely day out for all the family, a chance for children to meet the authors they love and, conversely, an opportunity for writers to meet the people who actually read their books.

Of course, it's no such thing. Mainly it's a chance for ramblers and hippies to gather in a field and convince themselves that everyone thinks the same way that they do. In essence, it's a competition each year to see who can dream up the most organically idiotic way of cleaning their teeth. Cow manure or nettles. The great debate.

Then there are the attractions. There's lots of movement and dance, a carbon gym and plenty of unnecessarily funky capital letters from the 2FaCeD DaNcE workshop. This year the *Guardian* had even built a House of Hay (geddit) out of what in Farringdon Road would undoubtedly pass for hay, but was, in fact, straw. It'd be an ideal building material for people who like rats and want to have breathing difficulties.

I have always thought that if I went along they'd pull my hair and steal my milk in the playground. But this year, with Boris in London's hot seat, a Tory looking after Crewe and Gordon scoring nought in the opinion polls, I figured – wrongly, as it turned out – I'd be safe. So I fired up the SUV and said: 'Come on, kids. Let's go and laugh at the lefties. It'll be fun.'

Annoyingly, the organizers had not sent any directions for those who were coming by road. Instead, we were told to use something called a train that would take us to Hereford – 20 miles shy of the books. If you didn't fancy this, you could come by coach. There were two options. A six-day trek from London via every market town in the land. Or an even longer journey from Bradford to Worcester, which is listed in my road map as being 'nowhere near Hay-on-Wye'. What you were supposed to do if you were coming from Crewe, it didn't say. Stay at home and watch Tom Clancy films on your plasma, probably.

To get around the festival itself, shuttle buses were provided. And, of course, these were very publicly running on biodiesel. Or, as I like to call it, a poor man's lunch. If you didn't fancy assuaging your middle-class guilt with that, you could use a bicycle, and three people had done just that. But because it was raining heavily, most had simply come in their stupid little eco-Fiat cars and turned 84 per cent of the surrounding countryside into a quagmire. Green? No, more a soupy Ypres brown, in fact.

Inside the tented village, many of the organizers were wearing tie-dye. One chap was sporting a kaftan. Beards were everywhere, and everyone was squelching around in sturdy shoes from the Street-Porter range. It looked like a scene from the Haight-Ashbury happy-clappy handbook on bonkers living.

But no. Behind the scenes, there was trouble afoot. Because the festival is now sponsored in part by a bank, and because all bankers, obviously, are the spawn of Satan, there's now a rival festival a mile or so down the road. This event, organized by someone calling herself the Poet, had invited Arthur Scargill to speak while the assembled druids ate bits of dirt from their smocks and mocked people at the real Hay festival.

So far, then, no books had actually made an appearance, but this came as no surprise since it is written that when one or two socialists come together they will immediately forget about the common goal and start squabbling over who's got the most environmentally friendly yurt. It's the Judaean People's Front all over again.

To try to give my children a taste of what life might have been like if their mum and dad had been lunatics, we bought them an ice cream made from sheep's milk. Nutritionally, they'd have been better off licking Arthur Scargill's hair. We did at least run into the children's author Georgia Byng, who took my youngest daughter's mind off the shit sheep ice cream.

My talk seemed to go quite well. The tent was full of families who'd paid £15 a ticket, none of which comes to me, incidentally; and so, in return, I tried to give them all a laugh – which they were unlikely to get from the ice cream or the Mexican diplomat's lecture on his conservation project to save the Latin American monarch butterfly.

But with each answer, I was inadvertently signing my own death warrant. There I was, jokily telling all the small boys in the audience that I'd once done 186 mph through the Limehouse Link in London, and that speed limits are for the weak. And backstage it was all being moulded by the eco-greens into a howling, sack-the-idiot press release.

I probably will be, and it's my own silly fault. I never saw it coming. I was expecting them to burn a pile of my books; I was ready for George Monbiot to leap on stage and arrest me for having a patio heater. I'd even taken a change of clothing in case a fat woman, full of root vegetables and hate, shoved a custard pie in my face again. It never occurred to me that I'd been invited specifically to shoot myself in the face.

Top Gear is back on your screens in three weeks. It'll be hosted by Bill Oddie and will feature lots of movement and dance. And how you can make a car out of straw.

Sunday 1 June 2008

It's just a dumb animal, Mr Oddie

It seems that Bill Oddie's fluffy *Springwatch* television programme has been in a spot of bother because it keeps showing pictures of animals and birds doing sex. Well, obviously I'm not especially given to defending the twitching weird beard but, honestly, all that birds and animals do is eat, sleep and mate. If you take the rumpy-pumpy out of the equation, what's left?

You can't even show them having lunch these days because a bird wrenching a worm from the ground would have vegetablists putting the producer's name on an internet hit list. Anyway, the sparrow porn, the rampant carnivorism and the ducky gangbangs are not the problem. No. It's the awful syrupy way that all nature's little creatures are judged and measured by human standards.

We are shown some footage of daddy swallow tenderly picking each of his little babies from the nest . . . and dropping them on to the floor, where they will gasp for a bit, in great pain, and then die. It's presented as though we are watching Josef Fritzl, but we are not. We are watching an ounce of feathers and bone killing its kids, not because it's stupid or psychopathic but because it's a bird. Are we supposed to think that all swallows kill their kids? Isn't that a bit like saying all human men wander about town centres at night stabbing one another with screwdrivers?

By all means tell me that a swallow can fly all the way from Africa and find the same barn in Norfolk that it left six months earlier. That is amazing. Or find one that can't. Because that would be hysterical. But do not try to convince me that swallows have some great intelligence that we humans lack. Because they don't.

It's much the same story with dolphins. Time and time again, nature presenters portray them as bright. But compared with what – a table lamp? A lobster? The fact is this: my dishwasher, by any measure, has a greater power of reasoning.

And anyway if it's suggested that a swallow could write a book if only it had hands, or build a box-girder bridge if you gave it a spanner, then when we see it indulging in infanticide, we will feel duty-bound to come round to the *Springwatch* bird box and wring its cruel and vindictive little neck.

Of course, we can get sentimental about animals. I like my dogs very much. Sometimes I talk to them as though they are my children. I've even trained them to fetch sticks and sit down. In other words, I've attempted to make them more human. But this is futile because they are not human. I know this because they spend most of their day in the paddocks eating horse shit. When they've had their fill, they come into the house and vomit on to every flat surface they can find. This has caused a great many arguments between my wife and me since we made a deal when the real children were young that I'd deal with the sick and she'd deal with the poo. I maintain, on this basis, that although the horse poo has come out of the dog's mouth and is therefore technically vomit, it is not. And that she must therefore clear it up. Normally, we end up taking out our rage on the dogs.

This is unfair. They do not know that if they must heave out the contents of their stomachs they should try to avoid the Bukhara rugs. A dog knows to bark at burglars and to be doe-eyed and sweet when you tickle its tummy; but don't get confused – it has no concept of Pakistani hand-knotted silks.

You see the problem. Because Oddie tells us that badgers are sweet and swallows are clever, we are unable to react properly when they vomit on our furniture or eat our children. Some people are so confused by the heart-wrenching nature of nature programmes that they have descended into madness and become vegetarians.

They point at me with hate in their eyes because I've killed a pheasant. But it's not a pheasant. It's lunch. What's more, I'll shoot any fox that breaks into my chicken coop and attempts to destroy my breakfast factory. And I'll stop only if one day foxy-woxy turns up with a bigger gun than mine.

Every time an Australian gets washed up on Bondi beach with one leg and half his head missing, there's always some shaggy-haired dopehead on the news saying the great white that attacked the poor soul was only being a shark. Absolutely. And we're only being human, which is why we're throwing hand grenades at the bloody thing.

The best way, I reckon, to cure people of their soft-focus, teary-eyed view of animals is to get them to imagine a nature programme made by dogs about humans. What would they make of people who collect stamps? Or people who ride motorcycles? Or vicars? Or people who devote their whole lives to helping others? How many hours would they devote to the fact that the most powerful people on earth now face the choice of electing as their leader a black man with a vision but no policies or someone who's so old that he needs to have his food mashed? They'd find us as strange as we, by rights, should find them.

And what on earth would Rover Attenborough say when he happened upon Kate Humble? 'Look at this one. She's adorable. Talented. Funny. And very cute. So what the bloody hell is she doing on television with a fat, hairy man who won't shut up, gets off on stag beetles having sex and becomes all sentimental when a swallow doesn't follow the *Daily Mail*'s instructions on being a good dad?'

Sunday 8 June 2008

Swim with sharks – it's easy money

Not that long ago it was very hard to make big lumps of money. You had to learn Latin, grow a side parting, wear a suit, play squash, do accountancy and get up extremely early in the morning. Friends had to be stabbed in the back and children ignored. Then along came the Greater London Authority, which, we're told, was a fountain of cash. It seems that all you had to do to get a huge grant was call Ken's Kremlin and explain that, as a Muslim polar bear, you were very concerned about the melting ice caps, the slave trade, Fairtrade potato crisps and, er, nuclear proliferation, and immediately your piggy bank would burst.

Sadly, though, when Boris took over, the gravy train for lunatics was halted and it looked as though the terminally lazy might have to go back to rubbing scratch cards or applying for a slot on *Britain Doesn't Appear to Have Any Discernible Talent*.

There's more grim news. When the government announced it was thinking of locking up men with beards for forty-two days, some people suggested that anyone who was not subsequently charged would be entitled to £3,000 a night for every night beyond twenty-eight days' detention. Excellent. You simply grow some facial hair and stroll into Terminal 5 with some wires poking out of your shoes, and Bob's your sugar daddy. You get three meals a day, a smorgasbord of drugs and you walk away after six weeks with £42,000 in your trousers.

Unfortunately, the whole forty-two-day thing now seems

likely to be a dead duck, but don't despair, because how's this for a money-making idea? Simply go on a scuba-diving holiday and get lost. Obviously, you don't want to be getting, ahem, 'separated from the dive boat' in Norway. Or in a gravel pit in Wakefield. It's best to go to a place where the sea is warm. This will make your 'ordeal' quite comfortable. And as an added bonus there will be sharks, which will sound great after you've been miraculously rescued and your story is appearing in *Hello!* magazine.

Don't worry – in lovely warm water the only sharks you'll see are so small, they wouldn't even classify as a hungry man's starter. When a newspaper talks of 'shark-infested waters', though, we all immediately think of cold-water predators biting Robert Shaw in half.

Now, some housekeeping. Don't, whatever you do, get yourself lost miles from land in some two-bit Third World backwater where all the rescue-boat captains are on heroin. You stand a pretty good chance of being out there for ever. Australia's good. They are all used to being eaten, and because of this, the authorities will most likely send a destroyer to the rescue. This will look fantastic on the evening news and will up your saleability immensely.

Oh, and do please remember to have something pithy but brave prepared for when they haul you on board. Crying like a girl is no good unless you actually are a girl. Tony Bullimore, the round-the-world sailor, set a pretty good benchmark in this respect. He really had been in trouble, miles from anywhere and freezing cold; he'd even started to eat himself. All absolutely excellent if he'd thought to flog his story. And then, when he'd been rescued by the Aussie navy and, of course, offered counselling, he said: 'What would I need that for? I've just been saved.' Brilliant.

Next, you must choose who's coming with you, and here

there's a big rule. No mingers. The girls must be prettier than a Caribbean sunset, partly because *Hello!* is not going to put someone who looks like Ann Widdecombe on the cover. The men, on the other hand, should be big and strong so that they can deal with any unfortunate attacks by cannibalistic fishermen or Portuguese men-of-war. But, critically, one must be a concave-chested prat whom you don't like very much. Because someone has to come home with a half-eaten head, after all.

Things to pack? Well, obviously you'll need some sandwiches so you have something to eat while you wait for the dive boat to go away. You'll also need some sun cream, a torch, a portable sat nav system, a harpoon gun and some condoms, in case one of the pretty girls falls for the 'Well, since we're going to die, we might as well' line.

Most important of all, though, you must take a camera with a flash. Last week we saw some incredibly dramatic photographs of a beautiful and healthy young woman swimming through 'shark-infested waters', at night, after she and some friends had been carried away by 'fierce rip tides' off Bali. This is textbook stuff.

The party of three Brits, a Frenchman and a Swede even came up with a fierce-looking dinosaur that had approached them when they did finally make land. It's called the Komodo dragon and billed as the largest lizard in the world, so we have in our mind a Tyrannosaurus rex, peering through the window of their broken-down Jeep. It all sounds terrifying, and we'll just gloss over the fact that it prefers carrion to live meat, and that they made it go away by throwing pebbles at it. Honestly, guys, it would have been more lucrative – not that you were going to sell your story, of course – if you'd scarified the Swede. We'd never have known.

Plus, it would have been better if, in the pictures you took as you sat on the island waiting for rescue, you hadn't all been smiling.

I do hope my simple guide to making a fortune while on a lovely holiday in the Indian Ocean will come in handy this summer. Because the only way you'll make more money is by sleeping with Wayne Rooney. And I really wouldn't fancy that.

Sunday 15 June 2008

Oi, get your hands off my lap dancers

The machine needs to be fed. When you have 650 members of parliament elected to make laws, and an army of 500,000 civil servants whose job is to make sure that those laws work, and more legions in Brussels making more laws, there is never going to be any respite. The machine can never rest until absolutely everything is illegal.

Whenever I let my mind wander, I become quivery-lipped and frightened thinking about all the things I could do ten years ago that I cannot do now. I may not smack my children, for instance, or talk on a mobile telephone while driving or put too much salt on my mashed potato or smoke at home if my cleaning lady objects or give my donkey a tender burial or encourage my dogs to kill rats. And if I put the wrong thing in the wrong-coloured dustbin, I'm likely to spend the next five years digging tunnels.

Outside my little world, things are even worse. Schools must ensure that their urinals are a certain height off the ground. Trawlermen must throw everything they catch back into the sea. The makers of beer must tell their customers to drink responsibly. And if Rowan Atkinson were to make a joke about gypsies, he would be digging tunnels too.

Today the machine is running out of people wearing high-visibility jackets to enforce its avalanche of new laws and so it is dispensing with the courts system and locking up people who may be innocent. And still it whirrs, announcing last week that it is going to ban people from becoming sexually aroused. At the moment lap-dancing clubs are classified in the same category as coffee shops and karaoke bars. Quite why coffee shops or karaoke bars need to be 'classified' by a government agent in a high-visibility jacket we are not told.

Nor is there much evidence that this classification system is working because, so far as I can tell, every single town in Britain these days is equally terrible – a vomit-stained centre full of estate agents, charity shops and building societies, ringed with a prefabricated, fluorescent sprawl of people in purple shirts trying to sell you Pentium processors and button-backed leatherette sofas.

At least a lap-dancing club brings a bit of individuality to a town, a bit of a respite from the endless chain stores and horrible pound shops. Sadly, though, the machine disagrees. It says that such places provide 'visual sexual stimulation' and as a result councils must be allowed to prevent new ones from opening and perhaps must even close existing venues.

Does this mean that anything that provides 'visual sexual stimulation' must be erased from the landscape? That would be a worry for Dorothy Perkins, as I know one chap who claims that its mannequins are extremely stimulating. And let's not forget, shall we, that some people are aroused by goats. I've even seen one photograph of a man making love to his Range Rover.

I struggle to see what's wrong with lap-dancing bars. I would object, for sure, if anyone suggested building an airport for Somalian rapists in my backyard, but a gentlemen's club? No. I don't like them much. I don't like the music or the volume it's played at. I don't like the businessmen who go there and I don't like sitting on velour. But, unlike the vast majority of the objectors, I base my opinions on experience. Extensive experience, in fact.

What do the do-gooders think goes on in these places? Do

they imagine it's a sea of opium, with men in macs playing pass-the-parcel with their embarrassing itches? Because it just isn't. Usually there is a handful of girls – all called Becki and all with unwise artwork on their shoulders and bones in their noses – sitting around wearing bits of chiffon and £1.99 underwear that was billed in the catalogue as 'erotic' but is no such thing. After a little while, a Becki will come over and tell you, usually in a Birmingham accent, that she likes to do les-bionics with her friends when the bar closes, in the hope that you will be so aroused that you'll give her twenty quid for a dance. It's not a dance that your grandparents would recognize. In fact, you don't dance at all. You just sit there, with your hands over your ears to drown out the music, while the girl takes off her mum's net curtain and puts two bagfuls of silicone near your face. This is like waving a steak in front of a hungry man. But the juices don't flow because you know that if you even look as though you're going to touch them, a bull elephant in a dinner jacket will arrive on the scene and break your liver.

Some clubs do allow the dancers to sit on the customers' knees but these are to be avoided, partly because some of the younger customers are so full of testosterone that phys-ical contact of any kind might cause them to burst. And partly because the Beckis who work in such places tend to be quite big. Get one of those on your lap and, if you're not careful, you're going to go home with gangrene.

I'm not stupid. I'm not going to say lap dancers aren't sex-ually stimulating. In fact there's one called Jennifer at a place in Dearborn, Michigan, whom I would describe as very sex-ually stimulating. But then so is the Polish girl who works at my local Caffè Nero. And so, I'm told, is Richard Hammond. Does that mean we should pixelate his little face on *Top Gear* tonight?

This new scheme is proof that the machine has gone off its rocker. And you know what scares me most of all? It's like the internet. We can never turn it off.

Sunday 22 June 2008

Dante's new hell: my work canteen

Where did you buy your ironing board? You didn't, did you? You were born with it. Everyone is, which is why everyone has one. I've seen tramps in Soho snuggled into shop doorways with nothing to their name except some string, a bin liner and an ironing board. My brother-in-law, who does not believe in possessions, stated proudly when I first met him that he owned nothing. But he was lying, of course. Like everyone, he had a wok. And an ironing board. What's more, nobody ever thinks: 'Ooh, my ironing board is getting worn out. I must buy another.' Nor does anyone suddenly feel the need to upgrade, as they might do with a computer or a mobile phone.

This is why I wasn't the slightest bit surprised to hear last week that Currys has seen a big fall in profits. Of course it has. It's ironing board central. If you were to win a trolley dash in one of its branches, you'd scoot off and – after a while – you'd think: 'Actually, you know what? I'll just take the trolley.' Every time I set foot in one of its branches, my head spins with the dreariness of it all. Indeed I came to the conclusion recently that Currys is the only shop in the world that sells absolutely nothing I want to buy. It turns out, however, that I was wrong . . .

Last month my BBC office was moved to something called a media village in White City, west London. It's a place where people in thin spectacles gather each day to try to make a difference. Designed by *Guardian* readers, for *Guardian* readers, it's a riot of impenetrable symbolism, concrete and sharp designer fountains, which would be arousing if you had mad hair and a degree in environmental poetry from a Fairtrade, organic peace workshop in Hackney. I don't see it like that at all, however. In fact, after just a few minutes I began to think that Dante got everything wrong. There are not nine circles of hell. There are ten.

After just one morning in this edgy, pedestrianized, eco-friendly cuboid, I was filled with an overwhelming desire to pile up some old tyres and set them on fire, using diesel. I don't like vandalism, but if someone were to decorate one of the buildings with a giant purple cock and balls, I'd be tempted to give him a pat on the back and a puppy dog.

Hopefully, I've now set the scene. Lots of women sitting around on Ozwald Boateng benches, working out how miserable their next programme can be and whether they can make all the interviewees cry on camera. And me, oiling my machine pistol . . .

Which brings me to the door of the village's grab'n'go takeaway cafe. The place where everyone goes for lunch.

Trust me on this. Currys has definitely lost its title as Britain's most out-of-step high-street retailer. Because I stood in this cafe for a full ten minutes and decided that the tastiest things in there were the tables and chairs. Maybe, if you were a budgerigar, you might have been excited by some of the offerings. But even then, you wouldn't know whether to put them in your mouth or use them as a lavatory. Finally I asked a pretty young waitress if there was anything on the shelves that, by even the loosest dictionary definition, might qualify as food. She looked perplexed. Is there anything in here that once had a face? Or anything with chocolate on it? Bewildered, she reached down and presented me with a plastic bowl full of lettuce. 'No,' I said, 'I am not a rabbit. I am a fully grown man. I am hungry and I want a kebab.'

Eventually she led me away from the Cellophane trays full of weeds to a rack selling what can only be described as Trill. I mean it. They were selling seeds to human beings. How insane do you have to be to think that'll work? And how certifiable do you have to be to think: 'Mmmm. Yes. Those'll keep me going for the afternoon.'

I would eat seeds, of course, but only if my harvest had failed and the soldiers had confiscated my goat. Why anyone would want to eat them in Britain, where we have pylons and plasma, I have no idea. So to find out I spent 50p on a small packet, opened it and made the catastrophic mistake of putting the contents in my mouth.

It turns out that these seeds are rich in magnesium, iron, phosphorus, calcium, selenium and zinc. In other words, you would get precisely the same nutritional benefit from eating a car. Taste-wise? Well, I'm no expert on these matters, but I'd say it was exactly like sucking on a box of matches.

Eager to make the nausea go away, I headed for the drinks counter – hoping for a Fanta or a Red Bull. But there is no place for these symbols of capitalist excess in a modern-day, west London media village, so I was offered a choice of elderberry juice, which is the first resort of the hippie and the druid, or something called wheatgrass.

It's hard to encapsulate the flavour in a sentence. Fans describe it as 'unusual' or 'strong', but I'd go further if only I could think of the right word. 'Vile' doesn't begin to get close. 'Horrendous' is wrong, too. A cancerous lung is horrendous. Wheatgrass is way beyond that. Combined with the phosphorus from the seeds, it felt like my mouth was hosting a bomb-makers' convention. Acid, metal, fertilizer, plastic, hate: all of these flavours swarmed round my head until, genuinely, I thought I might have to vomit all over the waitress.

I must therefore finish with a warning. You must never put this stuff in your mouth. If you are hungry, eat your ironing board.

Sunday 29 June 2008

Look, Mr McChap – you're part of Britain, so just get over it

If you were part of the Wimbledon centre court crowd on Monday, when Andy Murray came back from two sets down to beat Richard Gasquet, I hope you are thinking seriously this morning about doing the decent thing and committing suicide.

As I sat watching the revolting spectacle on television, I was – and this doesn't happen often – ashamed to be middle-class and English. Because there they were, 15,000 phlebitis-ridden Surrey women in their size 16 summer frocks, furiously banging their bingo wings together every time that poor Frenchie made a mistake. And raising what's left of the roof every time Murray, who looks like a piece of string with a knot in it, got a point.

This was not Britain versus France. It was two individuals who have worked hard to become their country's number ones, bashing it out at the world's premier tennis tournament for a chance to be flattened by Nadal. And because of that noise, and the whooping and the idiotic bias, the best man lost.

Sport is as much about mental attitude as talent, and it's hard to get your head in gear when you are faced with a sea of highlighted raspberry-ripple women waving their *Daily Mail*s at you and applauding every time you do a double fault. Rabble-rousing does not happen in other countries to anything like this extent. Because their tennis crowds have manners. And the thin-lipped, surgical-stockinged, Volvo-driving masses who descended on Wimbledon this year plainly do not.

I wouldn't mind but they were cheering for a man who has, in the past, made it plain that he is not English at all, or British. But Scottish. And that, for me, is becoming a problem. When we kindly gave the Scots their Stone of Destiny back, I thought that that would be that and Sean Connery would go back to playing golf. But no. Every day there's another rabid attack on the English from up there in the heather, another demand that we simply sever all ties and let them forge their own path in the world.

This I don't understand. I can see why the English might want independence from them. Scotland is a drain on our economy to the tune of about £10 billion a year. But them wanting to leave us? Isn't that a bit like the oxpecker spitting in the rhino's eye? They'd have to have their own embassies around the world. They'd have to get their own currency. And think of how much it would cost to set up a whole new state, especially in a country that managed to spend £414m on a parliament building. That works out at £1m for every man, woman and child still living there.

Scotland would even have to get its own army. Oh no, wait a minute. I've just remembered. They have one already. It's called the SAS.

There's more, too. Only last week there were calls from north of the border for a separate Scottish entry for next year's Eurovision song contest. What? The Proclaimers? Or just a random collection of men in dresses blowing into their tartan bags? Either way, I can't see them getting too many votes from Estonia.

It's funny. I've never had a problem with Scotland or its people. I recognize the massive contribution it's made to the world of inventions. I like haggis. *Local Hero* is my all-time favourite film. And in a rugby match, I've always supported the boys in blue so long as they weren't actually up against us.

Certainly, if I felt the need to poke a bit of fun at someone, the Welsh made much better targets. Now, though, things seem to be changing because, when I stop and think about it, I've never met a Welshman whom I've disliked. Apart from Piers Pughe-Morgan, obviously – and he claims to be Irish. Whereas, these days, every Scotchman rides into the room on a wave of bile and nationalism.

They have become the new Australians; unable to get through any conversation without bringing up a litany of English failures and embarrassments. Ask a barman up there for a glass of Scotch, and what you get instead is an essay on Culloden and Stirling and Bannockburn, and Murrayfield back in March.

All of this is fine when it's good-natured, but I have a sense these days that the veneer of friendly rivalry is being replaced with a mask of smiling anger. Sometimes I get the distinct impression that, if I mention Falkirk, the McChap will lean over the bar and pull my arms off.

I feel about this the same way that a mother might feel when her daughter, whom she's loved and nurtured and helped – with £10 billion a year – suddenly turns round and says: 'I hate you. And I'm going to get a flat on my own.' You know the poor child is going to have her heart broken and get into trouble and catch chlamydia.

So this column – it's a plea. Can you stop it? You lost. You're part of Britain. You've had 300 years to get used to that, and it's starting to look as though you're being stubborn.

The fact is that the union has been a good thing. We are grateful to you for inventing penicillin and the telephone, and you should be grateful to us for introducing you to proper food and trousers.

If you want to go, that's fine – but can't we at least part as friends? Because if we can't, next time there's a tennis match between Murray and Gasquet, I shall simply support the person who lives nearest to me. And that'd be the Frenchie.

Sunday 6 July 2008

Now we're for it: we've stopped behaving badly

There have been many very different reactions to Max Mosley's basement bunk-up. Some have been offended and some unmoved, but most people, since it's so *Carry On up the Khyber*, have read the reports and sniggered.

Hmmm. I wonder if I'm alone in having a bit of respect for the man. I mean, there he is, a sixty-eight-year-old pensioner getting it on with five girls in the middle of the afternoon. Fair play to you, fella.

I felt much the same way when I heard Prince William had put his chopper in Kate Middleton's back garden. Oooh, there was a lot of harrumphing – but come on, chaps. The man's a prince. All he did was borrow one of his granny's helicopters to drop in on the floozy. Wouldn't you?

David Cameron laid out a new set of guidelines last week to which all Tory MEPs must now adhere. They fill me with horror and dread because it means we're soon to be governed by a bunch of people who go to bed at ten, only drink ginger beer, never try to look up their secretaries' skirts and are quite happy to get paid £4.50 an hour. In short, we're going to be governed by bores and failures. Why is this a good idea? No one says of their friends, 'I chose them because they are all so kind to animals and they do good works.' We like people who like to laugh, to have fun, to break the rules once in a while. Trouble is, it's hard to find people like that any more . . .

In the olden days *Private Eye* was full of stories about journalists who'd ripped off their employers for forty grand and been in bed with a hooker when the story they were supposed to be covering broke. Now, it's just an endless parade of mild hypocrisy. Eighteen months ago the *Daily Mail* said this. And now it's saying the exact opposite. So what?

The maelstrom of expenses fraud and serial shagging has become a gentle eddy of honest-to-God mistakes. And whatever happened to the long lunch? Today, whenever I order a glass of wine in the middle of the day, people look at me as though I might be a Martian. And that's before I step outside for a cigarette.

This brings me on to Amy Winehouse. Has it occurred to anyone that she might be having a jolly good time? In the 1950s and 1960s, before the world became so po-faced, the rich and the famous would gather in Mustique and the south of France for debauched, drug-fuelled orgies and no one batted an eyelid. Today we tut because Russell Crowe has thrown a telephone at someone. And look what happens when an Old Etonian tries to make some governmental alterations in Africa. Instead of a statue in Trafalgar Square he gets thirty-four years in the slammer.

Imagine if we had someone like Winston Churchill in power today. A smoker. A drinker. A man given to Herculean bouts of depression. Under a hailstorm of criticism he wouldn't last a week. Look at poor old Charles Kennedy. Gone now and replaced with someone who, I feel sure, would get a dopamine rush from taking his dog for a walk.

It's the same for all of us. You can be ostracized by your neighbours for putting your refuse in the wrong-coloured bin, you can have your car vandalized if it has four-wheel drive and last week there were calls for cyclists to be jailed if they attempted to enliven this ludicrous means of transport by getting a move on.

Worse, the town of Redruth in Cornwall has imposed a nine p.m. curfew on all under-sixteens, which means that every fifteen-year-old boy must now be at home each evening with his parents watching Panorama. I fear the Cornish courts had better brace themselves for a massive increase in cases of matricide.

I look sometimes at the microcosm that is my own life and it's terrifying. Because in recent years I have been criticized for bumping into a horse chestnut tree; I've been called a berk, on the front page of a national newspaper, for using an iPod while driving. And only a couple of weeks ago I was 'blasted' for enjoying a gin and tonic while at the North Pole. There's a constant bombardment for me to sit up straight, eat my greens, comb my hair. It drives me mad. Honestly. Next time James May and I are at a Pole, we've decided he's going to mainline heroin and I'm going to shoot a baby polar bear in the face. For fun.

I fear for our future. I worry that bad behaviour is being erased from society, and that unless the trend can be reversed somehow we'll all have to go through life on the Planet Stepford, a rictus grin masking the boiling turmoil of desperation inside. I yearn sometimes when I encounter a neatly stacked pyramid of tins of beans to push it over. Don't you? Wouldn't it break the monotony of having to drive at 30 mph and eating a wholefood Fairtrade sandwich at your desk?

Recently Annie Robinson and I dreamt up a TV show that would serve as an antidote to the endless parade of hectoring and finger-wagging programmes we get today. Instead of running down the street after a cowboy builder who'd charged an old lady a million quid to build a fireplace, we would go after the victims. It was to be called *Sucker* and it would celebrate the ingenious while pointing the finger and howling with laughter at the stupid, the gullible and the fat. Never has the nation needed such a show more. And never has such a thing been less likely to get commissioned. Unless, of course, we could get Max Mosley to present it.

Sunday 13 July 2008

Working while on holiday is . . .
wow, just look at that

In the *Sunday Times* last weekend there was a huge story about how thousands of city families are now decamping to the countryside each summer. There were pictures of smiling mums with lovely teeth, under the wisteria, telling us how their children go on bike rides without being stabbed, and that because Nethercombe End is only 40 miles from the M5, their husbands can get up to the City for important meetings (with their mistresses, but it didn't say that) in just sixteen hours.

Right. Well, since I'm currently at my seaside cottage for the summer, let's see if it really is possible to combine a family holiday with work. Here we go.

The slate-grey sea trembles under a tempestuous sky. Waves: big green fists smash into the rocks and explode in a shower of crystalline white, whipped by the wind into a swirling ethereal moment when nature's savagery and power combine in an instant of shrieking glory.

Hang on a minute. I wanted to write this morning about Australia's immigration policy. But sadly, each time I look out of the window, I'm consumed by the view. This means that every time I try to send an e-mail to the *Top Gear* edit suite about cuts I need for next week's film, it always begins: 'The seagull's lonesome cry echoed eerily from the volcanic jaggedry . . .' and no one in Soho has the first clue what's got into me.

Anyway. Australia recently announced that all illegal immigrants . . . Oh, God almighty. I'm going to have to break off for a moment. It appears my son has fallen over on the rocks while emptying the lobster pots . . . and yes, there is a great deal of blood spurting from his left leg. I fear he needs to go to hospital.

He does. Back shortly . . .

Right. Australia's federal immigration minister Chris Evans, who is no relation to the biotech Welshman, announced last week that . . . holy Mother of God, I've just seen a whale. I'm not kidding. Was it a fin? Or a killer? There it is again. Bloody hell. It's massive.

I must go on the internet to find out. And that's going to take hours because here at the seaside, broadband is not the width of a human hair. It actually is a human hair, which feeds information at 35.7 kb per second. In English, that's 7 mph.

Two hours later. It was a minke. Fairly common in these waters, apparently. So anyway. Australia. Oh, hang on. Jane Moore's leaving. She's been staying for the past week, which means her column in the *Sun* will be all full of whales and tempestuous seas as well.

This is the problem with trying to work from a house at the seaside. Because none of your friends has one, they come and stay in yours, which means you can't do any work in the morning because you stayed up till three and your head hurts, and you can't work in the afternoon because you're drunk from lunch.

The coastguard's here. It seems a cyclist has careered through my field and six of our sheep were so frightened by his wizened face of hate they jumped off the cliff and into the sea. Three are dead. It's all hands on deck to rescue the survivors.

Four hours later. God, I hate cyclists. But where was I? Oh yes. Shafts of sunlight scream out of the leaden sky, piercing the endlessly swirling might of the ocean. No, sorry. What I mean is: for many years Australia has stood alone on the question of immigration, as immune to the body of world opinion as . . . the cheeky stonechat that's just landed on my gatepost.

Um. I've just been for a walk. I would never walk at home, but here it's different. I can pick samphire to fry up with a bit of butter. It goes well with the lobsters we catch. The powerful flavour helps to mask the taste of the twelve-year-old's arterial leg juice.

The people from the *Top Gear* office just called to talk about the interview in tonight's show. They're uncertain about whether we should go straight from the shot of the horse to the bit where Richard Hammond falls over. I told them I'd seen a minke whale. They weren't very interested.

What interests me most of all right now, much more than whether Australia really is full or whether there's a bit of space left over for most of Somalia, is whether to take all the children we have staying to Laser Blast this afternoon or whether we should stay here and play Risk.

Everyone's falling out over the issue. This is the problem. It's unfair, really, to drag your children away from their friends every summer, especially if you, like us, won't let them bring their PlayStations because they should be outside in the fresh air, cutting their legs off. So we ship their friends over here too. Hundreds of them. This means it's impossible to concentrate on the plight of Australia's Vietnamese boat people when there are only six Crunch Corners left and Isobel wants them all. And Arabella doesn't like anything green. And Tom will eat chips only if they are the shape of a 1973 Ford Mustang. And Dan's retching because of the samphire.

In an office in EC1, none of this ever happens.

You should see the cargo ship that just trundled by – its

huge diesel engine drumming the beat of international trade as its bluff prow waged an endless game of shudder-me-rivets with . . .

Sorry. Australia. Immigration. Er . . . I don't care. I'll worry about it when I get back to work. Here, by the seaside, I am on holiday, which is not the same thing. I'm therefore off for a beer.

Sunday 20 July 2008

By 'eck, our funny accents are the envy of the world

As I write, a team of researchers at Leeds University is working its way through £460,000 of our money, preparing a language and dialect atlas of Britain in the twenty-first century. Good. This is an excellent and important use of public money.

I can understand why the world started on the rocky path to civilization with so many different languages. Thousands of years ago, before the internet came along, it was extremely unlikely that a tribe in New Guinea would come up with the same word for a carrot as a bunch of Basques living in the Pyrenees. I can also work out why languages die. There is simply no point speaking a tongue that's shared by only four other people. It's a waste of paint on the signposts.

That said, I do not understand why English, which has been around since the Saxons put down their axes, has so many regional variations. And, more important, why those regional variations are still with us today, now that we all watch the same television programmes whether we live in Durban, Detroit, Darwin or Dunstable.

My youngest daughter, who seems to spend half her day watching pink animated crap from America, is part of the generation that thinks you dial 911 if you want the police and that 'colour' has no 'u'. You'd expect her therefore to sound like Paris Hilton. And yet when she opens her mouth, it's as though Joyce Grenfell isn't dead after all.

Then there's estuary English, concocted from a base of cockney and enlivened with constant use of the word 'like', which comes from Los Angeles, and the word 'fink' instead of 'think', which is a West Indian add-on; many say its spread across Britain is thanks to the popularity of *EastEnders*. This, however, can't be so because otherwise they'd speak it in Inverness too, and they don't.

It's not as if we cannot change the accents with which we were born. If you listen to the Queen on a recording made in 1956, it sounds as though she's speaking while trying to keep a peeled grape between her buttocks, and that her vocal cords are actually made from glass. Whereas today she sounds like any normal public-school games mistress.

Margaret Thatcher did the same thing and, if I'm honest, so did I. When I was eleven I was offered a part in a radio play, provided I lost my Yorkshire accent. I did, and it remained lost until I returned to the north after five years away at school, when, without my thinking, it came back. Then, when I moved to London, it was replaced, quite by accident, with an accent so Sloanily preposterous that I'm surprised I was able to buy anything in a shop without the man on the till being filled with an uncontrollable urge to leap over the counter and kick my head in.

Today I think I speak what most people would call BBC, or received, English. But no. The other day, a linguistics expert, not knowing anything about my early life, listened to me for a while and said 'Doncaster'. Not Barnsley, you'll note, or Sheffield. He was very specific and absolutely right. Apparently, it's the way I say 'one'.

This science of speech was much used when the police had a tape from someone they believed was the Yorkshire Ripper. Anyone could tell the voice was Geordie. Experts, however, could nail it down to a specific village. And they still can. Despite Paris Hilton and *EastEnders*, Kettering, for instance, still has an accent quite unlike the one used in neighbouring Corby.

According to the scholars, you can zigzag across America for a year and encounter only four different accents (I find that a bit hard to believe, but whatever). In Britain you can drive for just one day and each time you stop for petrol, the cashier will sound different. It's Punjabi in the morning, Hindi at lunchtime and Tamil in the evening.

I love this variety, although of course it can cause problems. I, for instance, would never employ anyone with a Brummie accent. I don't wish to be rude to the people of Birmingham, but I'm sorry, it makes you sound thick. Likewise, whenever I meet someone with a Somerset burr, I always imagine that in the next five minutes I'm going to be tied to a candlelit table, with a goat, and raped.

I'm not unusual in this respect. If you walk into a Glossop pub with a Stalybridge accent, someone is going to drop you. And if a Liverpudlian ever tries to get a job reading the national news, someone on the anti-racist, anti-ageist, pro-whale *Guardian* interview panel is going to say: 'The door is the wooden thing in the wall behind you.'

If, however, you have a Yorkshire accent, advertisers will want to give you huge lumps of money for voicing a television commercial because, apparently, it makes you sound honest. This explains why Sean Bean is currently trying to sell me absolutely everything.

And no. You cannot try to adopt a Yorkshire accent because unless you are from Yorkshire you will shorten the word 'the' to a 't', like Robert Carlyle did in *The Full Monty*. That's wrong. Dick Van Dyke wrong. Ray Winstone's *Cold Mountain Deep South . . . London* wrong. Sean Connery in everything he's ever done wrong. In Yorkshire the word 'the' is replaced by the briefest pause and a small nod of the head.

This small thing is important because when the world finally realizes French, German and, yes, even Mandarin

Chinese have no place in a modern English-speaking world, we can continue to have our national, and indeed regional, differences highlighted every time we open our mouths to order a McDonald's.

Sunday 27 July 2008

Peep in my wife's knicker drawer and see what you get

I should have written about Max Mosley last week. But I couldn't. I walked round the garden until my shoes were worn out, I looked at the view, I sucked half a dozen Biros dry and I was still sitting here, as the paper's deadline passed, unable to form a cohesive opinion.

Here's the problem. I like to think I am a journalist. I know the nation's proper journalists will harrumph at that and explain that three years on the *Rotherham Advertiser* and a certificate of competency in shorthand don't make me a proper hack, any more than a stint as a Saturday shop girl qualifies someone to run Wal-Mart.

But be that as it may, I trained to be a journalist, I love journalism. And I crave the company of journalists. So, wearing this hat, I am absolutely appalled by the implications of the Max Mosley outcome. I mean, here is a man whose strength of character is such that he thinks: 'No. I won't do any work this afternoon. I'll go to a flat in Chelsea where five prostitutes will check my hair for lice.'

Is it important that we know this? You're damn right it's important. This guy was effectively elected to his position at the FIA, the governing body of Formula One, by 125m people. He is therefore a public figure, and we can't have public figures bunking off for a bit of sex in German. It is also important we know that David Mellor was dressing up in a Chelsea kit while shagging some floozy and that John Major was bathing with Edwina Currie. Because if a prime minister can't keep his pecker in his trousers, then how do we know he can't keep his fingers off the button that fires the Tridents? If we have a law that prevents the press from investigating wrongdoing among public figures then it is carte blanche for the entire House of Lords to spend the rest of the year gorging on swan while taking it in turns to do man love on the woolsack.

But here's the problem. It is extremely rare that the newspapers these days go after genuine charlatans. Every day, I hear rumours of malpractice in charities, or fraud in business, but with dwindling circulations and advertising revenue in freefall, the press simply doesn't have the funds any more to chase leads. Woodward and Bernstein seem to have been replaced by a bunch of desk-bound journos who rewrite press releases from global-warming lunatics and run a couple of pap pictures of Madonna buying an ice cream.

Which brings me on to the dilemma. Because while I trained as a journalist, I wound up on television, which makes me a celebrity. Which means that, despite my best efforts to lead a quiet life, I am constantly photographed by a stream of two-bit losers who think my new shoes are in some way of importance to the nation.

On this basis, I found myself cheering wildly when the Mosley verdict came through. Because at last I knew the press could no longer come up my drive and take pictures of what's in my garage. The *Mirror* actually did that the other day. It opened my garage doors and took photographs. Which is exactly the same as opening my wife's knicker drawer and photographing what's in there. That's just out of order.

Then you've got Jonathan Ross. You can take it from me that he does not earn £6m a year. Nothing like. But the press can print that, amid stories that Madonna's had an affair, that Alan Davies has eaten a tramp and that Lily Allen has been swimming.

I do not know many people from the world of television. I have not been to Jonathan Ross's house. He's never been to mine. But those that I do meet, with the exception of Piers Morgan, are mostly very ordinary people with very ordinary lives. They do not shout: 'Do you know who I am?' at every train guard and maitre d'. They do not quaff champagne or gorge on peach and peacock. And mostly they earn much less than you think. And yet every single one of them is fair game for those members of the press that, deprived of funds to chase down proper stories, see them as the cheap option. I urge you all to think about that next time you're thumbing through *Heat* magazine and you come across a picture of some actress with stretch marks. Just imagine how that picture makes her feel. And how it makes her children feel.

Happily, however, Max Mosley, and Princess Caroline of Monaco, who won a similar case recently – although not involving any headlice – has finally put a stop to it. And if that means I can buy a cup of coffee without having my effing photograph taken every five seconds, I say hallelujah to that.

See the problem. As a journalist, I would say it is interesting for the public to know whether Madonna has had an affair but as a celebrity on her side of the fence, I would argue vehemently that it is not in the public interest. We have reached a point where newspapers will be disinclined to run any story on extramarital rumpy pumpy even though there is no actual British law preventing them from doing so. Just the interpretation of a tangential European law by one judge. What's more, there never will be a British law because if any politician stood up and proposed such a thing, everyone would jump to the conclusion that he's got a free private jet from the Syrians and a dungeon at home full of Thai ladyboys.

The only solution I can come up with is this: I am allowed to write what I want about whoever I want. But if anyone writes about me, I'll stick so many lawyers up their arses, they'll be able to turn a Vespa round in there.

Sunday 3 August 2008

Miss Street-Porter, I have a job for you in Cambodia

Since we're told charity begins at home, it's better, I've always thought, to give £1m to a hapless British person than 10p to an organization that provides sandwiches for prisoners in Turkey. Now, however, I have decided that, actually, charity begins in Cambodia.

Some people get all dewy-eyed about Africa. That's jolly noble, but I don't see the point because I fear that no matter how much money you pump in, the bejewelled pigs that run the place will pump it straight back out again, into the coffers of Kalashnikov and Mercedes-Benz. The only thing I'd send to the dark continent is a team of SAS hitmen to shoot the likes of Mr Mugabe in the middle of his face.

Others would say that we have enough problems on our own shores without getting all teary over the children of Mr Pot. I disagree, because these days, every time I think of underprivileged people in Britain, the hideous face of Shannon Matthews's mum pops into my head, all greasy, fat and stupid, and it's hard to summon up any sympathy at all. Cambodia, though, is different. It's a country of 14m people but between them they have only about 5m legs. In fact, there are 25,000 amputees, the highest ratio per capita of any country in the world. This is not because Cambodians are especially clumsy. It is because of landmines.

Nobody knows how many mines were laid during the endless cycle of warfare, but it's sure to be in the millions. What we do know is that since the Vietnamese invaded in 1979 and drove the madman Pol Pot into the hills, 63,000 people have trodden on one. One man has had his left leg blown off four times. They gave him a good prosthetic after the first and second explosions, but since then he's had to make his own out of wood. And it's still going on today. In most places in the world, you can get three rice harvests per year from your paddy field. In Cambodia, it's one. This is partly because the Khmer like a weird sort of rice that's harder to grow, but mostly it's because you set off with your plough and within minutes there's a big bang and your water buffalo has become a crimson mist.

As a result of the ordnance lying in every field, no one is fighting for a right to roam in Cambodia. They have no equivalent of the Ramblers Association. They have no concept of Janet Street-Porter. In fact they have no concept of England. Because the education is so poor, most people there believe the world is made up of four countries: Thailand, Laos, Cambodia and Vietnam. Everywhere else is France. All white people are therefore French. Angelina Jolie, who adopted a Cambodian baby, does much to help clear the landmines and has been made a Cambodian citizen, is French. I was French. And every night, most of the men settle down to watch Manchester United and Chelsea slug it out for honours in the French Premier League. I'd never met an adult anywhere in the world (apart from America) who'd never heard of Great Britain. In Cambodia nobody had.

What's more, you will never see a Cambodian person wearing sunglasses. Mainly this is because the average wage in Cambodia is less than £400 a year and so Ray-Bans are a bit out of range. But also it's because Cambodians all have flat noses. So sunglasses simply fall on to the floor every time you hop to the shops, and every time your buffalo explodes.

That's what did it for me. The sunglasses. Not the

education. Not the notion of living in a country where there is no Janet Street-Porter. The landmines made my eyes prickle, but my heart just mushroomed over the idea that they can't afford to wear shades. And that even if they could, they'd keep falling off.

I have therefore decided that I must do something. Unfortunately, however, we all reach a point like this when we decide we must help, and then it's so very hard to know what should be done next. Secretly we all know that for every pound we donate to a large charity, only 2p actually reaches the people we have in mind. The rest is spent on adverts for highly paid coordinators in the *Guardian* and expensive offices in London's glittering West End.

You always feel you want to go to the root of the problem. But in the bee that's come to nest in my roost, that'll be hard. Earlier this summer a team of Australian doctors happened upon a little girl in the town of Siem Reap. Her face had been horribly disfigured, by a bloody landmine I suppose, and they were overwhelmed with a need to help. They went to meet her parents, and her father was keen that his daughter be sent to Australia for plastic surgery. Her mother, however, went ballistic when she discovered the poor child would once again look normal. 'How will she be able to beg then?' she asked. And the Aussie medics were sent packing.

I can't even ring the Cambodian government for help because I fear it would be extremely enthusiastic and then all the money I sent over would be spent on fixtures and fittings in the finance minister's next luxury hotel. That's if I could raise any money in the first place. It's hard when money's tight here and everyone else has their own pet project.

I suppose I could write to Ray-Ban asking it to design a cheap pair of shades that can be worn by someone who has no nose. But I think it'd be better if I started work on some designs for the most brilliant mine-clearing vehicle the world has ever seen. I'm thinking of strapping some ramblers together, and then . . .

Sunday 14 September 2008

Hey, let's live fast and die when ministers tell us to

So, how are you going to die? It's a tricky question and unless you are currently on your way to an American airbase in Baghdad, while wearing a C-4 explosive vest, the chances are you haven't got a clue.

Certainly, if you'd asked Mrs Carol Colburn in May how she was going to shuffle off this mortal coil, she wouldn't have said: 'Well, tomorrow I imagine that I'll be scratched by a rat which will have traces of urine on its claws. Yes. That's how I'll meet my end.' But I'm afraid that's exactly what happened.

Similarly, if you'd asked the Greek playwright Aeschylus how he thought he would go to meet his maker, I bet you any money he wouldn't have said: 'Good question. And I think it almost certain that what will happen is this: I shall be out for a walk and an eagle will drop a tortoise on my head.'

We spend the first part of our lives imagining that we will not die at all, and the second part hoping that we will slip into the darkness of eternity, aged about 105, while fast asleep.

Undoubtedly, Kenneth Pinyan would have wanted this – but instead, in 2005, he received a spot of horse sex from his beloved stallion and, presumably a bit embarrassed by what had happened, chose not to seek medical help for the fatal injury that resulted.

Of course, if you choose to make love with a horse, you must have an inkling that no good will come of it. It's not like becoming so engrossed in a video game that you play nonstop for fifty hours and die of tiredness. That's what happened last year to a chap in South Korea called Lee Seung Seop.

That's the sort of thing that causes me to sweat. How many times have I done something apparently harmless that could very easily have killed me? How many times have I been unwittingly close to death in a car, or while wiring a plug?

How many times has an eagle dropped a tortoise where I had been standing only seconds earlier? And how do I know that right now, aged forty-eight, on a Saturday afternoon, my carotid artery isn't just about to rend itself asunder?

I hate the uncertainty. I hate the idea that later I might sit on the suction pump in my swimming pool and have my intestinal tract pulled clean out of my bottom. That happened to someone in America last year. Someone who'd woken up that morning imagining that it was going to be just another normal day.

Death also came unexpectedly to Isadora Duncan, who must have thought: 'I've taken the roof off my car, so because it'll be a little bit chilly, I'll wear this long scarf . . .' You see flowers at the side of the road these days, a petrol-station reminder that someone was just on their way home from work when the final curtain came slamming down. It makes me shiver with fear.

There's another problem, too. Because, like you, I harbour a vague notion that I'm not going to die until I've had a telegram from Buckingham Palace – or is it an e-mail these days? – I'm going to stay in to watch television tonight. I certainly wouldn't be doing that if I thought that in the morning I was going to trip while pulling on my trousers and break my neck.

Think. You are reading this now, on a Sunday morning,

and you probably have nothing on for the rest of the day. But what if you knew for sure that tonight you were going to explode? You'd get off your arse and try wing-walking. Or see how many baked beans you can eat with a cocktail stick in less than a minute. In short, you'd do something useful.

And that has given me a bonzo idea. We may be capable of living for 100 years, but most of the time we're not really living at all. We are wasting time, doing nothing in particular. And I'm sure this attitude would stop if we knew precisely when our time was going to be up.

So why doesn't the government introduce a law that forces everyone to jump off Beachy Head when they are sixty-five? This way, you would cram every single waking moment of every single day with stuff, adventure and excitement. It really would be a Brave New World.

And if you were unfortunate enough to die early, with, say, a stingray's pointy bit in your heart, you wouldn't traipse through the Pearly Gates thinking: 'Damn. If only I'd made love to a few more women.' Because under my proposals you'd have made love to them all. And, what's more, as the day of doom drew near, you'd have a chance to make sure that the local donkey sanctuary, and not your miserable family, was going to inherit all your belongings.

You'd also have the opportunity to say goodbye to your loved ones, a scene that was denied to Martin of Aragon, who, over supper one night and in rude health, died from an uncontrollable burst of laughter.

You'd also be able to choose to die with dignity, something that was not afforded to Evelyn Waugh, Elvis Presley or Lenny Bruce, all of whom went west, rather ignominiously, on the lavatory.

I can see the government liking my idea very much. Partly because ministers love bossing us about in life, so it stands to reason they'll also love telling us when to die. Partly because fewer people means less global warming. And partly because, with a looming pensions crisis, a number of economic problems would be averted if everyone got the gold clock and immediately hurled themselves on to the Central line.

Sunday 21 September 2008

Don't let banks lose your money –
do it yourself

A few months ago I was seated at dinner next to a banker and, as you can imagine, my watch immediately started going backwards. Minutes crawled by, and as he droned on about derivatives and sub-prime markets in America I began to wonder if it would be poor form to stab him in the eye with my lobster scissors. Instead I decided to try to will myself to death. But then I was snapped into hair-straightening consciousness when he casually mentioned that the giant Union Bank of Switzerland was in trouble.

UBS? That's where I'd plonked all my life savings. What do you mean, trouble? Are you saying that because some Mexicans can't afford to pay their mortgages I'm in danger of losing the fruits of a lifetime's graft? The answer, when translated and condensed, was yes.

The next day, in a bit of a flap, I rang the bank, which quite understood my concerns and offered to transfer the bulk of my savings to a company I'd never heard of. It was called AIG.

As you can imagine, the past two weeks have been most enjoyable. No wait. That's the wrong word. I mean blood-in-my-feet, dead-faint-half-the-time terrifying. As I sat there on that horrible Monday, watching the whole financial world on the brink of collapse, I thought back to all the midnight oil I'd burnt writing these columns, all the crappy hotels I'd stayed in while making various television shows. And how all of that revenue would be lost for a raft of reasons I simply didn't understand.

Of course I made strenuous efforts to get my money out of AIG as soon as the scale of its problems became apparent. But it wasn't possible. It had shut the fund in which I'd invested and it would remain closed for three months while it tried to sell the assets. 'We need to do this in an orderly fashion,' said the man on the phone, calmly.

Inwardly I was screaming. I don't give a shit about an orderly fashion, any more than a man in the trenches wants to look smart while running for his life. It's my money. I gave it to you. You've squandered it on a Mexican's house in San Diego and a stupid football team and that's your problem. Not mine.

It turned out, however, that I was wrong. It was my problem, so I decided to try to understand banking. And what I've gleaned from a two-week crash course is that it is completely unfathomable. There isn't a single person in the entire world who has the first idea how the system works. It's like the internet. An entity. Something that can be brilliant or terrible, depending on nothing that the human mind can grasp. But either way, it cannot be turned off.

This, for example, is what AIG had to say about the situation. 'Approximately $307 billion . . . of the $441 billion in notional exposure of AIGFP's super senior credit default swap portfolio represented derivatives written for financial institutions, principally in Europe, for the purpose of providing regulatory capital relief rather than risk mitigation. In exchange for a minimum guaranteed fee, the counterparties receive credit protection with respect to diversified loan portfolios they own, thus improving their regulatory capital position.' That's not English. So far as I know, it's not even human. It is rhyming slang for bank.

Then, for no reason that anyone can explain, news came through that the American taxpayer had rescued AIG. I was beside myself with happiness. I was also in California. So I turned off the CNN business report – the BBC was doing something on global warming, as usual – ran downstairs and, much to the surprise of the hotel doorman, thanked him and everyone in the lobby for getting me out of such a deep and confusing hole.

Sadly, however, it turns out I'm still in it. You see, I've just received a letter from an AIG assistant general manager – it has obviously put its top men on the job – saying that I can either have a fraction of my investment back in December, or I can take out a new fund – using imaginary money that obviously doesn't exist – and hope to get it all back at some unspecified point in the future. Now, I'm a gambler. I love the horses and playing cards. But this is a big one. This is keeping me awake at night. Can I really put twenty years of savings on red and hope that Carlos the Mexican sells his pick-up truck to pay off his mortgage?

My banker can't help. He, like everyone, is caught up in a whirlwind of uncertainty. I asked him a million questions and he hasn't been able to answer one. Advice? There'd been plenty in the good times – but now? I might as well have asked my dog for guidance.

It's the same story with the newspapers and the government. There is much finger-pointing. Blame is flying everywhere. It's the bankers. It's the Mexicans. It's capitalism. It's the price of oil. It's the Chinese. And, on the BBC of course, it's global warming. This is all very natural. But it doesn't really help.

And so it's up to me to come up with what I hope, for once, is a spot of sensible advice for those who are in the same boat.

Because there is no safe haven for your money, you need to give it to someone else. That way, it becomes their problem.

So, why not pay your income tax early? And call your kids' school to see if you can settle all forthcoming fees in advance. Need a new car? Why not buy one now?

Certainly I've decided not to send out any invoices right now. I simply wouldn't know where to put the cash. And so with that in mind, if you are the accountant at the *Sunday Times* and you are reading this, the payment I would like for this week's column is four lamb chops.

Sunday 28 September 2008

Fingers on buzzers, you bunch of ignorant twerps

Current plans to cut ITV's obligations as a public-service broadcaster would mean it'd have no need to fill the cracks in its open-the-box, come-on-down schedules every night with regional news programmes.

That would be excellent. I loathe regional news programmes. They're always full of fat women wearing 'Save our school' T-shirts that they've hurriedly pulled on over their normal clothes for the cameras, and pointless vox pops, and puffed-up councillors and green issues and plans for incinerators and recycled press releases, delivered with a solemn voice by a woman in an ethnic headscarf, in a bid to give them credence and weight.

However, while the demise of *Grantham Today* is a cause for celebration, I do believe this is yet another rivet removed from the aeroplane wings of civilization, and soon you'll turn on *Newsnight* to find Jeremy Paxman in clown shoes urging parties from either side of the political divide to settle their differences in a bout of mud wrestling.

Sadly I believe that television mirrors society. It was in black and white because we were. It made fun of West Indians when we did. It featured Terry Scott because we told lame jokes as well, and when we went to the pub, we didn't like all that 'foreign muck' on the menu either.

This is the problem with what's happening today. Because anyone with half a brain and speech genes that function properly is derided as a hoity-toity snob, all of television is aimed at the *Heat*-reading halfwits who literally don't know anything. We celebrate our ignorance of the Large Hadron Collider, we make sneery noises when someone from Fulham appears on a game show, and as a result, when we tune in to BBC1 on a Saturday night, Vanessa Feltz is being pushed into a swimming pool because she can't lie on the floor with her legs wide apart.

At the moment, television companies imagine that they must cater to the bovine masses or else their viewing figures and advertising revenue will dwindle to nothing. They know that when Jade Goody gets cancer the nation mourns and when Stephen Hawking speaks everyone laughs. So they fear that if they do not make shows for pig-ignorant northern lard buckets the nation will switch off the set and do something else with its time instead.

But what? The internet? Oh come on. This is a horrible place full of lies, hate, pornography and a billion apostrophes all in the wrong place. What's more, eventually it will cause you to end up in bed with someone inappropriate, or you will upset a German who will come round to your house and stab you in the heart. Or maybe the television execs imagine that we will all say, 'Well, Vanessa Feltz isn't falling into a swimming pool tonight so I shall read a book instead.' Really? Can you imagine Jade Goody saying that? Or Shannon Matthews's mum? Or anyone you saw in town today? Basket weaving, then? Or brass rubbing? Or maybe they think we'll all spend our evenings embroidering kneelers for the local parish church. Maybe in Simon Heffer's village. But not mine. Or yours. Or anywhere real.

Television companies need to be brave. They need to accept that, because there's nothing else to do of an evening, especially when money's tight, they may as well broadcast shows that enlighten us a bit. Unfortunately this is not going to happen, because shows are like nuclear weapons. Once one broadcaster is transmitting a Day-Glo bucket of primordial sludge to suit the average ignoramus, all the others have to follow suit. There can be no unilateral disarmament. They all have to agree to ditch Vanessa. Or it won't happen.

And so with that in mind I have come up with a proposal for Ofcom, the broadcasting regulator. Instead of removing the chocks of decency from the wheels of human degeneration you must stop thinking of TV as a mirror and insist it becomes a beacon.

Quiz shows should be designed to reward the bright and humiliate the stupid. Chris Tarrant must be banned from commiserating with the contestant who doesn't know anything and encouraged instead to look incredulous. There must be debates on Ibsen in every episode of Coronation Street, and Stephen Fry will be made to appear on everything. There will be peak-time Greek from Boris Johnson. QVC will be forced to drop the trinketry and sell fine English shotguns. And I want a show featuring Eton boys who go to a different northern city each week to laugh at the people who live there.

Ofcom must be made to remove the pink, the saccharine, the goofy, the idiotic, the cheap and the nasty and replace them all with Paxman. There will be no more traffic cops pretending that what they do is interesting and a lot more Kevin McCloud.

For guidance, I direct all of you to *Harry and Paul*, the latest BBC1 series featuring Harry Enfield and Paul Whitehouse. Here we find a couple of performers who presume the audience have a modicum of knowledge and a scintilla of intelligence. If you don't know what *The Duchess of Malfi* is or how the Sicilian Defence can be used, you won't get it. It is not aimed at Jade Goody. It's not even aimed in her general direction. It is, however, even though they've been jolly mean to me, the best television comedy I've seen since *Monty Python*. I'd like to think it's more than an island for the bright in a sea of purple and blue snot. I'd like to think it's a launch pad to fire a thousand rapier-sharp Oxbridge wits from the Footlights and into the comedians who strut about on TV these days imagining that they'll get a laugh if they climb on to Vanessa Feltz and make her eat a centipede.

Sunday 5 October 2008

Play it my way, kids, and you'll save rock'n'roll

Any slim hope we might have had of a Pink Floyd reunion tour was dashed recently by the death of the keyboard player, Rick Wright. Oh, sure, the remaining members could still settle their differences, find another keyboard player and get back on the road but, and here's the thing, would I go? Would I be watching Pink Floyd? Or nothing more than a facsimile of the outfit that provided a soundtrack to my life thus far?

We see much the same thing today with Queen. Or 'the Queen', as my dad liked to call them. They're out there now, strumming and banging their way through all the old favourites. They even have Paul Rodgers on vocals – and Paul, in my opinion, is the greatest rock singer of them all. But is it Queen without Freddie Mercury?

As you may know, I am a very big Who enthusiast. I saw them first in 1975 at the Bingley Hall in Stafford, and it was the start of something wonderful. But then Keith Moon shot into the next life through a puddle of vomit, and every time I've seen them since – it's thirteen and counting – I've always felt that, despite the best efforts of Kenney Jones and Zak Starkey, I'm not really seeing the band that gave us *Who's Next*. And now, with Entwistle gone, the problem will be even bigger.

Over the years, we have seen many bands hit by the untimely death of a member. The Pretenders were particularly unlucky. They'd been going only four years when James Honeyman-Scott died after a drug overdose. Then, less than a year later, the original bassist was dead as well. Meanwhile, being in the New York Dolls was more dangerous than taking part in the all-comers'-East-African-sex-without-a-condom competition. Recent plans for a second comeback tour were almost aborted when one of only three remaining members decided to up sticks and drop dead. Today, I'm told, Thin Lizzy continue to tour. Great. Until I tell you the band is actually made up of one bloke who played rhythm guitar on 'Whiskey in the Jar' and 'some other blokes'. That's not really Thin Lizzy, is it? And it's the same story, apparently, with the Four Tops, who really ought to be called A Top and Some Interlopers.

But we'd better get used to this sort of thing. At the moment, the *Daily Telegraph*'s obituary pages are full of Second World War heroes who charged into enemy lines armed with nothing but a pearl-handled butter knife. Soon, those guys will all be gone and, instead, we'll be reading about brave Joe Walsh, who became so fed up with fellow band members knowing he was about to break into their hotel room with a chainsaw that he bought a silent electric version. This way, they would still be in bed, asleep, when he came through the wall. In other words, the few rock stars who survived the heroin and cocaine will soon succumb to the misery of old age. And then what?

Trying to replace them is like trying to replace the foot from a beautiful old grandfather clock. Yes, you could have a craftsman knock up a new one, and it would undoubtedly do a splendid job of keeping the timepiece upright. But every time you looked at it, you'd know all was not right with the world. And, anyway, what's the point, when the clock face, the pendulum and the weights are about to give up the ghost as well? So what's to be done?

My wife insists that there is plenty of fresh talent coming along to replace the dinosaurs. She is wrong. The Franz Flighters, Car-sick Steve and the Frascatis are derivative and hopeless and I do not wish to listen to any of the noises they make. I certainly wouldn't pay even so much as one penny to see the Red Hot Chili Peppers, who, so far as I'm concerned, could not make a worse sound if they spent an hour attacking giant sheets of polystyrene with a flock of electrocuted cats. I hate them. I want to see Genesis and Yes and Pink Floyd. I want to see Stevie Winwood and Eric and Supertramp and Bad Company. But I have the most horrible feeling that I've already seen them all for the last time.

There is, however, a solution. At the moment, tribute bands have a fairly poor reputation. But I'm not sure why. When elderly people go to see Rachmaninov's Third, no one is ever disappointed to find that it isn't actually the man himself on the ivories. Indeed, many derive a great deal of pleasure in hearing how other musicians interpret the great man's work. In fact, when you stop and think about it, the London Symphony Orchestra is a tribute band. It simply turns up and plays music written by someone else.

So why can't we encourage this sort of thing among today's youngsters who wish to forge a career in the world of rock'n'roll? Instead of asking them to write their own material, which will be rubbish, we should ask them to interpret work by the masters: Camel, Gong and so on. At present, tribute bands try to reproduce exactly what their heroes did. Some are astonishingly good. I once saw a Floyd tribute band in Alaska who were semitone-perfect. But why can't they experiment? Try to improve on the original? As we saw when Gary Jules rejigged the Tears for Fears song 'Mad World', a modern twist can be extremely enjoyable and successful.

We see this with every performance of the Royal Shake-speare Company. We see it with every orchestra. And soon we will see it with rock music too. It's not the real thing. But it's the next best thing. And that'll have to do.

Sunday 12 October 2008

Ditch the laptop and suit if you wanna stay alive, Mr Corporate

It seems likely that in the next few months most businesses in the world will go bankrupt – so, to make sure yours isn't one of them, I've prepared a handy cut-out-'n'-keep guide on how to get ahead in the world of commerce. And stay there.

First of all, the laptop has to go. At present, the world's businessmen are physically incapable of sitting down at an airport for a moment without flicking open the computer and pulling a serious face while pretending that the machine is actually doing something. It isn't. You spend the first five minutes waiting for the damn thing to stop making Brian Eno chiming noises and the next twenty discovering that it won't connect to either 3G or the Edge, and that you cannot remember the password you chose for the T-Mobile hotspot. Then, by the time your son's birth date has been e-mailed to an account and you discover you can't access that either, they have called your flight and it's time to go.

So instead of pretending to be an international mover and shaker who cannot be out of touch for a moment, leave the damn thing at home and spend the time either thinking about stuff or reading a good book. Both of these activities will ensure you're a better, cleverer person, and that's a good thing because most people would rather do business with a chap who's read *The Power of the Dog* by Don Winslow than some nerd who reckons a widescreen iMac PowerTrip makes him look important.

Next. Your mobile phone. In the past few months I have

spent a great deal of time in airports and I've noticed corporate types have started to hold the handset with one hand and use the other hand to shield their mouth. This is absurd. In a Robert Ludlum novel there are a great many industrial spies who can lip-read, but in real life nobody can. So pack it in.

You can go ahead and have a normal conversation because the fact is we are not interested in what you are saying. You might like to think you look like an arms dealer who's negotiating with Kim Jong-il about the next consignment of nuclear centrifuges, but we know you aren't because you are called Steve and your clothes are from Burton.

Which brings me to the next point. Don't wear suits. It means you have to travel with a suit carrier, and that means you are shallow and stupid – i.e., more concerned about the creases in your trousers than the goods or services that you are trying to sell.

Oh, and when at leisure on a business trip, do not tuck your polo shirt into your trousers. This will make you look like an American.

Furthermore, when you are in the business lounge, do not drink orange juice. It is not big and it's not clever. Have a beer or some wine. In fact, since it's free, have a lot. Nobody likes a teetotaller. I would certainly not do business with any man or woman who walked into my office and asked for a glass of water. It's a sign that you are weak in the head.

And when staying in an international business hotel, do not go to the gym. Last week I was in Saigon, which is a fabulous city rammed with art, culture, bars and many restaurants where you can eat a snake's beating heart and tip its bile sac into a shot of vodka. And yet my hotel's gym was crammed with Steves lifting things up and putting them down again. For the love of God, what do you think you are doing? Get out of your shorts and go and see some paintings. You are blessed with a job that lets you travel. So don't waste your time drinking water, putting your stupid suit in a trouser press and lifting up stuff that's far too heavy. I know that you think it's a business thing to do, but it isn't. Forget your body. Think only about your mind.

That said, if you do go out, do not try to pick up a girl. Quite apart from the itches that will almost certainly result, you will look like a colossal berk sitting at the bar with a fourteen-year-old Twiglet running her bony little hand through what's left of your hair and claiming that you are a very handsome man. Don't be fooled. She will put her hand in your trousers, but only if she can subsequently get her hand in your wallet. Or, better still, your hand in matrimony and consequently a passport to come and live with you, briefly, in Guildford.

When you finally get to your meeting with the head of IT for i-IntelCorp (Far East division), don't kowtow. When Johnny Chinaman goes to see an American businessman, he doesn't wear a 10 gallon hat and ask the secretary to get him a Bud. So why do western businessmen do all that bowing and taking business cards with two hands? First of all, you're going to get the depth of your bow wrong, which is worse than not doing it at all. And worse, you're not being polite. You're being patronizing. You might as well ruffle the man's hair, for all the good it will do. So stop it. And don't sit on the floor. It may work in Japanese culture, but in this respect, Japanese culture is wrong. And don't play golf either.

Ever since the 1980s there has been a code of conduct for businessmen, and the result is a decimated stock market and the prospect of many years in the economic doldrums. This is because the people who should have been oiling the wheels of commerce have been in a gym or trying to impress their colleagues by owning an underwater laptop with millions of portals that connect to absolutely nothing at all.

There is a better way. Wear jeans. Read books. Talk normally on the phone. Make stuff that people want to buy. The end.

Sunday 19 October 2008

Take in a prisoner as a lodger and that's two problems solved

Disturbing news from the courts last week. A homosexual who killed and ate his lover was sentenced to thirty years behind bars. Which means, after he gets out a week on Tuesday, he's going to come round to your house, sprinkle you with some herbs and pop you in the oven.

Plainly, this is unacceptable and something must be done to keep cannibals out of our houses and our schools. But what?

Of course, I'm sure there are a great many people who think that if someone chooses one day to cook his best friend, he has demonstrated fairly clearly that he's resigned from the human race and must be shot in the forehead immediately, like a useless horse. However, I do not agree with capital punishment. I wish I did. Discharging 4m volts through anyone who has murdered, butchered or driven too slowly up the A44 would solve a great many problems, especially if carbon-neutral energy from wind farms were used. But because I find the idea of state execution abhorrent, I've had to spend the whole week dreaming up new ways of ensuring that people who can't behave properly are kept away from society for an appropriate length of time.

The problem right now is that all our prisons are full; and while there are plans to increase the number of cells over the coming years, few imagine for a moment that the supply will even remotely keep up with demand.

In Scotland, they are even talking of not putting anyone in jail for less than three months. This, say the Jocks, will free up space for those who really need to be there. It's a nice idea if you are a wishy-washy liberal, but it does mean that young men in hooded tops who run about town centres at night stealing mobile phones and pushing old ladies over cannot be punished at all. You can't fine them, because they have no money. You can't confiscate their belongings because everything they have is stolen anyway. You can't give them an electric ankle bracelet because that is seen as a mark of respect. And if you can't send them to prison, society is completely stuck.

The obvious solution is to build more prisons, but for a number of reasons, this isn't possible. First, Alistair Darling has given all our money to Mr Barclay, Mr Lloyd and Mr Rock, so there's none left. And second, the new prisons would have to be built somewhere. And everywhere is someone's backyard.

In the olden days, when I was rash, I dreamt up a plan that involved many more prisoners being housed in the jails we have already. The idea, in a nutshell, called for 'massive overcrowding'. If there are currently four to a cell, shove in another thirty, and don't worry about the cost of feeding them. Simply fit a window box and explain that they can eat only what they can grow. And if the harvest fails for any reason, well, they could take a leaf out of the cannibal's book and eat each other. The lavatory would be a bucket, the central heating would be the bucket, too, and for entertainment, there would be bullying on a grand scale.

I'm afraid, however, that I went off this idea because I actually know quite a few people who've done some time, and I don't like the idea of them sitting around all day trying to stop someone from eating their thighs.

Don't worry, however, because now I've come up with

another plan – and it's brilliant. At present, the government is doing a great deal to ensure that people who are struggling to pay their mortgages are not evicted from their houses by the recently nationalized banks. This is very noble. But the idea that you can borrow money to buy a house and then not pay it all back undermines the very essence of capitalism. People must be made to understand that, if they have dug themselves into a financial hole, they have to earn their way out again. And so, I believe the government should pay these people a small rent each month, which can go towards covering their mortgage, if they agree to have a prisoner staying in the spare room.

I admit this is a bit of a lottery. You could get a cannibal from Leeds who creeps into your bedroom every night with a knife and fork and some mango chutney. Or you could get Otis Ferry, who's on remand only because he wants to chase foxes. I'm not sure, though, that this is any different from the chance you take when you hire an au pair. You could get a moose who wants to practise her drop-kicks on your children or you could get a raving nymphomaniac who has an allergy to underwear. And anyway, let's be honest, it's a lottery for the prisoner as well because he could end up at my house, chained to a radiator for twenty-six hours a day in the Terry Waite suite. Or he could end up staying with a woman who bakes him cakes, lets him out for walkies and on Sundays allows him to chew on her bingo wings.

Plainly, an idea this radical needs to be tested before it's rolled out on a national scale, and I'm happy to be a guinea pig. Simply send me the chap from AIG who took my money and gave it to Wayne Rooney and now won't give it back, and I'll be happy to see how he likes being a prisoner in my spare room for a year or two. I should imagine, after the savage beatings and the dog sick, he'll be fully rehabilitated and able to go back into the world of international finance without feeling compelled to give any money to Wayne Rooney ever again.

Sunday 26 October 2008

Wake up and smell the coffee – tea is for morons

I quite understand why people choose to be communists or Australians or tattooed. I may not share your opinions, but I know why you have them and I would fight for you to be able to express them in public. Obviously not to the death, though. There's no way I am going to die so that a green person can climb up a chimney and write 'Gordon' on it, for instance. However, while I understand why people want to drive an electric car or cut the Queen's head off, and even why some people decide to emigrate to Spain, I do not understand why people continue to drink tea.

Recent figures show tea consumption is shrinking, especially among young people, yet Britain is still by far the largest consumer in the world per capita, with each person in the land drinking, on average, four cups a day. This is baffling. I quite like a cup at around 5 p.m. because this is 'tea time', but the figures suggest that many people are drinking it at 'coffee time' as well. Some, since there is such a thing as 'breakfast tea', must also be drinking it first thing in the morning. This is as mad as starting the day with a prawn cocktail – and it all has to stop.

First of all, asking for tea in someone's house is extremely antisocial because, if you take it with milk and sugar, this is a complicated, four-ingredient request. It's exactly the same as being offered a biscuit and saying, 'Ooh, thanks, but actually I'd prefer a Sunday roast.' Seriously. That means meat, potatoes and two veg. And there is no difference between this and tea, milk, sugar and boiled water. In fact, it's worse, because your host will have to find a teapot that hasn't been used since their wedding day and is at the back of a cupboard behind the equally dusty fondue set. In fact, the only thing I hate more than people asking for tea is people who ask for a gin and tonic. Why can't you just have a beer like everyone else? Because now I've got to hunt down not just the gin and the tonic, but also the lemon and some ice. At least with coffee most people have a machine that can deliver a refreshing and invigorating brew at the touch of a button. Furthermore, coffee drinkers, being more travelled and therefore intelligent, will take it in the European style. Black with nothing added.

Of course, you may say that coffee causes your teeth to go brown and your heart to explode. But tea, if we're honest, is as healthy as sucking on the pointy end of a machinegun. Eight per cent of a tea leaf is toxic, around 25 per cent is irrelevant, 2 per cent is nutritious caffeine and most of the rest is acids, arsenic, chlorophyll, salts and tannins – which are useful only if you want to give your stomach lining the texture of a horse's saddle. If I were to use the model dreamt up by environmentalists when discussing climate change, I could very easily argue that tea will cause you to lose control of your limbs and that you will have to spend the rest of your life in a wheelchair. Which could happen, for all I know.

Herbal varieties, however, are even more dangerous because if you come round to my house and ask for peppermint tea I will punch you in the mouth. Herbal tea is for nonces. At best, it is pointless. At worst, it is an affected piece of Hyacinth Bucket snobbery designed for the sort of people who spend half an hour deciding whether the wine they've been given is all right. And chai tea? Have you tried that? Well, don't – because you can achieve exactly the same effect, for a lot less, by drinking your own urine.

Of course, I dare say that some of you at this point are

wondering why I am writing about tea in these troubled times. And thinking that, surely, with Peter Mantelpiece back on the front line and the financial markets in disarray, there are more important things to worry about. Not so. Because when you stop and think about it, how many French or Italian banks have gone bust? And while we wobble, Spain's Santander bank is stalking the globe like one of the country's gigantic trawlers, sucking up the broken minnows.

This is because they are all coffee drinkers. They wake up, have an espresso; then, invigorated, they go to work quite literally full of beans. We, on the other hand, expect to be able to operate on a stomach full of wet leaves. Tea, in actual fact, caused our banking crisis. And before you point out that America is in a mess and they drink coffee, I should explain that they don't. They put half a granule in a Styrofoam bucket and call it coffee. But it's not. It's just a cup of warm water, and you can't operate on that either.

The most popular tea in Britain is the sort favoured by workmen. They like it because it takes an age to make and is far too hot to drink when it's ready. It is, in short, nothing more than an excuse for not doing any actual work. That's why it was so popular with empire-builders. They needed something time-consuming to fill the long, yawning hours. For the same reason, they played endless games of cricket.

Today, tea drinkers are clinging on to a way of life that's gone. Tea break. Tea time. Tea clippers. It's got to stop. Tea should be viewed in the same way as we view coal. Something from the past. Something that is no longer relevant. Something for those who see the world in monochrome, through the eyes of Terry and June.

In an espresso MTV world, tea no longer has any place.

Sunday 2 November 2008

Into the breach, normal people, and sod the polar bears

Greetings from the bunker. As I write, the MP for Ipswich is running around the country calling through his beard for me to be sacked. And the English Collective of Prostitutes is out for blood as well.

But let's be honest, shall we? There are more important things to worry about than what some balding and irrelevant middle-aged man might have said on a crappy BBC2 motoring show. Such as the war in Congo, the dramatic interest rate cut, the second coming in America and – most important of all – the gradual transformation of Scotland from a country full of deer and inventors into an enormous golf course.

Just last week an idiotic-looking American man whose hair is on back to front was given permission by cash-strapped Scottish politicians to build what sounds like the single most ghastly development the world has ever seen on top of what appears to be all of Aberdeenshire. Donald Trump, owner of the Miss World pageant and believed – by me – to be the world's largest consumer of onyx, says it will be the greatest golf course in the world. Can you even begin to imagine the depths to which he will sink in pursuit of this billion-dollar goal? How many pillars will there be? How many giant stone dogs will guard the entrance? It'll be McLexus Central.

And, really and truly, is it necessary? There are already, by my calculations, nearly 600 golf courses in Scotland. And since most of the residents live in Westminster these days, that works out at one for every two people. I simply cannot see why there's any need for another.

As far as I'm concerned, a golf course, with its random splashes of unnatural emerald green and its Rupert Bear trimmings, is more of a blot on the landscape than a pig farm or a power station. Scotland is properly beautiful, but already – if you look at it on Google Earth – it appears to have been dribbled on by a radioactive dragon. When Trump has finished it'll look even more stupid than his hair.

Unfortunately, if you wanted to try to stop Trump making things worse, you had to join forces with either the Rambling Association – which couldn't concoct a sensible thought if you gave every member a typewriter and a million years – or the environmentalists, who seemed bothered about only the possible effect on the area's sand dunes. Oh, and then the Royal Society for the Prevention of Birds piped up and said the new course would damage a warbler, which seemed a bit far-fetched.

This, almost certainly, is why the hateful proposals have been passed. Because sensible people who recognize Trump as a man who probably has bath taps in the shape of swan's wings couldn't possibly side with Mr Porritt, Mr Oddie and a bunch of purse-lipped, ramble-crazed mental cases.

At the moment, as far as I can see, all commercial planning applications are considered on just two issues: the economic benefit versus the man in the dirty trousers who's found a rare snail on the site and wants it to be protected. The Newbury bypass was a classic case in point. On the one hand you had the government, which wanted to free up the log jam of traffic, thus improving transport links between the Midlands and the south coast. And on the other you had that part-man, part-ape called Swampy who kept chaining himself to diggers and pointing at all the butterflies that were going to be squashed. You never heard from the people of Newbury who just thought: 'Yes. Build the damn thing

because then I'll waste less of my life in a bloody traffic jam.'
In other words, you never heard from anyone who was not
motivated by greed or rage.

We see this problem all over the world. The American
election came down to a two-way choice: a white man or a
black man. There are only two arguments on climate change:
you think you're to blame or you don't. You think Jonathan
Ross is brilliant. Or you think he should be sacked. No weight
or platform is given to the silent majority, for whom the third
way is rather more than some Blairite vision that existed only
in a New Labour speechwriter's wet dream.

I wish it were different because then the bright and the
informed, the people who couldn't really give a stuff about
warblers or sand dunes and have no desire to trample around
in other people's gardens just to keep alive the spirit of Lenin,
might conceivably have been able to convince the Scotch
government that Trump should be kept in America, where
his chintz and his patterned carpets go down well.

Certainly I believe there should be a third way when it
comes to all planning matters of this type. I believe we should
be incentivized enough to get off our bottoms and fight the
good fight – not because of a butterfly or a polar bear or
because we stand to make billions, but because golf courses
are awful and anything Donald Trump does sits like a golden
bogey on the unsullied face of a newborn child.

I want this to be a movement. A movement for normal
people. And I even have a leader in mind. Kevin McCloud
from *Grand Designs* on Channel 4. He should be forced by
law to appear in all planning committees where large projects
are being considered, so that he can argue the case from the
point of view of you and me.

For now, I suppose there is some good news to be gleaned
from the sorry saga of Trump's plans to turn Scotland into

Benidorm-by-the-Noo. One day he'll come over on his hideous private jet and open his terrible new golf course. And I cannot wait to see what the notorious winds in Aberdeenshire do to his barnet.

Sunday 9 November 2008

The daddy of all idiots at your child's school sports day

If I felt inclined, and I don't because I don't want to be robbed every night and stabbed over the breakfast table every morning, I think I'd make a rather good foster parent. Unfortunately, despite my fondness for reading Winnie-the-Pooh stories and having big coal fires to keep everyone warm at night, I would not be deemed suitable, because various well-meaning councils have determined that it's bad to place a child in the care of someone who is fat and who smokes. Sorry then, Lee. No Pooh and tickets to *Top Gear* for you, my lad.

This spotlights an interesting new development: that the government we elect to build street lamps and erect park benches now has a view on what makes a good parent and what makes a bad one. Fat's bad. Smoke's bad. Predatory vegetablism, though, is fine. And so is keeping the house at −42°C for environmental reasons.

Certainly, any parent who turns up to watch their kid play in a school sports match would be deemed 'extremely good', even though I've just returned from watching my son play rugby and it seems that absolutely no dad in Britain can do this properly. I do not know what it is that causes normal, bright and funny people to lose their grip on reality as soon as they find themselves standing alongside a school sports pitch. But since everyone does, what I've done for you is to prepare a handy cut-out-'n'-keep guide to what's acceptable and what's not.

First, parents must remember that they are an embarrassment to their children.

Mick Jagger is an embarrassment to his kids. I am an embarrassment to mine. You are an embarrassment to yours. Everything you do. Everything you say. Everything you wear. It's all completely wrong. So here's a tip when on the touch-line. Be normal.

If your child's team scores a try, you may applaud but do not – and this is something I witnessed just two hours ago – run on to the pitch, bellowing like a wounded animal, with a red face, a jugular vein standing 6 in proud of your neck and your arms held aloft like a triumphant boxer. Because after you have reached the middle of the pitch and sunk to your knees in a puddle of gratitude and happiness, you will realize you are the financial director of a leading advertising agency and you have just made yourself look like an idiot. Massive demonstrations of pride are acceptable if you are a Chelsea supporter and Didier Drogba has just slotted his eighth of the afternoon past Liverpool. But when you are watching a bunch of muddy twelve-year-olds running about like star-lings, they are not.

Also, no matter how knowledgeable you might be about the sport you're watching, do not feel free at any point to offer loud and hectoring advice. This will make everyone on the team want to kick you in the head and, since it's against school rules to attack visiting fathers, they will simply wait until they are in the showers after the game and kick your child instead. You may not smoke around your children to protect their lungs. You may feed them only brown rice to keep the cancer away. And you may give them only warm and fuzzy video games to preserve their minds. But if you shout on the touchlines you will end up breaking their noses by proxy. I guarantee it.

Furthermore, offering helpful hints at the top of your voice will irritate the ref, who may at some point come over and ask you to be quiet. This – and I've seen it happen twice – can end in a fight. And no one wants to see the divisional manager for a supermarket chain rolling around in the mud trying to punch his son's history teacher in the face.

You can always tell when people are likely to behave like this because they will be supporting the other team and will have taken a day off work and driven hundreds of miles to be there. This means the person in question is extremely enthusiastic – and that means he will suddenly lose track of what you are saying to him and start jumping up and down shouting 'Man on' and 'Face the ball' and other unintelligible things. And the next thing you know, he'll be wrestling in an undignified middle-aged way with Mr Jenkins from IVb.

If you find that someone has come from far away, walk off and talk to one of the women who turn up without a spouse in tow because they will be grateful for the company. I know this because any man who puts 'supporting my son in rugby matches' below the line of things he's prepared to do in the way of parenting is plainly hopeless as a husband. And there-fore his wife will want to have an affair with you. This is why almost all women on the touchline at rugby matches are dressed up to the nines.

However, and this is critical, when you have become engaged in small talk with a pretty mother and you are arrang-ing to meet for tea afterwards, do not get so distracted that you miss your child scoring a try. He doesn't want you there. He doesn't want you to make a noise. But trust me on this: he wants you to be watching at his moment of glory. So pay attention.

Now for the tricky part. When it's your own child who's put the team in front, for Christ's sake, keep calm. Do not shout, 'That's his eighteenth of the season so far,' because everyone will hate you. What I do is claim that it's his first-ever try and then, to hammer the point home, pretend to faint. One day I'm hoping this will make the pretty mother I'm invariably talking to give me the kiss of life.

Of course, this might irritate your boy if he were to turn round and find his dad being snogged by Fortescue minor's mum. But since just standing there will annoy him anyway, you may as well give it a try.

Sunday 16 November 2008

I'm a Tigger, he's a Piglet, and you must be a Pooh

Genetically speaking, you are almost completely identical to every other living thing on the planet. I mean this. If I could break into your house tonight and alter your DNA by just 2 per cent you would wake up in the morning as a cauliflower or a mighty Scotch pine or a worm.

At one end of the human spectrum you have the Polynesians. At the other you have the Basques. And all of us, all 6 billion of us, fit in between. Which means we cannot all be different. There simply cannot be 6 billion permutations of human being, any more than there can be 6 billion permutations of a cocktail stick. We know there are not 6 billion, or even six dozen, ways of being a hunting dog.

David Attenborough tells us this all the time. He says hunting dogs do this and hunting dogs do that. And then he goes under the Pacific Ocean to tell us that all salmon find the spot where they were born, and have sex and die. There is never a salmon swimming the other way, smoking a cheroot and wearing a big hat. Attenborough couldn't generalize like this if he were to make nature programmes about humans. He couldn't say: 'All humans are German photocopier salesmen and they all have Audis.' If he did, he'd get a letter from one of Sting's mates in Brazil, saying: 'I've got a dinner plate in my bottom lip. I do not have a photocopier and all I know about Germans is that they taste nice.'

I have never met anyone who is like me. And you have never met anyone who is like you. But it's a mathematical certainty that there are several of you out there and several of me. Scarily, that means there are several Piers Morgans as well.

Astrologers such as Mystic Meg will tell you that they've known this all along. That the human race in actual fact breaks down into twelve distinct groups that have nothing to do with nature, nurture or DNA. Mrs Meg says the positioning of the stars is why all Pisceans will give themselves a Brazilian this evening and why all Sagittarians will fall down the stairs. Plainly, however, this is nonsense. The Italian actress Claudia Cardinale is an Aries, like me, but I have never been asked for her autograph. And no one has ever exclaimed to me: 'How can you not be Elton John? You're so alike.'

Astrology is a hopeless way of subdividing our species. And so is the idea put forward by marketeers. They say that if you have a gigantic flatscreen television and like eating chips you are a C or a D, and if you are Nicholas Soames you are an A. It's all very Huxleyesque, but I'm afraid it's also rubbish because I have a massive telly and I eat chips, but I also shoot pheasants in the face and I enjoy driving quad bikes on the road. Perhaps this is why my junk mail invites me to buy tartan zip-up slippers and handmade English shotguns.

Then you have those who split the human race into tribes, saying that there is such a thing as 'the French' or 'the British'. No there isn't. I have nothing in common with Valerie Singleton and even less with Shannon Matthews's mum.

So how do we break down the human race into groups? This has occupied the minds of some of the greatest thinkers throughout history. But actually I suspect the answer was found in the middle of the last century by A. A. Milne. Yup. I gave this some serious thought in the bath this morning and I have decided that we are all either Pooh, Piglet, Tigger, Kanga, Roo, Wol, Rabbit or Eeyore.

Let us take the example of my colleagues on *Top Gear*. James May is Wol. He thinks he is very serious and very clever, but actually he can't even spell his name properly. Then there is Richard Hammond, who is Piglet. And though I have a big stomach and a fondness for elevenses whether it's eleven in the morning or four in the afternoon, I am Tigger. Think of anyone you know and I guarantee that, while they may not be pigeonholeable by race, star sign or socio-economic classification, they'll slot neatly into one of the characters from Winnie-the-Pooh.

Clement Freud? Eeyore. Lorraine Kelly? Kanga. Ant and Lard? They're Roos.

I believe the Winnie-the-Pooh stories are the funniest things ever committed to paper. Even today I cannot get through the tale of Richard Hammond taking Eeyore a balloon for his birthday present without collapsing on to the floor in helpless mirth. However, if you look beyond the tears and the life-threatening convulsions, you will find that all of human life is here.

Knowing this will be of huge benefit to marketing people. Digitas, for instance, can target the Eeyores while the nation's beekeepers can direct-mail the Poohs. It will also help the divorced. Instead of advertising for a Leo, which means you could end up with Alexandre Dumas or Alan Shearer, why not advertise for a Tigger? Then you'd know exactly what sort of person will be waiting for you at the Harvester with a red rose and a copy of the *Financial Times*.

Employers too will be able to cut through all the lies and the nonsense on a CV. There is, for instance, no point taking on a children's entertainer, no matter how well qualified he may be, if he is an Eeyore. And there is no point taking on a plasterer if he is a Tigger.

Funny, isn't it? If you laid out all the permutations for a

Rubik's Cube, the list would stretch for 261 light years. There are 519 quintillion alternatives for one of those cubes. And yet it turns out that for the human race there are just eight.

Sunday 23 November 2008

Sorry, worms, you won't be getting a piece of me

Being dead used to be ever so easy. They'd put you in a box, lower you gingerly into the ground and let you rot in peace. Or, if the ground in your town was full, they'd throw you on a fire and let you spend the rest of time in a vase, on your mother's mantelpiece.

Now, though, in the same way that you can get married underwater or during a parachute jump, you can choose how you wish to be disposed of when you have done dying. Just this week, for instance, a former navy diver called Derick Redfern was attached to the nose of a torpedo, which was then detonated on the sea bed off Plymouth. This means that now, and for all time, Mr Redfern is a part of the Gulf Stream.

Meanwhile, in Spain, officials at the Catalunya circuit near Barcelona announced on Monday that motor-racing fans can now be laid to rest at the track. Quite how this will work I don't know. It'll certainly be a big nuisance for Lewis Hamilton next year if he skids in the final corner on Geoff Simmons of Batley.

Perhaps they mean that a dead person can be used as part of the tyre wall. Or maybe to soak up oil spills.

Some may argue that if you are used as a crash barrier or detonated on the sea bed, some of death's dignity is lost. I'm not sure this is so, because I don't see much dignity in lying in a box with your eyes leaking out of your face either. Far better, surely, to use your liquefying body as a soft landing for racing drivers. And if you wind up in the Atlantic con-

veyor, at least you get to see the Caribbean once in a while –
something that's not possible if you are lying under 6 ft of
Surrey.

I've always said that when I die I want to be buried, because
if it turns out there is a heaven, it'll be hard to enjoy its boun-
tiful magnificence if I've been cremated. Seriously, you're
never going to pull an angel if you look like the contents of
a Hoover bag. It's for this reason I'm nervous about donor
cards. I don't think it'd be much fun in the land of milk and
honey with no liver.

However, now that it's possible to make all sorts of odd
requests, I'm reconsidering my post-Reaper strategy. This
needs serious thought. I know this because I have watched
people try to scatter the remains of their loved ones near my
holiday cottage on the Isle of Man. It sounds lovely, but
because it's always windy, the bereaved family normally ends
up going home with bits of their dearly departed dad in their
hair. This means that, far from ending up on a lonely rocky
outcrop, he winds up being washed down the plughole amid
much sobbing.

I see the same sort of problem with those who scatter the
ashes of loved ones in their back garden. Schoolboy error,
this, because one day it won't be a back garden any more. It'll
be a branch of Tesco or a Travis Perkins depot. And that
means your dad could end up as a breeze block. Or in the
sandwiches of someone he disliked.

Space is tempting because there's no wind, and it doesn't
change, and I'm delighted to report there is indeed a company that will blast your ashes into orbit for just £250. A
word of warning, though. While the company managed to
get bits of Gene Roddenberry, the creator of *Star Trek*, into
orbit, it made a bit of a hash of things when it came to getting the *Enterprise*'s chief engineer up there. The first time it

tried, the rocket crashed and Scotty ended up not in the Andromeda Galaxy but just outside Santa Fe, in New Mexico. Happily he was found, and earlier this year he was launched again from a Pacific atoll. But that went wrong too when the rocket exploded, sending the Canadian actor into the sea, where, one day, he will probably crash head-on into Derick Redfern. Almost certainly, this is not what either man would have wanted.

I should also explain that, if you do manage to get your husband into low orbit, he will be a hazard to navigation in the years to come. So don't come crying to me when what used to be your spouse's left leg punches a bloody great hole in the side of a space shuttle, killing everyone on board.

Let me therefore give you some other ideas. Your dust could be mixed with paint and used to create a piece of art. This means you could spend the rest of time as Angelina Jolie's left breast. Or the front bogie wheel of a steam locomotive. Or whatever subject you choose. I know I'm preaching to the converted here, as a recent study found that only 5 per cent of British people want to be laid to rest in a churchyard. You could become part of a football pitch or a bit of the M1. Or you could be turned into a diamond. This is surprisingly easy. You simply heat your ex-husband to 1500°C and keep him at this temperature for several weeks until everything that isn't carbon has oxidized. Then you mix him with a bit of metal and a diamond seed crystal and then apply a pressure of 800,000 lb per square inch. After a period of several years, your husband can be cut and placed in a ring of your choosing. You may even opt to wear him as a stud in your navel or, dare I say it, lower down. He'd like that, I'm sure. But remember to remove him if you get remarried.

Me? Well, I've decided exactly what I want my family to do

with my body when it's become meat. I want them to take it round to Peter Mandelson's house and leave it in his front room. This is my wish, and, as my servant, Lord Mandelson is forced to oblige.

Sunday 7 December 2008

The BBC's letting loonies gag
me with mink knickers

Last week Nigella Lawson went on the television and said she'd like to shoot a bear and turn it into a coat. Nothing wrong with that. We hear all the time from people who would never wear a fur coat, so why should we not occasionally hear from someone who would? Unfortunately, however, in the current climate it is no longer possible to express an opinion on TV because you are bound to upset a pressure group that then runs around waving its arms in the air and calling for you to be sacked or shot or turned into a hat. Nigella, for instance, has enraged an organization called Viva!, which stands for Vegetarians International Voice for Animals. And another called Peta, which stands for People for the Ethical Treatment of Animals. Neither is very big or very important. I'd guess they have even fewer members than the Church of England. But they have websites, and they have spokeswomen, and they are always prepared to come up with a quote when contacted by reporters.

I tripped over a similar bunch of loonies recently when I made a throwaway line on TV about lorry drivers murdering prostitutes. This was branded a sick joke by something called the English Collective of Prostitutes, whose job is to be angry when contacted by a member of Her Majesty's press looking for a story.

You could give me any subject matter: paving stones, cabbages, your next-door neighbour, dogs – anything that took your fancy – and I bet that after half an hour on the phone I could come up with someone who was prepared to be cross about it. If it got their name in the papers.

It's not just weirdos in attics either. Harry Enfield and Paul Whitehouse were hauled over Ofcom's coals in October for showing a scene in which a man tried to mate his pet northerner with someone's Filipina maid. Somehow this managed to infuriate the government of the Philippines, which made all sorts of agreeing noises when asked if it wanted Harry and Paul to be killed and eaten.

The problem is simple. If you say, in public, that you would not shoot a bear or you would not support an attack on Iraq or you would not buy a Range Rover because of climate change, you are offending nobody. Because you are saying, 'I will not do something.' But if you say you would do something, like shoot a bear, then someone in an attic with a website and a silly acronym for their micro-organization (membership: three) will jump on your case and not let go.

The situation has become worse in the wake of Jonathan Ross and Russell Brand's telephone call to Andrew Sachs's answering machine. Everyone is after petrol and kindling to keep that fire going until Ross returns to the airwaves in January. That's why poor old Chris Moyles was splashed across the papers recently for talking about prostitution and then talking about Poles. 'Aha,' said someone in a loft. 'You see. You see! The BBC is out of control. They are employing a man who thinks all Polish people are hookers.' And it's why I had to get legal on various newspapers that were trying to suggest I'd given the finger to an American policeman in a recent edition of *Top Gear*. I hadn't, but it looked that way, and that's a big enough stick for those who are professionally angry.

It's now reached the point where the BBC has drawn up a new procedure to make sure no one in its employ ever says anything that could possibly offend anyone. This is an enormous undertaking. With four television channels broadcasting twenty-four hours a day, along with five national radio stations, and forty local stations in England alone, it amounts to 8,232 hours of broadcasting a week. That means 89m words every seven days, not one of which can offend anyone.

Impossible? Well it's not like they're not trying. News reports featuring mildly grisly scenes have to come with health warnings. And I have to tell two people what I'm planning on saying. If I don't, I am summarily dismissed. And if either thinks there's someone out there with a website and an acronym who might find the remark offensive, it has to go. The procedure, scarily, is called 'compliance'. Sounds like something a Dalek might say to some captives: 'Comply. Comply.' It has to stop. Because what the BBC is doing is pandering to the wishes of extremists. I mean it. There is no difference in my book between the spokesman for Viva! and suicide bombers who fly planes into tall buildings. Both believe they are right and, crucially, neither wants the other point of view to be heard.

It is their right to eat weeds rather than food. I support them in that. I wish them well and I would gladly give them a platform on TV to express their views, no matter how pallid and drawn their badly malnourished faces may be. So how can they possibly object to someone saying: 'I like a chop'? And how can we have reached a point where we castigate Harry and Paul for their extremely funny sketch? I even saw some hopeless MP on TV saying we should go back to the days of proper comedy like *Fawlty Towers* . . . in which I seem to recall Basil pretended to be Hitler and made some Germans cry. I promise you this: that scene today would not be broadcast because out there somewhere is a Kraut in an attic with a bad temper and a big mouth.

To sum up, then. We all know you can't use the f-word before nine, the n-word unless you're Quentin Tarantino and the c-word ever. We sort of know what's funny and what's sick. We know something is offensive only if offence is meant. We know the rules and we really cannot have them redrawn by the English Collective of Prostitutes, the government of the Philippines, the *Daily Mail* and a bunch of people who don't reckon it might be fun, just occasionally, to go out at night in a pair of mink knickers.

Sunday 14 December 2008

Ambulance, quick – some idiot's had a brainwave

You must have noticed the change. You used to be able to get a good night's sleep in a British city centre, but these days you are woken from your dreams every five minutes by the siren of a passing ambulance. And figures out last week show this is no illusion. In London, the number of calls received by the ambulance service has rocketed from 3,000 to 4,000 a day. And in the West Midlands it's a similar picture, with 8,000 calls being received last weekend – a 30 per cent increase on the same weekend last year. So what's going on? Obviously some people need an ambulance in these troubled times because they've been stabbed or shot or they've ingested a bit too much ketamine and are walking round the garden whinnying.

There are many reasons why the number of calls has jumped so dramatically and so quickly and I'm sure the NHS will be having many meetings, with biscuits, to try to work out what they might be and what might be done to bring the situation under control. Doubtless, the *Daily Mail* will have a few ideas as well, probably to do with immigrants and Princess Diana. Or people attempting suicide because they've just read a story suggesting that cornflakes give you breast cancer.

Happily, I have been giving the matter serious thought as well and I've come up with some ideas of my own. One of the reasons more people need the services of an ambulance driver is because of politically motivated weather forecasting.

The Met Office, which claims to know what the weather will be like in a hundred years but cannot tell what it will do tomorrow morning, now seems to be incapable of saying what it was like yesterday either. It announced last week that thanks to patio heaters and *Top Gear*, the past decade has been the warmest on record even though temperatures have been falling since 1995 and Britain has been suffering from the coldest start to winter for thirty years. And because the weathermen tell us it's warm outside and will get warmer still until we all burn in hell, people get dressed in a T-shirt and shorts and then die of hypothermia while scraping 6 ft of sheet ice from the windscreen of what the Met Office calls a polar bear-killing, Arctic-melting, carbon-emitting, greenhouse-creating star-destroyer but you and I know as a Ford Fiesta. That said, I don't blame the Met Office for all of the ambulance service's woes.

No. I suspect the main reason there has been such a dramatic leap is that Britain is now fuller than ever of people who are technically stupid. In the olden days (i.e., before last week), it was a big story when someone dialled 999 in hysterics because they'd broken a fingernail. But now it happens so often, it's no longer news. Just last night in my local supermarket a woman became so hysterical about a hair she'd found on the outside of a packet of bacon that she called the police. Had I been armed, I'm fairly sure I'd have shot her in the back of the head. Certainly, I thought quite seriously about clubbing her to death with my shopping basket.

And this is just the tip of the iceberg. In the West Country a woman called for an ambulance because her television remote control was out of reach. Then there was the young man who reckoned he needed emergency care because he'd sniffed some deodorant by accident. And on the very day the ambulance service made its announcement, it had a call from a twenty-two-year-old woman who'd squeezed a blackhead and it wouldn't stop bleeding. One pensioner told an ambulance crew she'd summoned to wait for forty minutes because she was baking a cake. The crew gave her a stern warning about wasting their time and left, but the warning plainly wasn't physical enough because exactly forty minutes later the daft old bat told a second crew that her cake had risen nicely and she was ready to go to hospital.

The stories are endless. The people with shampoo in their eyes. The people who think they've caught a virus from their computer. The people whose brains are so tiny and so ineffectual that they cannot determine what is a nuisance and what is an amputation.

From an early age, I've told my children that they may come rushing into the house wailing only if they can actually see bone poking out of their skin but, plainly, other parents are not so wise. Even when their child has nothing but a minor flesh wound, they mollycoddle it so that they end up rearing a pathetic imbecile.

So, now that we have uncovered the problem, we must decide what to do. Many would call for better education but this is expensive, it won't make an impact for fifteen years at least and I can hardly see where it would fit in the curriculum now that children have to spend so much time learning how to have oral sex and why the Range Rover is boiling Johnny polar bear.

I have therefore decided that the carrot-and-stick approach is best. Only without the carrot. This works for dogs and so I see no reason why it should not work for life forms that have less intelligence, such as northerners.

In short, ambulance crews summoned to the assistance of someone whose head is still attached to the body and who does not have gangrene or Ebola should be allowed, if they see fit, to burn the person's house down. Or, if they are kindly souls, to take an item that has roughly the same value as the call-out, so that it can be sold by the NHS on eBay.

In the meantime, perhaps the Met Office would be good enough to consult its supercomputer for the weather forecast instead of telling us what Jonathon Porritt thinks.

Sunday 21 December 2008

Save the high street – ditch bad service and ugly sales girls

I fear I may have seen Vietnam for the last time. As the jet lifted off from Saigon in September, I looked out of the window and thought: 'I'm forty-eight. I'll probably never get the chance to come back here again.' And it made me sad.

I'm also sad that, in all probability, I shall never again fly in a jet fighter or ski down a black run or make fumbling lurve in the back seat of a car. In fact, the list of things I've already and unwittingly done for the last time is endless and, if various reports are to be believed, includes shopping.

According to the men in braces who put our money somewhere and can't quite remember where, up to fifteen big high-street retailers will disappear from town centres in the coming months. And if my local town is anything to go by, they will undoubtedly be joined by all those little boutiquey delicatessen bijou cubbyhole shops that smell of sun-dried tomatoes and potpourri. The ones run by stick-insect blonde women and paid for by their husbands to stop them running off with the gym instructor.

Each town will be left with nothing but two giant retailing cathedrals in which you will be able to buy everything from smoked salmon to soil. The meat will be scarlet, the prices will be low and they won't be shops as we know them.

They'll be filling stations for the stomach. They'll be horrid. They'll be American. I shall never set foot in one. I shall simply buy everything I need from the interweb.

And that's sad too.

And so what I thought I'd do today is provide a handy

cut-out-'n'-keep guide for the high-street moguls of this world, and the stick-insect women, explaining what they've been doing wrong, what might be done to stave off their demise and, with it, the demise of every town centre in the land.

Because let's face it, the pubs are going too, and the estate agents and the building societies.

First of all, then, we must address the problem of the physical purchase. At the moment, when I buy something, a man in a nasty suit sits me down and asks all sorts of impudent questions about where I live and my telephone number. Wrong. I know that this has nothing to do with my guarantee and everything to do with you profiling your customers so you can get a man in India to call up at an antisocial hour in six months' time to sell me a washing machine. Pack it in. Take my credit card. Give me the product. Get me out of there as quickly as possible and do not sell my details to anyone in India or I will come round in the middle of the night and burn your shop down.

Next. Have everything in stock. I know this is expensive and complicated but I really don't like going to all the bother of trying on a pair of shoes, only to have the silly girl emerge after ten minutes from a non-existent storeroom to explain that she doesn't have the style in my size and would I mind coming back in a week. Yes, I would mind very much.

Retailers need to understand – and they really don't – that while there are a great many people, usually those with bosoms, who enjoy mooching about in the shops because it's safer and less complicated than shagging the gym instructor, the rest – those with zips down the front of their trousers – do not enjoy it much at all and would like the whole process to be over as fast as possible. Speed, then, is everything.

Now we get to the question of price tags.

And I'm talking to you now, Mr Tiffany.

I walked into your Bond Street shop the other day, took one look at the counter full of jewellery, noticed that nothing had a price tag and promptly walked out again.

This is because I knew exactly what would happen if I hung around. I'd point at a brooch. The sales assistant would get it out of the cabinet. I'd have to ask how much it cost and she'd say, through a loudhailer so everyone in the shop could hear, '£250,000.' And I'd then have to shrug and try to look nonchalant, which is jolly difficult when your knees are knocking. I buy jewellery like wine, on price. It is the only thing I want to know. I don't care about the setting or where the diamond came from. I just want to know whether it costs 5p or £800m. Knowing this speeds up the transaction and saves me from embarrassment, and any jeweller who doesn't realize this has only himself to blame when the bailiffs drop round for tea and buns.

Retailers should also know that men can only ever buy what they want 'now'. It is why, whenever I'm sent to a supermarket to do the weekly shop, I only ever buy what I want at that precise moment. So instead of getting six bumper packs of bog roll and four trays of dog food, I come home with one tube of Smarties. I am allergic to buying a bumper pack of anything. When I need a shave I only need one razor. When I want lunch I want one pizza. So sell them singly, please. And while we're at it, Dolmio, smaller pots, if you wouldn't mind.

Finally, and I hope this is helpful, pretty girls cost the same to employ as ugly ones.

There's a shop in St James's Street, London, called Swaine Adeney Brigg that sells lilac riding crops for £900. I have no use for anything like that but I buy one a week because the assistant is so pretty. In short, nobody likes to be served by a boot-faced crow. Or, and this is for you, PC World, a man in a purple shirt.

That is the end of my column and if retailers pay no attention to it, it will be the end of their shops as well. The rest of you have a happy new year and for heaven's sake enjoy it. It might be your last.

Sunday 28 December 2008

Ring a ring o' clipboards – we all fall down

When I was a keen young reporter on a local newspaper, I was dispatched to the council house of a young woman who'd called and said her home had been overrun by cockroaches.

Home turned out to be the wrong word. It was a structure of sorts containing nothing but upturned boxes and several children who looked like they'd walked straight off the set of *Kes*. As we tried to sort out a family picture, it transpired that the woman had absolutely no idea which kids were hers and which ones belonged to what I'd taken until that point to be a puddle of lard but was in fact her sister. Nor did she have the first clue what cockroaches were. 'You know what they do?' she said. 'They burrow into kiddies' heads, lay their eggs and the kiddies end up with a head full of spiders.'

That was thirty years ago, and you might imagine things on the sink estates of grim northern towns were much better these days. But no. Over the Christmas holidays we read about the Mansfield couple who went on a seven-hour drinking binge with their sick-encrusted baby. The father was an extraordinary-looking creature who appeared to be part mouse, part pipe cleaner, and the mother had six previous drunk-and-disorderly convictions. Plainly, then, they are entirely unsuitable parents, and unless the social services continue to keep a close eye, their poor child will wake up one day in a box under a bed and it'll be Shannon Matthews all over again.

I was therefore delighted to read last week that the government is going to take action to make life that little bit better for the children of this great nation. However, it is not talking about increasing its vigilance on children who are made to eat only what they can find in the heroin-laced stairwells of the tower blocks in which they live, or those who are sent out to exchange stolen car radios for six-packs of Rohypnol. Instead, it will be employing a vast army of men and women with clipboards who will come round to your house when your child is two to make sure it can speak properly. This is bound to be a worry if you are Glaswegian or the love child of Ant and Dec.

The initiative is being developed in response to a report that found some two-year-olds were unaware they had a name, let alone what it was. And that one in ten of all children in deprived areas didn't know a single nursery rhyme.

Hmmm. I've given this some thought, and I can't see the problem. Nursery rhymes are cruel and terrible things full of stories about dismembered sheep and the bubonic plague. You have Simple Simon, who was obviously a retard, Hickory Dickory Dock, which is just rubbish, and Wee Willie Winkie, who ran through the town in his nightclothes, peering through the windows of children to see if they were in bed. Clearly, the man was a paedophile, and the less two-year-olds know about such things, the better.

In fact, I applaud any parent who hides these sordid and frightening stories and encourages their children to play Grand Theft Auto instead. But I very much doubt the parka army with its clipboards will share my views. Nor do I expect it will concentrate its efforts in areas where children are in real need of help. In the same way that airport security people blunderbuss their anti-terrorism efforts across the board, which means they are just as likely to jab a digit in the back of Harry Potter as they are a sweating Afghan with wires poking out of his shoes, social workers are just as likely to target the local vicarage as they are the sink estate.

Indeed, they've already said as much. Someone called Jean Gross, who is spearheading the government's drive to make children learn nursery rhymes by the time the umbilical cord is cut, says that such problems also affect middle-class families, especially if their under-twos spend long periods in mediocre childcare while both parents work hard to pay off a big mortgage.

I find this a bit terrifying because I remember, when my children were young, having them examined by someone who didn't know them, didn't know us and could summon, with the stroke of a ballpoint, a government machine that could at worst take them away and at best give them a problem with a Latin name that they'd spend the rest of their lives trying to overcome. And all because they didn't know Humpty Dumpty was not an egg, or a fatty, but a civil war cannon. I actually know one couple who, quite wrongly, had their child taken away. And could have it back only if they lived in secure accommodation with twenty-four-hour surveillance. It remains the most barbaric example of a useless and dangerous system that now is set to get even worse.

When it comes to the rearing of a child, there is no definitive right and wrong. Social workers – whom I admire for the most part – will continue to be too cautious in some cases and too heavy-handed in others. Mistakes will continue to be made, which is fine if you are a shelf-stacker or you pick vegetables for a living. But when your mistake devastates a family, it is absolutely not fine at all.

If we go back to the children I encountered thirty years ago in that cockroach-infested house, it's entirely possible they are all now in jail for selling ketamine to toddlers. But it's also possible (just) that they are university professors.

And let's finish with the example of a young girl whose father was an abusive alcoholic and whose mother became so fed up that she shot him dead in front of the child. Every rulebook in the world would say she should be taken into care. She wasn't. And she grew up to be Charlize Theron.

Sunday 4 January 2009

The world will never be safe until Scrabble is banned

News from the dusty bit at the back of the toy shop. In the past twelve months, sales of Trivial Pursuit have tripled, Monopoly is 13 per cent up and Scrabble is twenty-three times more popular than it was in 2007. Naturally, the sort of people who like long walks in the fresh air see this as an indicator that Britain is reverting to traditional family values and that instead of going out at night to sniff glue and stab a policeman, the nation's children are all at home in pinafore dresses, whittling chess pieces round the fire with Mum and Dad. They see the resurgence of the board game as a good thing.

I'm not so sure, though. Take Monopoly as an example. To begin with it's good fun but, like the banking and property system on which it is based, there is a flaw. It never ends. You go bankrupt so you borrow money from your mum, who has loads. Then you go bankrupt again. So you borrow more money from the bank. And then, when there is no more money left in the box, you write out an IOU and keep on borrowing by which time it is Thursday, everyone is bankrupt and you have realized that unchecked capitalism doesn't work whether it comes in a stock market or in a box. That's if you're lucky. If you're not, there will be a 'bad loser' around the table who will land on your hotel in Northumberland Avenue and in a hysterical rage will burst into tears and throw the board, his dog, your iron and all your dad's houses into the fire.

In theory Scrabble is much better and yet it, too, is flawed. Well, it is for me because I always end up with seven vowels.

So while my opponent is writing 'underpass' across two triple word scores and claiming it's a game of skill, I'm getting five for 'eerie'. Again. And they are looking at me as though I might be a simpleton.

I have a similar problem with backgammon. So far as my wife is aware, dice have six faces all of which feature six dots. I, on the other hand, have only ever thrown a two and a one. Even without a player coming the other way, it would take me about eighteen months to get all my pieces to the other side of the board.

To eliminate the element of luck, I always suggest chess but this doesn't work either because the only person who knows how to play in my family is my son, who's twelve and consequently charges around the board on a wave of testosterone, endlessly leaving his queen in silly places and then mocking when, out of kindness, I pretend I haven't seen the danger it's in. Or that he's just moved his castle diagonally or that, for the past two hours, he's been one move away from checkmate.

In fact, playing any game with children is hopeless. Charades, for example. They sulk when you give them 'The Beastly Beatitudes of Balthazar B' or 'Versailles: The View from Sweden' and you, in turn, get cheesed off when they endlessly mime their way through a film which has two words and sounds like Carry Hotter.

Even Tri-Tactics – the only board game I really enjoy – is ruined when your opponent is under sixteen. Because you sit there thinking: 'Oh, for God's sake. How are you able to text a friend, talk to half the world on Facebook and watch some American drivel on television, all at the same time, when you cannot remember that the piece you attacked thirty seconds ago with your puny little destroyer is still my aircraft carrier?' Board games, then, do not bring a family closer together.

They rip out its heart in a seething cauldron of rage, hysteria, accusations and hate. And I fear they have a similar effect on world peace.

To understand this new and interesting theory, we need to look at the world since Pong. This was the first commercially available video game; it featured two bats, a square ball and lots of irritating noises, it came along in 1972 and since then the western world has, for the most part, been at peace. We can therefore conclude that Pong and other games of its ilk ended the Cold War because, for the first time in history, leaders had something better to do than rush about threatening to bash one another's heads in.

I realize, of course, that this doesn't apply to Tony Blair or George W. Bush but that's because they were too busy reading the Bible to play Space Invaders. I, on the other hand, played a lot of Space Invaders and I've never wanted to invade anywhere.

When we look at the world's trouble spots today – the Gaza Strip, Somalia, Sri Lanka and so on – we find large chunks of the population which have no possibility of playing Grand Theft Auto. This means they are bored. They could play Dover Patrol or Mousetrap but choose instead to hold up oil tankers or cut off their neighbour's arms.

The board game was invented about 5,000 years ago and it didn't quench anyone's thirst for activity. People continued to invent stupid new religions and have wars because they knew that getting an axe in a face was better, by miles, than a game of Cluedo. Look at Hitler. He could have played Risk but because it can only ever be won by the person charged with the task of conquering Australia and North America, he decided to make up his own rules and play them out for real. Would he have done so if he'd been given a PlayStation and a copy of Call of Duty V? I seriously doubt it.

The fact is this. Since science harnessed the electron and turned it into a Cylon or a Nazi paratrooper with a realistic machine pistol, the world has unquestionably been a better place. And so, too, is life for the family.

I'm writing this at our seaside cottage where there is no PlayStation and no Wii. As a result the children get up in the morning, play something old-fashioned and then bicker about it till bedtime. Tomorrow we will be back at home, which is full of gruesome, vicious, bloodthirsty electronic games. Peace, contrary to the teachings of those in tweed, will be restored.

Sunday 11 January 2009

Run for cover – Pooh the Dark Knight is coming

I've just watched the latest Batman film, *The Dark Knight*, and it is very far removed from the original television show I used to watch as a boy. For instance, instead of biffing and kapowing his way through the tracing-paper plot in a body-hugging supersuit, our hero is a brooding and complicated character, tortured by inner demons, a sense of his own worthlessness and perhaps a touch of shame about what he and Robin used to get up to in the bath together back in the sixties. In short, Batman has become what film marketing people call 'dark' or 'gritty', and we see a similar problem with today's James Bond, who has lost the one-liners and the gadgets and become 'brooding' and 'complicated'.

It's the same story with the plot. In *Quantum of Solace* I was left utterly bewildered by what on earth he was up to half the time. Was Mathis a goodie or a baddie? I have no idea, and if I have no idea, what chance is there for the small boys whose fascination with 007 has kept the brand alive for so long? Even the car chase was impossible to follow. It was designed to be the longest, and best, in all of movie history, but what we actually saw in the cinema was a savagely edited facsimile. Why was it cut down? Presumably so they could shoehorn in more shots of Daniel Craig smouldering.

And deeper insights into his inner being.

In the olden days, Bond would get some orders from M and then embark on a series of fights, interspersed with some light sexual intercourse, until eventually the baddie and his entire operation exploded. It was as easy to understand as a boiled egg. But today, we're told, 007 is more in keeping with the character from the original books. We have to be told this, of course, because no one has ever actually read one.

Frankly I wish he'd just get back to the days when he head-butted Curt Jürgens in the face, blew up Donald Pleasence's volcano and went to bed with Barbara Bach.

It's easy to see what's going on here. After a character has been around for forty years, the people who created him become bored with blowing up Pinewood every two years. So they start to employ directors and actors who want to explore the hero's roots and his motivation. Which means that, instead of getting Superman to fly about and make the world go backwards, they ask what being a superhero does to a man's soul. Can he ever love someone? Can he ever be at peace? Does he ever develop a deity complex because there is simply no answer to the eternal question: why me? Oh, for God's sake. Just kick Lex Luthor in the wedding veg and let's have another explosion.

Depth of character is fine in a film such as *Shadowlands*, but it is emphatically not fine in *Die Hard* or Bond or Batman, which have endured precisely because, in an action film, lead characters have to be shallow. We don't want to know why they never go out without a machinegun, just so long as they use it as often as possible.

Taking a cartoon character seriously is going to kill the golden goose in much the same way that the appeal of a real goose would be lost if you looked at the life it led, and the goslings it reared, before it was shot in the head and buried in gravy. And that's why I am extremely alarmed to hear that after an eighty-year pause Winnie-the-Pooh is making a comeback. Yup. The people who manage the estate of the author A. A. Milne and the artist E. H. Shepard have allowed a publisher to commission a new book called *Return to the Hundred Acre Wood*, and while I'm sure it will sell jolly well and make lots of money, I fear that it will be impossible to rekindle the magic.

First of all, A. A. Milne – unlike most people who shorten their byline this way – was an exceptional writer: of that there can be no doubt. And while I don't doubt for a moment that the new author, David Benedictus, is an exceptional writer as well, it would be impossible to expect that he'd get the tone exactly right. And a Pooh story that's off by even 5 per cent may as well be *Tess of the D'Urbervilles*.

What makes Pooh engage even today – apart from the genius of the writing and the joy of the illustrations – is that the stories are so exquisitely simple. It was Eeyore's birthday. Pooh felt he should have a present. Piglet – surely the most unpleasant character in fiction since Judas Iscariot – decided to get there first so he'd be credited with the idea. He fell over. The present exploded. He got his comeuppance. The end.

And there's the second problem. It is hard nowadays to get away with something so elemental. We'd have to know why Eeyore was so miserable all the time, and inevitably that would lead us to his upbringing on a sink beach in Blackpool. Then we'd be invited to explore why Piglet is such a nasty piece of work. Perhaps it has something to do with his height. Maybe he's bitter and nasty because he has SPS – short pig syndrome. Maybe there could be a lesson here, as there seems to be in all children's literature, about the effects of bullying.

Speaking of which: Christopher Robin. Way, way too white. He'd have to be Somalian and the forest to which he escapes with his friends would have to be a park full of dog dirt in Hackney. I bet there are meetings going on today in which someone at the publisher is wondering whether

Winnie-the-Pooh ought really to be a black bear called Winston-the-Pooh. Maybe the next book could be called *Pooh: Dark Knight of Solace*.

Pooh, Batman and Bond have endured because they were brilliant ideas. And what I wish is that the custodians of these good ideas would refrain from meddling. Where possible, stick to the original concept. And where it isn't possible because, say, the author was everything and the author is dead, move on and come up with a new brilliant idea.

Sunday 18 January 2009

Get another round in, lads – we've got some pubs to save

Bad news from the tap room. It seems that in the past two years 3,382 pubs have closed, and so far this year they have been shutting at the rate of one every four hours.

Now I should make it plain from the outset that I dislike very much what is usually called the traditional pub. I hate the low beams, the horse brasses, the V-necked jumpers, the jovial back-slapping freemasonry of the regulars, the tankards, the unfunny hunting cartoons in the bogs, the peer pressure to drink a pint of Old Fuddlecome's Bottom, the urine-spattered peanuts, the patterned carpets, the wheel-back chairs and the overpowering sense that absolutely everyone around you is there mainly because they hate their wife and children. I also hate theme pubs because the theme, no matter what it says on the door, is almost always 'fighting'. And I really hate gastropubs because of the way they always make fans out of their paper napkins.

However, as I'm well aware that everyone else enjoys pubs a lot, I feel duty-bound to address what might be done to stop the anvil of death coming down with increasing velocity on what people in *The Archers* like to call the beating heart of the village.

Obviously, the drinks industry is quick to blame the economy for the problems but, plainly, this is nonsense. I have absolutely no idea what beer costs, but I bet you can buy two pints and a packet of pork itchings for less than the price of a parking ticket.

Plainly, then, it's not money that's keeping people away,

which leads us directly to the fact that the one thing you cannot do in a smoking room is smoke. There's no doubt that this has had a profound effect on the licensing trade, and David Cameron must make it a top priority to overturn the ban the moment he takes office. In the meantime, however, publicans must stop whining and carefully study the anti-smoking rulebook to find a loophole. There will be one. I guarantee it. This is a government document, remember, so it's bound to be festooned with mistakes big enough to drive through in a pantechnicon.

I've given the matter only a moment's thought and already I've come up with some proposals. You could claim your 'lounge' is a theatre and that all the customers are actors. Then they can light up. Or you could make your pub an embassy. Or, best of all, sell fine cigars, which makes you a tobacco specialist. And then the ban doesn't apply.

Next, we must address the problem of food. I appreciate of course that there is extra cash to be earned from serving meals, but unless you know what you're doing, and, let's be honest, if your chef is a school-leaver from Darlington, he does not, I wouldn't bother. He'll only end up making a shepherd's pie from actual shepherds.

Once you have ditched the menu, fired the gormless oaf you employed to murder the chips, done away with the fancy napkins and edged craftily through the smoking ban, you must then turn your attention to the most important point of all, the main reason pubs are shutting down so fast: the idiotic notion that you should be encouraging your customers to drink 'responsibly'. So, instead of displaying a sign that says you will not serve anyone who appears to be intoxicated, accept the age-old business practice that you will serve absolutely anyone, even if they've crawled to the bar on their hands and knees, leaving a trail of sick in their wake. You are in business to make money; not to send your customers home with the liver of a foetus.

The government says the average adult male should not drink more than three to four units of alcohol a day. And to judge by the 'drink responsibly' slogans that now appear as part of a gentlemen's agreement on all alcohol products and advertisements, the booze industry agrees. Small wonder they're in a mess and all the pubs are closing down. How can you possibly expect to make a profit if you are displaying a sign asking customers to buy less? It's madness. Think about it. Three units is one large glass of wine, and for all the effect this has on a 16-stone man like me, I may as well suck the moisture from a clump of moss. I drink at least a bottle of wine a night. And before going to bed I have a small tumbler of vodka enlivened by the addition of some sloes I found last year growing by a railway line.

This is my business, and the drinks industry, if it had half a brain, would be encouraging me to keep it up. The government, meanwhile, should ask what on earth it's doing telling the people it claims to represent how much of what they should put in their mouths. Genuinely, it staggers me that with all the problems facing the nation right now, some of my tax money is being used to work out how much wine I should drink before supper. What next? An enormous Prora-style holiday camp on the east coast where smiling families in lederhosen will be ordered to do star jumps from dawn till dusk? Drinking to excess is what separates us from the Greeks. Being drunk is what separates us from the beasts. And what's more, drinking makes me happy. Not drinking makes me unhappy. Which means if I do as I'm told by Gordon Brown, I'll be sad all the time.

Publicans must fight this 'nanny knows best' interference. Yes, there is alcoholism and, yes, its effects on people are catastrophic. I know this only too well, sadly. But why should the many be made to cut down on one of life's greatest pleasures because of the few? Speaking of which . . .

My final suggestion for the pub trade is this. If you suspect that one of your customers may be boring, ask him, using a blowtorch if necessary, to be quiet.

Sunday 25 January 2009

Come quick, Nurse – the NHS
is going frightfully green

Last Saturday started off very normally. I had a hangover and was staggering around the house in loose robes, trying to find some restorative tomato juice. My wife, meanwhile, was picking one child up from a sleepover and taking another to some form of cello-based horse-riding activity. And then my son came in from the garden, where he'd been playing football with his mates, to say he had a headache.

'Pah,' I said huffily. 'You don't know the meaning of the word. They're hosting the Glaswegian round of the world pile-driver competition on my forehead as we speak, son, so go back outside and stop complaining.' The thing is, though, he really did look dreadful. He was hot too. And what's more, he said he couldn't stand the crack of light coming through the blind I'd drawn to stave off the hammering in my own head. And then he was explosively sick.

I put him to bed, wobbled down the stairs again and began to read the newspapers, where my eye alighted on a story about meningitis. Cases are up a whopping 25 per cent this year and it mostly affects young boys – especially those who, like my son, have recently had flu. Helpfully, the journalist had included a number of symptoms every parent should know about and I read them with a growing sense of unease. One stood out. The sufferer often has a stiff neck. Hurriedly, I sought out the boy and asked if he could put his chin on his chest. 'Ow,' he said pitifully. 'My neck hurts.' Being a modern sort of person, I went on the NHS Direct internet site, keyed in the symptoms and was told, in the blink of an electron, to dial 999 immediately.

I didn't. Fearful of being labelled one of those people who call the emergency services because they have broken a nail, I rang the doctor's surgery and was directed to a helpline number where, after a few minutes, a man came on the line, listened to the boy's problems and said: 'Call for an ambulance straight away.' I still didn't. An ambulance would have to come 20 miles to my house and then go 20 miles to the nearest hospital. That's an hour at best and with meningitis you often don't have that long. So despite the hangover and the possibility I was in no legal state to drive, I bundled him in the car and, twenty minutes later, we were skidding to a halt at A&E.

Four hours later, after he'd been poked, prodded and hit on the knees with hammers by what felt like everyone in all of Oxfordshire, and I'd read all the *My First Alphabet* books in the waiting room and built a rather good Lego jet fighter, we were given the good news. It had been a migraine.

So, now that I've experienced the NHS first hand, I'm well placed to make some helpful suggestions on how the service might be improved. And you know what? I'm a bit stumped. Yes, it would have been nice if some of the books in the waiting room had been more adult in nature; and in the same vein, I do think that some of the prettier nurses could have been wearing stockings. But that's about it.

If I were running the NHS, frankly, I'd give everyone a hearty slap on the back, fire a few managers and tell everyone to carry on. Sadly, though, I'm not in charge. Some lunatics have that job and their suggestions for the future of healthcare are extremely alarming.

First of all, they are going to reduce the amount of meat and dairy products on offer on their menus. They say this will reduce a hospital's carbon emissions but, because that makes quite literally no sense to me at all, I can only imagine the real reason is that they want every patient to be cured of their animal-killing, right-wing hunting bastard past.

It gets worse. They say that if the NHS were a country it would be the eighty-first biggest polluter in the world, between Estonia and Bahrain in the league tables, and that as a result people will be discouraged from going to hospital in a car.

Right, you pig-ignorant tossers. I'm at home. I think my boy has meningitis. Do you think I'm going to take him there on the bus to help protect the plankton? Or do you think I'm going to wait for an ambulance that you've converted to run on melted-down Tories? Well I'm not. And if you turn all the car parks into allotments, I shall simply drive my Range Rover through the plate-glass windows and park in the foyer.

They also want hospitals to get their power from wind turbines, which will be a great comfort on quiet, still days to those who rely for their next breath on a life-support machine. And they say that patients should drink less bottled water, presumably so that they have no option but to drink from the MRSA-infested sinks.

You think this is all nonsense? Well, you're right, but sadly they haven't even got started yet. They want equipment to be reused. What equipment? Needles? Nappies? Rubber gloves? And get this. They also say hospital staff should be encouraged to work from home. I'm sorry, but what good is a nurse when you need some more painkillers and she's at her place, feet up and watching *Countdown* for all you know? The problem here is that the government announced recently it wished to cut the output of carbon dioxide in Britain by 80 per cent by 2050. That cannot be done, but of course it has to be seen to be trying, which is why the NHS now has a Sustainable Development Unit – the department behind all these idiotic ideas.

Its quite frankly deluded boss, Dr David Pencheon, says that in a low-carbon future, healthcare will not look anything like it does today. You're damn right, sunshine. The hospitals will be full to overflowing with people who are dead.

Sunday 1 February 2009

I dare you to visit Johannesburg, the city for softies

Every city needs a snappy one-word handle to pull in the tourists and the investors. So, when you think of Paris, you think of love; when you think of New York, you think of shopping; and when you think of London – despite the best efforts of New Labour to steer you in the direction of Darcus Howe – you think of beefeaters and Mrs Queen. Rome has its architecture. Sydney has its bridge. Venice has its sewage, and Johannesburg has its crime. Yup, Jo'burg – the subject of this morning's missive – is where you go if you want to be carjacked, shot, stabbed, killed and eaten.

You could tell your mother you were going on a package holiday to Kabul, with a stopover in Haiti and Detroit, and she wouldn't bat an eyelid. But tell her you're going to Jo'burg and she'll be absolutely convinced that you'll come home with no wallet, no watch and no head. Jo'burg has a fearsome global reputation for being utterly terrifying, a lawless Wild West frontier town paralysed by corruption and disease. But I've spent quite a bit of time there over the past three years and I can reveal that it's all nonsense.

If crime is so bad then how come, the other day, the front-page lead in the city's main newspaper concerned the theft of a computer from one of the local schools? I'm not joking. The paper even ran a massive picture of the desk where the computer used to sit. It was the least interesting picture I've ever seen in a newspaper. But then it would be, because this was one of the least interesting crimes.

'Pah,' said the armed guard who'd been charged with

escorting me each day from my hotel to the Coca-Cola dome, where I was performing a stage version of *Top Gear*.

Quite why he was armed I have absolutely no idea, because all we passed was garden centres and shops selling tropical fish tanks. Now I'm sorry, but if it's true that the streets are a war zone, and you run the risk of being shot every time you set foot outside your front door, then, yes, I can see you might risk a trip to the shops for some food. But a fish tank? An ornamental pot for your garden? It doesn't ring true.

Look Jo'burg up on Wikipedia and it tells you it's now one of the most violent cities in the world ... but it adds in brackets 'citation needed'. That's like saying Gordon Brown is a two-eyed British genius (citation needed). Honestly? Johannesburg is Milton Keynes with thunderstorms. You go out. You have a lovely ostrich. You drink some delicious wine and you walk back to your hotel, all warm and comfy. It's the least frightening place on earth. So why does every single person there wrap themselves up in razor wire and fit their cars with flame-throwers and speak of how many times they've been killed that day? What are they trying to prove?

Next year South Africa will play host to the football World Cup. The opening and closing matches will be played in Jo'burg, and no one's going to go if they think they will be stabbed. The locals even seem to accept this, as at the new airport terminal only six passport booths have been set aside for non-South African residents. At first it's baffling. Why ruin the reputation of your city and risk the success of the footballing World Cup to fuel a story that plainly isn't true? There is no litter and no graffiti. I've sauntered through Soweto on a number of occasions now, swinging a Nikon round my head, with no effect. You stand more chance of being mugged in Monte Carlo. Time and again I was told I could buy an AK-47 for 100 rand – about £7. But when

I said, 'Okay, let's go and get one', no one had the first idea where to start looking. And they were even more clueless when I asked about bullets.

As I bought yet another agreeable carved doll from yet another agreeable black person, I wanted to ring up those idiots who compile surveys of the best and worst places to live and say: 'Why do you keep banging on about Vancouver, you idiots? Jo'burg's way better.' Instead, however, I sat down and tried to work out why the locals paint their city as the eighth circle of hell. And I think I have an answer. It's because they want to save the lions in the Kruger National Park. I promise I am not making this up. Every night, people in Mozambique pack up their possessions and set off on foot through the Kruger for a new life in the quiet, bougainvillea-lined streets of Jo'burg. And very often these poor unfortunate souls are eaten by the big cats.

That, you may imagine, is bad news for the families of those who've been devoured. But actually it's even worse for Johnny Lion. You see, a great many people in Mozambique have Aids, and the fact is this: if you can catch HIV from someone's blood or saliva during a bout of tender love-making, you can be assured you will catch it if you wolf the person down whole. Even if you are called Clarence and you have a mane. At present, it's estimated that there are 2,000 lions in the Kruger National Park and studies suggest 90 per cent have feline Aids. Some vets suggest the epidemic was started by lions eating the lungs of diseased buffalos. But there are growing claims from experts in the field that, actually, refugees are the biggest problem.

That's clearly the answer, then. Johannesburgians are telling the world they live in a shit-hole to save their lions. That's the sort of people they are. And so, if you are thinking about going to the World Cup next year, don't hesitate. The exchange rate's good, the food is superb, the weather's lovely and, thanks to some serious economic self-sacrifice, Kruger is still full of animals. The word, then, I'd choose to describe Jo'burg is 'tranquil'.

Sunday 1 March 2009

Class-A cocoa, the powder of choice on my crock'n'roll tour

Ever since I was a teenager, I've wanted to be a rock star. I used to look at the pictures in *Melody Maker* of Paul Rodgers getting on to Bad Company's personal Boeing 737 and think: 'What in the name of all that's holy will be going on in that thing after it takes off?' None of it, I suspected, would involve accountancy or mineral water.

I'd hear tales of Keith Moon fire-axeing his way into Peter Frampton's bathroom so that he could cut old Goldilocks's hair with a pair of garden shears. Or of Joe Walsh buying an electric chainsaw so that no one would know he was coming until he arrived through their bedroom wall. Or of one notable drummer snorting cocaine off a famous guitarist's dog. And then I'd stop daydreaming and find my careers master was still droning on about the joys of estate agency.

However, standing like a swollen river between me and my dreams was an unfortunate fact of life. I could not play a musical instrument. And when I sang, it sounded like I'd been kicked in the testicles. I realize that this never stopped the Bee Gees, but they had lovely hair by way of compensation. Mine looked like Brian May's in a spaceship.

Last year, however, someone came up with the bright idea of making a *Top Gear* stage show and taking it round the world. We'd have to charter 747s for all the props. There would be roadies. Special effects. An endless parade of hotel rooms. Maybe even some groupies. It would be rock'n'roll, except I didn't need any talent. I signed up like a shot.

And so we arrived on Waiheke Island midway through the

tour. We'd done ten sell-out shows in South Africa and narrowly avoided being fried in Australia. Next on the tour of countries we used to own would be Hong Kong, but for now we were taking a couple of days off in a rented house.

There were four guys and three girls. There was a pool. There was a beach. There was a 65 ft cruiser tied up to the jetty, a Range Rover Sport on the lawn and two helicopters in the garden. We only needed one, the Twin Squirrel, but I'd decided to act like a rock star and had insisted on my own personal Hughes 500 – the best, fastest, most agile chopper in the world. We had, therefore, all the ingredients you need for a bit of serious rock'n'rollery, even though this was New Zealand, where, if you ask someone for drugs, you get a packet of Disprin. No matter. There was beer. There was champagne. And I'd brought my own personal cutlery made from giraffe bone.

Unfortunately, because we'd already done twenty shows, I was a bit tired. And since there were seventeen more to go, I didn't want to get too wasted, so we decided to play Risk. We tore that house apart looking for the box – well, when I say we tore it apart, we looked carefully in all the cupboards, because we didn't want to make a mess. But to no avail. So one of the pilots was ordered to fire up his Squirrel and go to Auckland to get it.

I'd love to say this gave me a thrill, a sense that we'd marched up to the fringes of extreme and kept right on going. But all the while, I had this horrible feeling that someone was paying for that chopper – and that it might be me. To take my mind off the cost, we decided to see who could throw a girl the furthest down the swimming pool. I picked the lightest but sadly, on my first attempt, I felt my back go. So I left the others to it and went to bed with some class-A cocoa.

The next day I was stung by a wasp. When my arm became

thicker than my thigh, I decided that I was almost certainly going to die and that it was a rather hopeless way for a rock'n'roll star to go. Most career through the pearly gates on a burning motorcycle with half a gallon of heroin coursing round their arterial route map. Not from an insect sting.

I tried, as the tour thundered onwards, to act like a rock star. In Hong Kong I thought seriously about having a wee from the helipad on top of the Peninsula hotel – to see if I could finish before the first bit hit the ground. But I thought I might get into trouble.

Then, later in the day, I decided to drive a 50 ft powerboat through the harbour at full tilt to see if the wash might roll over a Star ferry. But there's an 11-knot speed limit. Which seemed sensible, so I stuck to it, vigorously.

Girls? Yes, there were loads, but when you have the British tabloids breathing down your neck, it was better, I figured, to ignore them.

On the last night we had a party. A big one. And I decided to make it through to the dawn. But I had three shows to do the next day and a long flight home in the evening. And I was pretty tired, so at two I called it a day.

And therein lies the problem. When you are forty-eight you just don't have the stamina to push the outside of the envelope. And your moral compass is sufficiently well developed to keep you, and your car, out of the hotel swimming pool.

Make no mistake, I loved every minute of the whole exercise – but I would have loved it so much more if I'd been eighteen. So listen up, children. Forget about getting a job. There aren't any. And forget your Facebook too. Just do your piano practice. Get good quickly – there isn't a moment to lose.

Sunday 8 March 2009

I'm starting divorce proceedings in this special relationship

Back in the eighties, a French industrialist described Britain as an American aircraft carrier off the coast of Europe. And then last week Jacques Myard, a member of the French assembly, mocked the special relationship we claim to have with the US, hinting, with a rather cruel smile, that when it comes to foreign policy, they are the masters and we are the lapdogs, wagging our tails whenever they throw us a biscuit. Which isn't very often.

It would be easy to scoff at this Gallic arrogance, arguing that, while Monsieur Myard can sit under his wisteria enjoying some lovely cheese, his country's antipathy towards America means that all the pop music on French radio is rubbish and that his government cannot afford a new aircraft carrier. However, if you look at Gordon Brown's recent trip to Washington, Johnny Frenchman would appear to have a point.

Gordon gave Obama Barrack a penholder carved from the timbers of an anti-slavery ship. The sister ship, in fact, of the one that was broken up and turned into the desk in the Oval Office. Barrack, meanwhile, gave Brown *The Graduate* on DVD. Which smacks of an 'Oh, Christ. What shall we get him?' moment at the local petrol station.

Then we have the issue with crime. The British authorities have to present a robust prima-facie case to the American courts before we can extradite someone to the UK. Whereas an American cop can drag you across the Atlantic if he even so much as thinks your beard is a bit dodgy.

Trade? Well, I spoke over dinner the other day with the boss of a large British engineering company about the benefits of the special relationship when you are doing business in America. He snorted so explosively that large chunks of lamb and mashed potato shot out of his nose. 'Special relationship!' he chortled. 'There isn't one.' Certainly this was true during the Suez crisis, when America sat on its hands. It was also true when Harold Wilson refused to get involved with Vietnam.

And let's not forget John Major either, who got all cross when Bill Clinton had Gerry Adams round to the White House for tea and buns.

Or how Bill got the hump with Major after details of his time at Oxford University were leaked to the press. Special relationship? Sounds more like a session at Relate to me.

Sure, Tony Blair was close to George Bush, but this, I fear, had nothing to do with Churchill's dream and much to do with America's need to claim its efforts in Iraq were 'international'. A claim that was helped enormously by Blair's wonky grasp of history. 'My father's generation went through the Blitz. There was one country and one people which stood by us at that time. America and the American people.' Er. No they didn't, Tony. They were too busy bankrupting the empire by charging £8 billion for two clapped-out First World War destroyers: the USS *Weak* and the USS *Colander*.

On a personal note, I find no evidence of a special relationship when I go to America. There is no fast-track lane through immigration for visiting Brits. The customs man always looks at me as if I've just chucked his tea into Boston harbour. And we have to answer questions about whether we've ever done genocide, just like everyone else.

Of course, it is hard for a civvie to say whether the special relationship exists in military circles. But certainly the troops

I speak to tend to suggest not. When they're asked what US forces are like in theatre, the answer is mostly unprintable, apart from a liberal use of the word 'useless'.

To be fair, I can't imagine that the Americans find us much cop as allies either. I mean, I can hardly see them queuing up to borrow our snatch Land Rovers or our Nimrods or our lumbering Sea Kings or indeed any of our hardware at all. They probably think they are going into battle with a bunch of keen and well-trained soldiers . . . from the Stone Age.

As further evidence, consider this. How many British bases are to be found on American soil? It's, er, um, hang on . . . none. And how many US ones are to be found over here? To get an idea, try driving through Suffolk one day, past Mildenhall and Lakenheath. There are so many American cars on the road, you could be forgiven for thinking you were in Iowa.

Maybe we don't help ourselves. Maybe we come across as a bit arrogant. According to Rowland White's amazing new book *Phoenix Squadron*, when the first four Brits were sent to the new Top Gun academy in California, they didn't much care for the 'Maverick' and 'Iceman' style of call sign adopted by their American counterparts. But their hosts insisted, so they came up with 'Cholmondley', 'Dogbreath', 'Alien' and 'Spastic'.

Interestingly, however, when I went to a US air force base in North Carolina a few years ago, I was shown the spec sheets for the F-15 fighter. Alongside each component was a box explaining which countries could know its secrets. And there was only one country that was entitled to see the details of all of them. Not Israel. Not Saudi Arabia. It was us. Even though – or perhaps because – the RAF doesn't actually have any F-15s.

The best way, I think, of understanding how the special

relationship works is to answer this question. When a visiting American actor comes here and makes nice noises about Britain, do you feel all warm, gooey and proud? I bet you do. Now think how it works the other way round. When a British actor goes over there and makes nice noises about America, do you think they even notice? Honestly? I believe it's time we stopped deluding ourselves about our relationship with America, which since the late 1940s has produced virtually nothing. And tried to make friends with the French. Because the last time we did that, the world got Concorde.

Sunday 15 March 2009

You're a bunch of overpaid nancies – and I love you

Over the years I have argued that football is a stupid game in which twenty-two overpaid nancy boys with idiotic hair run around a field attempting to kick an inflated sheep's pancreas into some netting while an audience of several thousand van drivers beat one another over the head with bottles and chairs.

Nor could I understand how someone from Tooting could possibly support, say, Manchester United, a team sponsored by those hateful bastards at AIG and made up of players from Portugal, France, Holland and, in the case of Wayne Rooney, Walt Disney. Where's the connection? What's the point? I have also suggested that it's preposterous to have football stadiums in the middle of cities. Why should anyone be delayed by match traffic just so a handful of thugs can watch a Brazilian man falling over? And as for those people who can't cope if their team loses. Give me strength. If you get all teary-eyed just because someone from Latvia, playing in a town you've never been to, for an Arab you've never met, against some Italians you hate for no reason, has missed a penalty, how are you going to manage when you are diagnosed with cancer? I have always hated football, but then one day, out of the blue, my son announced that he had become interested in Chelsea.

This was a living nightmare. If he'd said that he'd become interested in smoking, I could have made all sorts of threats. If he'd said he'd become interested in homosexuality, we could have talked. But a football team? I had no answers. I didn't even have any questions.

However, because he spent so much time watching football on television, I started pausing to watch. And I began to think that actually it's a very beautiful game when it's played properly. And that the offside rule, really, is no more complicated than the average power station. And then I started picking up bits of information from the commentators, which meant, for the first time ever, that when conversation with friends turned to football, I could join in, instead of sticking my fingers in my ears and singing sea shanties.

This meant that pretty soon people started asking if perhaps I'd like to go to a game. And that's why last weekend I was at Stamford Bridge watching Chelsea demolish a team I used to call Manchester City. But that I now know is called Useless Money-Wasting Scum. This was my first Premier League game and, ooh, it was good. When you're there, rather than watching on television, you get an overall view, which means you can see how the game works. You notice that Frank Lampard is like a blackbird, always looking around to see where the hawks are. You see that Carvalho runs with his arms up, like a begging puppy, and you work out that Michael Essien always seems to be able to find a piece of the pitch that the Useless Scum either hadn't noticed or were frightened of.

The other advantage of being there is that on television the microphones are positioned so you can't hear the chants. I'd heard, of course, about this mass spontaneity over the years, usually when a team is playing Liverpool. 'Sign on. Sign on. With a pen in your hand. Cos you'll ne . . . ver get a job.' Or: 'The wheels on your house go round and round. Round and round. Round and round.' There are others too. Plymouth Argyll refer to any team they play as northern bastards. Then you have the Charlton fans who travelled down the M4 to Reading recently and, having failed to think of any suitable abuse, came up with: 'What's it like to live in Wales?' The Chelsea fans topped all this last Sunday with a non-stop song, the lyrics of which were: 'F*** off, Robinho. F*** off, Robinho. F*** off, Robinho.' I joined in wholeheartedly, even though I wasn't entirely sure who Mr Robinho was and why I wanted him to eff off so much.

No matter. It was all so brilliantly working class. Or it would have been, had I not been seated in a private box just outside the no-jeans-allowed Armani Lounge, where I'd feasted on smoked salmon and quaffed bucks fizz before kickoff.

But I got a reminder of footballing's outside-khazi and jumpers-for-goalposts roots when Chelsea scored. I turned and smiled a patronizing smile at the man sitting behind me, the former *Independent* editor and all-round crap driver Simon Kelner. It turned out he was a big fan of the Scum and, honestly, I thought he was going to kick my head off. I wouldn't have blamed him. I used to be surprised that football fans fought one another. Now, though, having experienced the white heat of pride and tribalism first hand, I'm surprised they don't any more.

After the game I was taken to the Chelsea dressing room so that I could admire all the players' penises – many were very enormous indeed. I talked to Roman Abramovich, who was charming, and Lampard, who, having just run around for ninety minutes, still found the energy to get the entire team to sign my boy's Chelsea shirt. I don't do that for kids who come to the *Top Gear* studio and I'm supposed to be the public-school-educated toff.

So there we are, then. I am now a football fan. I know this because in one afternoon I learnt I'm not a football fan at all. I'm a fan of Chelsea. Chelsea are the only team that can play. Chelsea players have by far the most impressive reproductive organs. Stamford Bridge is my church. The men who play there are my gods.

In short, I have a team, and that's what's always been missing. Because I was born in Doncaster.

Sunday 22 March 2009

Stand still, wimp – only failures run off to be expats

God tells us that there are ten rules in life: Sir Thomas Beecham, the conductor, maintained that there was only one – try everything except incest and folk dancing. Most people, however, reckon there are two. Never meet your heroes. And never turn your hobby into a job.

There is, however, a third rule. It's a big one. It's bigger than the one that says you should never meet Chuck Yeager, the US test pilot who became a hero for breaking the sound barrier, because he'll turn out to be deeply unpleasant. It's bigger than the one about not coveting your neighbour's wife. It's even bigger than not doing morris dancing. It is known simply as Rule Three and what it says is this: do not, under any circumstances, become an expat.

You may be thinking of moving to South Africa because some communists have smashed the windows in your agreeable home. You may imagine that you should go to New Zealand because the police have found a builder with a broken bottom in your swimming pool. Or you may consider moving to a cave on the North-west Frontier because you have knocked over some skyscrapers. But don't give in. It is always better to stay where you are and face the music.

Even if the music in question is the tinkling of your broken sitting-room window or the screams of other prisoners in the showers or the gristly, gooey sound of your fingernails coming out.

The fact of the matter is this: every single person who ever moves to another country – with the exception of America where you go to grow – is a failure. Seriously, no one has ever woken up and said: 'I am completely happy. I have a lovely family, many friends, a great job and plenty of savings. So I shall move to Australia.' It's always the other way around. 'My wife has left me. My children don't want to know. The divorce cost a bundle and I don't have any mates. So I shall move to Oz.' That's why they call us whingeing poms. Because the poms they get do nothing else.

Of course, I have been to a great many palm-fronted island paradises and I've thought, as I've watched the sunlight dancing in my rum punch, how lovely it would be to live in a place where you just wear shorts and read books.

But I know two things. First, home is not where you live; it's where your friends are. And second, within a week, I'd be a raging alcoholic. I'd start by trying not to drink before twelve. But then it'd be ten and before I knew it I'd be pouring gin on my cornflakes and my nose would be enormous and covered in what look like barnacles.

Then the drink-addled bitterness would set in. I'd realize that my existence was shallow and pointless and that every girl I ever met would either be made from leather or interested only in men who had 65 ft cruisers in the harbour. Not noses that looked like the bottom of a battleship.

To keep myself sane, I'd have to keep reminding myself, by reminding absolutely everyone within earshot, constantly, that I couldn't possibly live in Britain because it's full of bloody foreigners who hadn't bothered to learn English. Then I'd summon Manuel and, in English, order another pint of gin.

I was in Majorca last weekend, which is jammed full of British expats, all of whom would begin their explanation of how they got there with the same thing: 'Well, after I sold the cab . . .' There they were, in their chips and footie bars with their desperate eyes and their booze-ruined noses, regaling everyone with their stuck-record views on life back in Blighty.

'Don't know how you can live in Britain. Bloody weather. Bloody Muslims. Bloody Brown,' and then, after a wistful pause, '. . . you don't have a copy of today's *Telegraph* do you?' I've always felt desperately sorry for expats and now, of course, life wherever they may be is even worse than ever because, all of a sudden, their hacienda is worth less than the plot of land they built it on ten years ago, and they can't let the holiday flat they bought to supplement their pension. Which is now worthless as well.

It's proof really that there is no God. Because no one who's supposed to be a force for good would keep on hitting people like that. 'I'm going to make you so miserable, lonely and friendless that you break Rule Three. And then I'm going to take away your home, and your income until you are a homeless drunk in a land where you can't speak the language and you're vomiting gin into the gutter through your barnacle-encrusted nose at three in the morning.' You'd have to be a complete bastard to inflict that much pain on someone.

Sadly, I fear that in the coming months, as deflation takes hold, a great many people will begin to wonder if life wouldn't be happier on the sunny side.

I urge you all to think carefully. Even if they've taken your land and your homes, they cannot take your friends. Or your family. And no matter how infrequently your children drop by now, you can trust me on this: if you live abroad, you'll probably never see them again. Ever.

You will sit there in a bar, in your stupid Hawaiian shirt, pretending the waiter is a friend, reading the barcode on a two-year-old copy of *The Week*, trying desperately to convince yourself that you are happy. But you won't be, because abroad is where you go on holiday. Britain is home.

And you know what? Yes it's cold. Yes it's run by idiots. And yes, I wasn't bothered about Jade Goody either. But at least we don't throw our donkeys off tower blocks and we don't cook our food in the garden.

And because it's always 57 degrees and drizzling, we are less inclined to sit outside all day getting sloshed.

Sunday 29 March 2009

It's pure hell in the mountainous Cotswold region

Forbes, which is a magazine for American people who wear loafers with no socks, has said that the best place to live in Britain and, indeed, the sixth-best place to live in Europe is the pretty Cotswold market town of Burford. They reckon it's better than Barcelona, better than Paris, better even than Rome. Its reasons for suggesting this are that it lies in a 'mountainous region' and that it's home to a wealth of celebrities including the Tory leader, David Cameron, Kate Winslet, Kate Moss and various members of the rock band Radiohead – a group of people who, interestingly, are linked by one common bond: none of them lives anywhere near Burford.

Whatever. The result will infuriate my colleague James May, who has stated very often that the RAF should be instructed to wipe Burford from the map. Burford, in fact, is about the only word in the English language that can make him even remotely excitable and animated. He loathes its tweeness, its gingham-lidded, horse-brass-and-knick-knack, backward-looking smugness and maintains that its haywain, 'Morning, Vicar', low-ceilinged, 'pint of best' pace of life belongs on a postcard, not in a modern society. Sixth-best place to live in Europe? May would argue that it's the sixth circle of hell. And he's right. But for the wrong reasons.

A lot of people would imagine that living in the countryside is easy now that there are tarmac roads, no tithes and no plague and you can't be executed for being a witch. But actually it's harder now than at any point in history.

The first thing that will happen if you move to a land of clean air and big skies is that, immediately, some ramblers will come and sit in your kitchen claiming that they've done so for twenty-one years without let or hindrance and that, if you complain, you will have to spend all your life savings in legal fees.

Eventually you will lose and Janet Street-Porter will bring all her mates round to sit by your Aga, explaining that it churns out six tons of carbon dioxide every year and you are a murderer. But you won't notice because you'll be too busy attempting to rid your garden wall of slogans urging you to go back to London and thus free up property in the country-side for the glue-sniffing, pimple-faced locals.

You might try pointing out that no one ever complains about the army of country folk who come to the capital every year and buy up all the flats that could have been used to house inner-city kids. But I wouldn't recommend this unless you want to know what it feels like to be hit in the face with a shovel.

Next, we should look at the case of Mike Batt, who wrote the music for *Watership Down* and is said to love rabbits. Last week it was reported that he employed a marksman to go out and shoot thousands of them in the face. There are good reasons for doing this. Rabbits ruin trees, poison the soil and eat so many crops that each year it's reckoned they cost the agricultural industry more than £100m. But, of course, if you shoot a bunny-wunny between the eyes, a million vege-tablists are going to jump up and down claiming that you are a fascist and should be ashamed of yourself.

So now you'll have Street-Porter, some glue-sniffers with paint cans and all of the League Against Cruel Sports in your garden. And, as a result, you won't dare go outside to shoot the magpies that have been such a nuisance of late.

Wrong. Wrong. Wrong. You may not kill rabbits or badgers or foxes or crows but the vegetablists announced on Thursday, just a day after Mr Batt was lambasted for killing Hazel and General Woundwort, that they want you to kill as many magpies as you can. Bag a bunch and the RSPB will send you a special achiever's badge.

Confused? Oh, you wait till you try to find a post office or a bank. Or just try popping into Burford to try to buy something you might actually need. They can sell you a teapot in the shape of a Norman church and some local shortbread. But a packet of bog rolls? Some cat food? Not a chance.

Then there's the problem of socializing in the countryside. Because there are no buses, no taxis and no trains, you are faced with two options when you go out at night. Drink bitter lemon or drive home drunk. The only good news if you choose to drink and drive is that you won't get caught by the police – because there aren't any. And you're more likely to find a dustman than a doctor.

Other problems? Well, yes, a few. You won't be able to hear the birdsong because of all the motorbikes, your view will be ruined when a masonic handshake seals the deal on a light industrial unit at the end of your garden and every time you go for a walk you will come home dead, having been run over by a drunken yobbo in a Citroën Saxo.

And your dog won't fare much better because it will have been shot by a farmer.

Pretty soon, then, you will do what most people do in the countryside at some point: commit suicide.

Still, it could be worse. You could have ended up in Gaiole, the Tuscan town that *Forbes* reckons is the best place in Europe to live. Here you will be woken at four every morning by some walnut-faced peasant with a strimmer and driven mad all day by barking dogs. And then you will come home one day to find that your wife has put on 3 stone, grown a moustache and decided to spend the rest of her days cleaning the front step.

Sunday 19 April 2009

What a difference now I've stopped drinking fish fingers

As we know, the government has been waging a campaign of hate against the middle classes for many years. It's never the fat and the lazy, with their ancient cars and their unlagged lofts, who are targeted in the war on climate change. No. It's people with Agas and Range Rovers and patio heaters at their second homes in Gascony.

It's the same story with obesity. In my experience it's the dim and the gormless who have become enormous in recent years, but rather than telling Colleen and Lee to walk to the working men's club every night and stick to orange juice, our glorious leaders have produced a guide on how you can provide your dinner party guests with less alcohol in such a way that they don't notice. Mainly, it involves serving what I like to call beer-free beer and not topping up everyone's glass quite so frequently. They also provide some handy cut-out-'n'-keep recipes for low-alcohol cocktails ... which will ensure that at midnight the few remaining guests will still be talking about property prices in Fulham and school fees.

Plainly all this advice from Mr Brown's taxpayer-funded dinner party advisers is rubbish but to make sure we all understand the need to lose friends and alienate people, they recently announced that one glass of Chablis contained the same amount of calories as four fish fingers. I found this a bit far-fetched and so, on your behalf, I decided to conduct a simple experiment. I would give up drinking, to see what effect it would have on my planetary waistline.

This is a big deal because, as I've explained in the past, I drink a lot. On my recent holiday I would have two beers before lunch, a bottle of rosé with it, a banana daiquiri for pudding, a snooze in the afternoon, four rum punches before dinner, another bottle of wine with that and then some piña coladas to get me in the mood for more sleeping. It works out, if the government is to be believed, at 3,500 calories a day in booze alone.

First of all, I'll explain the rules of my experiment. I would continue to eat as normal and to sit down as much as possible during the day. There would be no jogging or cycling, and no low-fat yoghurt or weeds instead of chops and chips. The only change would be the drink.

And the results are . . . drum roll, please . . . after seven days I have lost precisely 1lb.

This makes no sense because if I really was getting through the equivalent of fifty fish fingers a day, you would imagine that after a week of no fish fingers at all I'd have the body mass index of Jon Bon Jovi and the torso of Willem Dafoe. And yet all that's happened is that I've gone from 224 lb to 223 lb. At this rate of decline, I'd be about 657 years old before there'd be any visible difference at all.

And am I prepared to go that long without a drink? Well, strangely, the answer is: probably, because actually it's not so bad. I certainly see no point in cutting down on alcohol because drinking one glass of wine has about the same effect as adding one grain of sand to the Sahara desert. I don't even notice it. So it's either forty or none at all and I've gone for the zero option.

DefCon 1.

The first problem was finding something as enjoyable as wine to drink after a day at work. Water obviously is useless because it's just liquefied lettuce. You may as well drink helium. So what I've done is rediscovered a fondness for

Robinsons lemon barley water and, I have to say, it's nicer than any claret.

With that problem out of the way, we move on to the next – not drinking in the company of those who are. God, drunks talk gibberish, usually at a volume that can crack rock. Then they fall in the bin, blame Gordon Brown and emerge with a set of opinions that hovers somewhere between Genghis Khan and the *Daily Mail*. Trying to talk sensibly when all around have lost their heads, and their ability to sit on a chair, is like trying to do applied maths while being keelhauled. I've often wondered how my teetotal friends have managed to stay on the wagon when they are surrounded by booze and boozers. Now I know. You begin to see drink not as a relaxant or as a stimulant but as a problem that doesn't screw with your waistline. Only your mind.

There's more good news. Last night I drove to London, had supper with friends and then did something I've never done before. I. Drove. Home. Again. Not with one eye in the mirror and my heart in my mouth. But with gay abandon and a reckless attitude to the speed limit. Come and get me, rozzers. Let me blow in your bag. Bring it on.

Even better, I've started waking up feeling an unusual compulsion to draw the curtains and play table tennis with the children. I no longer have to spend the morning clinging on to things. And do you know what? I haven't had a lumpy yawn for a whole week now. Perhaps that's why I'm still fat. I've stopped vomiting.

Of course I cannot imagine even for a moment that this will be a long-term experiment but I do recommend you give it a bash. Contrary to what the government says, you won't lose much weight, but you really will feel – there's no other word – 'better'.

If that sounds appealing, then I can assure you that giving

up drink is a damn sight easier than the alternatives. Doing without roast potatoes, and skipping.

What's more, avoiding alcohol won't make you a bore. It'll make you the exact opposite.

Sunday 26 April 2009

Gordon the ass is stomping over everyone's pets

As Mr Darling and Mr Brown continue to ruin the economy, people are having to ponder on what they can no longer afford. And many, according to the Royal Society for the Prevention of Animals, have decided the family pet must go. Apparently thirty animals a day are being abandoned at the moment. Almost 60 per cent up on last year.

This is understandable. I mean, if I had a tiger and I lost my job, I'd think seriously about getting rid of it. And it'd be much the same story if I had a whale or a bear of some kind. Certainly, I've made it perfectly plain to my donkeys that if Harriet Harman gets her way and I'm replaced on *Top Gear* by a Somalian lesbian, they'll be off to the sausage factory.

There is no doubt that some pets are extremely expensive to run. My labradoodle requires a professional shampoo and blow-dry after every rain shower. My golden lab is kept alive with nothing but cash. And the electricity bill for the fox-zapping fence that rings my chickens' enclosure means that every egg they produce costs roughly £1m.

And then we get to the horses. I have spoken to my wife about turning them into glue but she maintains they are not luxury items at all, and that the only reason she burns the various equine bills is because they are too trivial and small to file away and keep.

Hmmm. They have sweet itch constantly and as a result are always draped in yashmaks that must cost £800,000 each. Plus they need new shoes every two days, and a visit from the psychiatrist every time they see a paper bag in a hedge. And that's before we get to the fact that their absolute favourite food is the wooden post-and-rail fence that keeps them in the paddock. In a single night, they can eat about 500 yards of it. And fencing is unbelievably expensive to replace. To stop them doing this, I have painted the new sections with a virulent chilli oil, but it turns out that what they like even more than wooden fencing is wooden fencing smothered in chillies.

I would estimate that the cost of keeping the horses where they belong, preventing Brer Fox from eating the hens, running a lab to hatch the eggs, blow-drying the dogs and retrieving the sheep that ramblers like to chase into the sea at my holiday cottage is about £4 billion a year. I definitely spend more of my earnings on animals than on my cars. Far more.

And so I can quite understand why someone who has been made redundant might turn to his wife and say, 'Honey. I'm sorry. But the llamas have to go.' I noted last week that Harrow school, presumably suffering, like everyone else, from Darling and Brown's insanity, is having to sell its enormous collection of butterflies. Which have been dead for a hundred years.

However, I was extremely alarmed to see that someone had abandoned a tortoise. I'm not joking. He was handed in to a rescue centre in Bolton because his owners couldn't afford to run him any more. Now, leaving aside the question of why Bolton needs a tortoise rescue centre, we really must ask how bad things have to be before you say, 'Well, I'm sorry, kids, but Tommy the tortoise has to go.' I realize, of course, that it's much easier to abandon a tortoise than various other animals. You're forever reading about people who've driven from Scotland to abandon their dog in Exeter and three weeks later it's homed and is back on their doorstep. Cats can do this as well. Unless you drown them first. Whereas a tortoise cannot. Take it to the end of the road, and even if it has a homing gene, you and your children will be six feet under before it's back.

However, I can't see the point of getting rid of one in the first place. Experts say that tortoises require a diet that contains just the right balance of calcium and phosphorus and that they should be provided with a heated kennel. Then they undermine their authority by saying that tortoises can dig under fences or climb over them and are vicious. I think maybe they've got tortoises somehow muddled up with prisoners of war.

The fact is that a tortoise is unbelievably easy to keep. Sure, it may not be very cuddly, it's completely useless at retrieving sticks and it won't bark at burglars, but even if it loses a leg, there's no need to call the vet: simply attach a caster, which can be bought for £2.49 from B&Q.

Apparently the tortoise that was handed in at the Bolton centre had kidney stones because of dehydration. Again. Not a problem. Just give it some water. It doesn't even need to be Hildon or Evian. What's more, tortoises are tough little bastards.

When I was a kid I had two. Gilbert and Squeak (Sullivan and Bubble died) both escaped one night into a neighbouring field of wheat, where they survived a combine harvester and the burning of the stubble.

Naturally, I have a tortoise today and I have calculated how much he costs to keep every year. In the summer he lazes about in the garden eating dandelions, and in the winter he sleeps so soundly that I use him as a chock for my classic Mercedes. The final bill, then, is nought. Actually, it's less than nought because without him I'd have to get the Merc's handbrake repaired. Henry is in fact saving me money.

And best of all, he will live to be 1,000, which means we won't face the same sort of sobbing we had from the children when the vet, for just £30, said the pet mouse had a tumour and would surely die.

For many reasons, then, the tortoise is the ideal recessionary pet. Your other animals, I'm afraid, will have to be left on the central reservation of the M5. It's something I've known for a while. The sort of socialism being practised now by Darling and Brown ultimately kills people's dogs.

Sunday 3 May 2009

Change fast, before we all gag on the fabric of British life

Last week a million dewy-eyed fools were celebrating the fiftieth anniversary of the Mini, the small car that symbolizes everything that's been wrong with Britain since Hitler poisoned his dog.

I do not wish to dwell on cars here but it's important to stress that, back in 1959, for all sorts of oily reasons, the little Austin was very clever. France had its Citroën 2CV. Germany had its Volkswagen Beetle. Russia had its ox. And we had the Mini, the best-packaged, most fun personal transport module of them all.

And then the British did what the British did best. Nothing. The Mini was therefore crap by 1965, but despite this it was still being made as the twenty-first century dawned, by which time it was as out of date as a Norman keep. And I have the distinct impression that, if BMW hadn't bought the company, it would still be churning them out today. Gramophones in a flatscreen world.

It's much the same story with the Land Rover. Designed just after the war, it is still being sold to farmers and the British Army, where it sits in the modern theatre like a medieval trebuchet. So why hasn't it been replaced with something that has space for a driver's shoulder? Oh, because that would be like tearing down Anne Hathaway's cottage. It's part of the fabric of British life.

Of course it is. Anything becomes the fabric of your life if it hangs around long enough. Your old dog with its anal warts. The leaky pipe in your spare room. Even syphilis can become part of the fabric of your life if you don't go to the doctor's.

Look at the Royal Navy. Tony Blair announced in 1998 that we needed some new aircraft carriers. But there was so much fannying-about that the contract to get the process going wasn't signed until 2008. Ten years later. You'd imagine of course that before the ink on the paperwork was dry, the companies charged with building these new carriers would be up and running. But no. Here we are in 2009 and there's still no keel. And of course, pretty soon, parliament will turn round and explain that our old carriers, which chug around on one engine to save fuel, have become part of the fabric of British life and, as such, cannot be decommissioned.

Look round the back of any public building and you'll note the plumbing, and the paint, was installed in about 1951 and has not been upgraded since. Battersea power station is still there, producing no power, or indeed anything at all. And the next time you're in a London taxi, wonder why the rear suspension has to be made from corrugated iron. I'll tell you why.

Because it's always been made that way.

I was examining some photographs of Sandringham House this morning and, oooh, it's a monster. It should be pulled down immediately and replaced with something much more attractive. But can you even begin to imagine the hulla-baloo if Mrs Queen even mentioned such a thing? Even when change comes, it's half-arsed.

I mean, look at the House of Lords. Mr Blair, the great modernizer, decided it was unfair to have the country ruled by people whose only qualification for the job was a great-grandad who'd killed lots of Turks. So did he abolish it? Did he hell. He just replaced the Bufton Tuftons with a bunch of people whose only qualification is a hatred of meat and a chip on the shoulder.

And what plans are in store for London's next bus? Why, it's a bloody Routemaster.

A particular bugbear for me is the red phone box. It was cramped, draughty, prone to vandalism and used mostly as a lavatory. So we should have rejoiced when mobile phones made it redundant. But oooh no. You can't get rid of London's red phone boxes.

And there's the problem. If we form an emotional attachment to every single thing that comes into our lives, pretty soon the whole country will become clogged up with stuff that doesn't work any more.

Woolworths was a classic case in point. When it went out of business, everyone ran around saying it should be saved because it was 'traditional'. No it wasn't. It was a terrible shop, selling awful things that even ghastly people didn't want to buy. Woolworths was useful only for sheltering from a Second World War bombing raid.

You should look around your house for more examples of this stupid sentimentality. For sure, your dining-room table may have originally belonged to your grandfather. But if the legs have woodworm and the surface contains traces of diphtheria, then why not replace it with a new one? Just because something is old, it is not necessarily good. The Victorians, for instance, couldn't paint horses. They always looked like Devon Loch, with their legs sticking out all the wrong way. So why have a Victorian hunting scene in your lavatory when Hallmark can sell you something that is better for less? Of course, I would not suggest we erase all of history from the British landscape. And certain things that should be preserved cannot be displayed in a museum or encapsulated well enough in a history book. Burford, for instance, or the Queen. But we, as a nation, must stop getting teary-eyed about the death of something we hold dear. The wet British summer. The traditional ketchup bottle. The long-playing record. The busby.

With that in mind, I think there should be a national referendum, maybe with an accompanying TV show, where participants are invited to nominate one thing from British life that should now be put in the dustbin. I'd like to kick things off by nominating the Labour party.

An apology: last week, I said the tortoise was an ideal pet because it costs nothing to keep and will never upset your children by dying. Unfortunately, on Monday, perhaps because we spent nothing on it, ours did just that

Sunday 10 May 2009

Okay, you've got me bang to rights – I'm a secret green

Last week, in this newspaper, I was outed as a recycler, a man who composts his tea bags, eats wasps and spends most of his days tutting in supermarkets at the Day-Glo orangeness of the carrots. Or, to put it another way, a damned hypocrite.

Well, I'm sorry, but if the newspaper is going to publish these accusations, then I am surely allowed to reply. Yes, I do recycle. Yes, I do eat wasps, if they've burrowed into my apples. And yes, I do get so angry in supermarkets that often I leave my half-filled trolley in the spices aisle and come home empty-handed.

There's more. On Wednesday I spent most of the morning demanding to see the manager of a restaurant in which each individual sugar lump was wrapped in its own plastic sleeping bag. 'Why,' I wailed, 'do you buy sugar this way?' Using plastic to wrap sugar just means more litter and ultimately less diesel for my Range Rover.

And there's the problem. Because these days the rules state that you are either completely green or you are not green at all. The whole movement has been hijacked by lunatics who want everyone to live in crofts and Facebook trees.

Excuse me, but I have yet to be convinced that man's paltry 3 per cent contribution to the planet's bank of carbon dioxide affects the climate. And furthermore, I do not share the view that a rise in global temperatures is necessarily a bad thing. For instance, I believe a parrot would be a more interesting Cotswold garden bird than a sparrow.

As a result, I'm still the same man who dreams of running

amok on the set of *Mamma Mia!* with a large-calibre machine-gun. I'm still the man who wondered what my dead tortoise would taste like. And I'm still the man who lights his patio heater in April and leaves it burning non-stop till Bonfire Night.

However, I am also the man who likes to poke restaurant managers in the forehead when they bring me individually wrapped sugar lumps. And I will continue to fill supermarket trolleys and then leave them for some halfwit to unload again after I've stormed out in disgust at the sheer quantity of entirely unnecessary packaging.

Wal-Mart reckons that a third of all consumer waste in America comes from packaging and says it is committed to reducing its use by 5 per cent. That sounds noble, but why only 5 per cent? Why not completely? Why do we have to buy apples in a polythene bag? Why do all toys have to come in their own moulded plastic display box? And why, if they do, does the plastic have to be of such thickness that many car firms would not even use it to make a bumper? I recently bought something called a Black Widow slingshot. It's a catapult that fires ball bearings with devastating force. I was very much looking forward to blatting a few pigeons with it. But I cannot get through the plastic case in which it was sold. Scissors just break. My Strimmer became jammed. And dynamite is ineffective. I would very much like to meet the man who chose to seal his product this way, and kill him.

The list of my issues is endless. Why is milk served in a plastic thimble and not a jug? What's the matter with grease-proof paper for sandwiches? Why do hotels serve jam in one-cubic-inch jars? And why do DVDs come in an impregnable Cellophane wrapper? It's not like they're going to rot.

It's not just packaging either. I am particularly partial to a radish, and as a result I grow my own, in my own vegetable garden. Well, obviously, I don't grow them. A man does. But it's my bit of land and I'm the one who nourishes it by composting coffee grounds and old copies of the *Guardian*. Anyway, the radishes I grow may be full of worm holes and covered in mud but pop one into your mouth and it feels like your tongue is stuck in a gin trap. Peppery is too sprightly a word to describe the savagery of their kick. This is how a radish should be. And watercress.

And now we get to the miserable offerings sold by supermarkets, in plastic bags. They taste of absolutely nothing. You would be better off eating the plate on which they are served. They are nothing more than cross-trainers for your mouth, something to do when you're not smoking.

I would like to meet the people responsible for this. I would like them to try one of my radishes and one of my chicken's eggs, and I would like them to eat watercress straight from the beck in Appletreewick. And then I would like to stand, with my hands on my hips, and demand an explanation.

Make no mistake. I hate anything labelled organic. I deliberately won't buy Fairtrade crisps. Or anything with a pithy nuclear-free, multicultural slogan. I loathe the movement, but I love, with all my heart, the destination. And this from a man who blasted his taste buds to kingdom come with nicotine by the time he was twenty-six. This from a man who cannot tell the difference between chicken and fish.

So yes, I recycle and I grow my own eggs, and I harvest my barley field from the inside out, so that any of the birds in there have a chance to flee. But all of these things are my choice. I would not dream of banning supermarket radishes or the bags in which they come. I would not set up a website for like-minded individuals. I would not go on a march.

I get on with these little things quietly, because if I made a noise and a fuss I would be labelled an environmentalist. Which is a terrible, hideous, beardy label for unwashed communists.

Nobody wants that, and this highlights something rather interesting. If the eco-ists would only shut up, I wonder if the sound of their droning would be replaced by the sound of normal people fitting solar panels and making soup from nettles and twigs.

Sunday 17 May 2009

I'll be right there, Sir Ranulph – must conquer the sofa first

Sir Ranulph Fiennes explained last week that he reached the summit of Everest by imagining it wasn't there. He said he was prepared simply to 'plod for ever', never once allowing himself the luxury of thinking about where he was going, what he was doing or whether he was halfway to halfway yet. In other words, Britain's greatest adventurer achieved his goal by adopting the mindset of everyone else. 'Plodding for ever' is what almost all of us do almost every day. We get up in a morning, we trudge through the day, with no sense of purpose or ambition, and then we die.

Just this morning, after an enormously long time, the lift doors finally opened in my London apartment block to reveal a middle-aged woman who apologized for the eternity I'd been kept waiting. 'I like to go up and down in here,' she said. 'You sometimes meet quite interesting people.'

So while Sir Ranulph walks from pole to pole, goes to his shed to amputate bits of his body that have become a nuisance, climbs the world's highest peaks, has a heart operation and then runs seven marathons in seven days on seven continents, we have a woman who amuses herself by going up and down in a lift.

I'm no better. I amuse myself by getting up in a morning, going to Guildford, driving round corners a bit too quickly, while shouting, and then driving home to bury whichever pet has died that day. On Tuesday it was the mouse. Or, to be more accurate, the tumour with a mouse growing out of it.

I envy Ranulph Fiennes. I envy his drive. I envy his quest-fulness. Certainly, I know for sure that if I were enraged by a big American movie company that dammed a trout stream to make a feature film about talking animals, I'd sit at home and do nothing except write imaginary letters to my MP. Fiennes, on the other hand, nicked some explosives from the SAS stores and attempted to blow the Americans back from where they'd come.

If I'd got frostbite by trying to retrieve my tent and cook-ing equipment from the jaws of the Arctic Ocean, I'd whimper and wait for the doctor to work his miracles. Fiennes simply broke out his saw and did the job himself. He did. He cut bits of his own hand off because 'it was annoying me'.

The rest of us are so very different. I, for instance, want to learn how to play the piano. But that means buying one, get-ting someone to bring it round, finding a book full of tunes that I like and that don't have too many sharps or flats in them . . . and, all things considered, I can't be bothered. I want to start collecting butterflies, but that means reading books and buying a net, and, frankly, it's easier to watch tele-vision instead. There are so many things I want to do, so many ways I want to push my body and expand my mind, but it's always easier to carry on plodding.

Gardening is a classic case in point. Last year, in a flurry of square-jawed determination to do something worthwhile, I bought a tree. It was delivered on the back of a lorry, in a huge pot, and plonked by the garage. Which is where it sits now because it's just too much of a faff to move it.

It's much the same story with my fountain. Three years ago I arranged for a plumber and an electrician to do the groundwork, but then I decided that not finishing it off was easier than finishing it off, so today my back lawn still has an unsightly pipe and some wires poking out of the grass that I really should cut this afternoon. But I won't because I'll be too busy watching the Monaco Grand Prix. Not live, obviously. That would have meant organizing tickets and finding a hotel and getting childcare and going to an airport, and, honestly, it's so much easier to watch it on television. Unless the weather holds, in which case I'll just stay in a chair in the ruin that could be a garden. But isn't.

My latest project is bonsai trees. While everyone else at the Chelsea flower show last week mooched about wondering why there were so few shooting invitations this year, I became transfixed by the display of miniature topiary. The pine trees with their gnarled trunks and wind-blown lean looked exactly like the fully grown examples you might find on a cliff in southern Spain. But they were just a couple of feet tall. The detailing was exquisite. And I found myself swooning in the conjoining of nature's infinite bounds for beauty and man's ability to make everything better still.

Bonsai-ists are the same as Yorkshire's dry-stone wallers, who bring the countryside to life, and the thirteenth-century cathedral builders, whose vision provides a focal point in our temperate flatlands. I spoke for a while with a fellow bonsai enthusiast, who explained about how it's essential to concentrate on the roots rather than the plant you actually see, and how to change the fertilizer and ensure a steady flow of phosphoric acid, and how to prune the leaves and to make sure there is precisely the right amount of sunshine. And I'm afraid my eyes started to glaze over as I realized it would be much easier to fire up the PlayStation and spend an hour or two shooting my children in the face.

For this reason, I'm never going to build the fantastic train set that exists only in my mind. I'm never going to hang the pictures I haven't bought yet. And I'm never going to clear

Cambodia of landmines. And neither are you, because you're sitting around reading the papers, same as you did last week and the week before.

I know we can't all be Ranulph Fiennes.

We can't do everything. But don't you wish that sometimes you could find the time from the drudge of the humdrum . . . to do something?

Sunday 24 May 2009

Letting beavers loose in Scotland is a dam-fool idea

As we know, the economy is stagnant, we are up to our shoulders in debt and things are likely to get worse. So imagine my surprise to find the government has decided to spend £275,000 on eleven Norwegian beavers that will be freed to roam wild in Scotland. As this works out at £25,000 each, I'm wondering if the money could have been better spent. Because I've done some checking and it turns out that for the same kind of cash they could have bought an extremely rare white lion cub, half a dozen house-trained chimpanzees and a brace of albino pythons. A striped Bengal cat, which looks very much like a small monochrome tiger and is created by mating an Asian leopard cat with a domestic tom, can be bought, according to a *Forbes* magazine survey, for as little as £500. Extremely good value for money considering that I should imagine many of the couplings end with the domestic tom inside the female's stomach.

Of course, the people responsible for choosing the beaver instead would argue that Scotland is not an appropriate place for mutant tigers or pythons – I think they're wrong on this – and that they went for the big-toothed rat because it used to live there before man invented toast and wanted something to put on it.

Needless to say, the scheme has met with considerable opposition from the likes of Jeremy Paxman and Sir Ian Botham, who say that beavers will eat all the fish they were hoping to put back, and from locals who think they will catch cryptosporidiosis – an incurable ailment that causes such uncontrollable diarrhoea that sufferers have been known to excrete their own lungs.

I made that up, in the same way that alarmists have made up the threat levels. Beavers do carry a range of parasites – as businessmen on trips to east Africa know to their cost – but the chances of becoming ill after a walk in the glens are nil.

For me, the problem with reintroducing beavers to Scotland, where they haven't lived for 400 years, is that pretty soon the Highlands will be a broken and desolate place full of nothing but poisoned oxbow lakes, dead deer and grouse moors that look like the UAE's empty quarter.

To understand the problem, we need to go back to the nineteenth century and the creation of Yellowstone, the world's first national park. Obviously man knew best, so to make sure it was as diverse as possible, bears and wolves were not encouraged with quite the same fervour as various deery things. Which meant that pretty soon the whole place was awash with elk. Lovely. Unfortunately, elk absolutely love aspen trees, which meant that soon enough they were all gone. And that was a problem for Johnny beaver, because without the aspens he couldn't dam the rivers and streams. So he moved out. And without the dams, the water meadows dried hard in the summer months, meaning there was no grass for the deery things to eat. So they started to move out as well.

Unwilling to accept they'd made a mess, the authorities blamed the migration on carnivores and started a cull of wolves and bears. Which meant their numbers started to fall, too. Until in the 1950s pretty much all any visitor could see on a trip to Yellowstone was about a million bored elk wondering if the fender from Wilbur and Myrtle's Oldsmobile would keep them going till the aspen trees came back.

And then came the clincher. Unlike the Indians, who had regularly burnt the region, the whitey eco-ists had steadfastly waged war against all forest fires. This meant the ground was littered with tinder-dry fallen twigs and branches. So when the lightning struck in 1988 and the fire started, it burnt close to the ground rather than in the trees. This meant it burnt hot and could not be extinguished and the result of that was simple. The soil in the entire park – all 2m acres of it – was rendered sterile and useless.

That's what will happen to Scotland. Oh, they may say the beavers will be monitored and they'll be good for the tourist industry. But that's what Dickie Attenborough said about Jurassic Park just before the T-rex ate his children.

I'm not suggesting that the beavers will eat people who go to see them, although if they are ramblers that would be no bad thing. But who's to say the trees they chew don't contain some unknown bacterium that stops sheep becoming man-eaters? Who's to say the floods their dams create won't swamp Glasgow? Who's to say the Loch Ness Monster isn't an ancient beaver experiment that got out of hand? Of course, the beaver enthusiasts will dismiss all this as non-sense and point to the red kites that were successfully reintroduced in the Chilterns a few years ago. Absolutely. I love to see these majestic birds soaring over the cut on the M40 as I drive to London. They lift my spirits. But did any-one notice the RSPB findings last week? The sudden and dramatic decline in the number of lapwings, wood warblers and fieldfares? Could this have anything to do with the sud-den re-emergence of the airborne raptor? Then we have foxy woxy. Now that the hunt is not allowed to (legally) kill them, everyone's chicken run is full of nothing but feathers and feet. Mine looks like a voodoo preacher's wet dream. And that means we have to buy our eggs from the supermar-ket, which means we'll all catch salmonella and die in great pain.

I have this advice for Scotland's eco-ists. Don't try to manage nature. Embrace it. Make it a part of you. Eat it. Forget the beavers, which, while cute and clever compared with, say, a rock or an apple, are expensive and mostly invisible. If it's tourists you're after, look at the giraffe. Children would love to see them on the glens, they won't hurt Sir Botham's salmon, they carry no unpleasant diseases, they are cheap and no one will steal their eggs.

Sunday 31 May 2009

Say cheese, darling – I'll stick on your horse's ears later

One of the things I'd most like to do is force the people on *Desert Island Discs* each week actually to live on a desert island with nothing but the music they select. Then we'd be able to see how wacky and interesting they feel after twenty years of 'Two Little Boys' by Rolf Harris and the 'Love Song' from *Sanders of the River*.

We see a similar problem with those who make wild and stupid claims about what they'd save should their house suddenly be on fire. By all means tell your mates over dinner that you'd rescue the onyx cufflinks bought for your eighteenth birthday by a long-lost girlfriend. But don't come crying to me when the firemen are removing the soggy and charred lump of meat that used to be your dog.

I've always said that, if a giant meteorite were to be heading for my house, I'd save my copy of *Monty Python's Big Red Book*, which was signed in 1976 by every member of the team. That, however, is a lie, designed mostly to reveal that I have such a thing. The truth of the matter is that it would be left behind. Because what I'd actually save are my photograph albums. If they were to burn I would feel a biting sense of loss. And that's strange because I haven't looked at them since 1979 and I'm fairly certain I never will again. In fact, I'm pretty sure that I haven't looked more than once at any picture I've ever taken. And I bet you haven't, either.

How many people – hands up – have ever watched their wedding video? That's, let's see ... none. And think how much effort you made on the big day. You paid a man in a cheap suit to come along. You allowed him to jostle your friends and relatives out of the way. You sacrificed an hour of perfectly good drinking time so he could get some nice angles of you on the swing, under the weeping willow tree in the churchyard. And where's the video now? I bet half of you don't even know.

It's the same story with pictures. In the olden days our SLRs were the size of Bibles, but we'd lug them around with an assortment of spare lenses and flash guns and we'd move people out of the sun and make everyone smile and we'd take the film to the developers and we'd pay a bit extra for a fast turnaround because we were desperate to see how everything had turned out. And then we'd leaf through the finished shots in ten seconds, put them in a drawer and never, ever, look at them again.

Today, things are very different. Because you have a digital camera on your phone, you take pictures of absolutely everything, and on YouTube every day's a wedding day. You used to come back from your holiday with twenty-four pictures, because that's how many were on the film. Now most people come back from a trip to the shops with about a billion. The other day I took a picture of the sky simply because it had no clouds in it.

And yesterday I caught my daughter taking a picture of a pair of scissors. Our new tortoise, meanwhile, has had more portrait work done on it than the Queen.

Because cameras are in effect free and because there is no longer any developing, photography no longer has a cost. And without a cost it has no value. It's much like the music you can buy on iTunes. It's not music at all. It's just millions of people making a noise. You may say this is a good thing. You may say it was unjust that in the days before photography only the rich could afford to immortalize themselves on paper. And now everyone can. But down the line I can see this causing all sorts of issues.

Let me explain why. This morning I decided to transfer all the pictures of the sky and our kitchen scissors from my iPhone on to my computer. This is easy enough if you have about four spare weeks, the temper of someone who's actually dead and a master's degree in American business-speak.

The problem is that over the years I have owned many phones and many digital cameras. So when the computer detects that it's been presented with some pictures, it stores them in the electronic equivalent of a dusty box in the cellar, behind the gun safe. Finding them again is a nightmare. But find them you do, and then what? Do you delete the ones that have no meaning or that are out of focus? No. You either leave them all where they are, in which case they will be lost for all of time when your hard drive crashes. Which, one day, I assure you it will. That, of course, is not as disastrous as losing a photograph album, because you will also have put them on Facebook in the mistaken belief that the rest of the world will somehow be interested in what you did on holiday. Frankly, I'd rather look at someone's piles than their holiday pics. Or you carefully move them to a disc, which involves going into town, buying a packet of three, coming home, finding out you've bought the wrong ones, going back into town again and then finally getting everything transferred. It would be easier to set up an easel and break out the oils.

But before you do any of these things, I bet you have a little fiddle with the computer's Paint Shop program. You start out imagining that you'll put everything the right way up and maybe get rid of everyone's red eye. But pretty soon you will be giving your children massive noses and making your family pets sepia. I always give my wife some horse's ears, which makes her very angry.

And therein lies my problem with all this. At the moment, when a historian or a genealogist uncovers a faded picture from Victorian times, he will know it was a special occasion and that the person with his unsmiling face and ramrod back must either have been important or have done something worthwhile. But what will he be able to deduce when he leafs through the pictures we take today? Nothing. Except that we had machinegun-trigger fingers, enormous comedy noses and monochrome pets and we all got married in a fog of Vaseline on a swing.

Sunday 7 June 2009

Now there's a first – my elephant has just exploded

Recently, a friend bet me that I would never begin a newspaper column by suggesting that the musical score of *Ondine*, a little-known ballet, is virtually identical to side one of *Works: Volume One*, the Emerson, Lake and Palmer double album from 1977.

I don't normally go to the ballet. I usually have better things to do than sit about watching men standing on one leg for two hours. But last weekend I was taken by my ten-year-old daughter to the Royal Opera House to see *Ondine*. And here goes: I couldn't help noticing that the score is virtually identical to side one of *Works: Volume One*, the Emerson, Lake and Palmer double album from 1977.

Now, we know Keith Emerson was not averse to dropping a bit of classical pomp into his prog-rockery. For *Brain Salad Surgery*, he lifted chunks of Hubert Parry's score for 'Jerusalem', and on *Pictures at an Exhibition*, Mussorgsky is credited as a co-writer. I was always under the impression, though, that side one of *Works*, a towering classical achievement, was all Keith's work. The album sleeve notes certainly suggest that. And yet there I was, in the ballet, not just recognizing phrases and chords, but predicting precisely what would come next. Because I'd heard it all before.

It would be wrong, of course, to suggest that Keith, a talented songwriter and knifeman, thought to himself: 'The music from *Ondine*, a little-known ballet, has not been used to advertise tyres or chocolate. And chances are, no one who goes to the ballet will ever listen to ELP. So I'll nick it.' That would be a moral and legal outrage. So there must be another explanation. And there is. On a piano, there are only around twenty-five types of chord, each of which has twelve possible roots and can be inverted in a number of ways. Do the maths and it works out at around 8,400 possible combinations.

The simple fact of the matter, then, is that by about 1963, all those combinations and all the combinations of stringing them together had been used up. It is therefore inevitable that some pieces of music are going to sound pretty much identical to something that has gone before. And as a result of that, it is pointless for bands to record new music. We've heard it all before.

There is a similar problem with exploration. Obviously, every mountain has already been climbed, which is why, nowadays, you need to reach the top of Everest in the nude to make waves. Sometimes, when I am up in the Scottish Highlands, or in the middle of Iceland, I wonder if any human has ever trodden on the same piece of earth that I'm treading on at that precise moment. It's nice to think I'm the first. But, realistically, it is improbable.

In all forms of artistic endeavour, we see similar issues. Surely I am not the only person to have noticed that Ron Howard's *Frost/Nixon* is identical in every way to *Rocky*. Or that every modern bespoke, architect-designed house is the same as all the other modern bespoke, architect-designed houses. Or that every painting for sale on the walls of my local pub is identical to all the paintings for sale in your local pub. There are very few ways of painting a cow in a meadow. And they've all been done already.

It's rather depressing to think that, no matter what you do or where you go, you will always be Scott of the Antarctic, the plucky chap who came in second. Or that you can spend years writing an epic, only to have some artistic dunderhead think: 'You've stolen that from a ballet.'

However, there is one area in which every one of us breaks new ground every single day. We do it every time we speak.

Recently, while filming an episode for the new series of *Top Gear*, which starts again next Sunday, incidentally, I turned to Richard Hammond and said: 'Oh no. I've just shoved this anarchy flag through my water lilo.' And I can be absolutely sure that no one has ever said such a thing before. 'My elephant has just exploded.' No one ever said that either. Or: 'My word, Gordon Brown's doing a good job.' Or: 'Caroline Flint. Mmm. Tasty.'

Last week we learnt that there were now exactly 999,999 words in the English language. Actually, a spokesman for the Global Language Monitor claims there are a million, but since the millionth entry is 'Web 2.0', it must be discounted on the basis it is an existing word with a number tagged on to the end.

Then you have the *Oxford English Dictionary*, which claims there are in fact 616,000 'word forms' but only 171,000 that could be called current.

Whatever the true figure, I calculated recently that the BBC alone transmits around 87m words a day, all of which manage to offend the *Daily Mail*, and while I accept that most people only ever use a few hundred types of word in the course of a lifetime – unless they are estate agents, in which case it's about a billion, none of which makes any sense – we cannot ignore the fact that there are 400m people in the world for whom English is the first language.

That's 400m people saying, on average, 1,500 words a day. Week in, week out. You'd imagine, then, that every single combination would have been used up years ago, and yet we can be certain no one has ever said: 'I name this ship HMS *Vulnerable*.' Or: 'The thing I love most about my husband is his herpes.' Or: 'Look at that maniac in that Saab.'

We can also be certain that making a whole newspaper column out of the similarities between *Ondine* and Emerson, Lake and Palmer has never been done before. Definitely not by anyone who could be £10 better off as a result. But then, I need the money because, according to the *Daily Mail*, all BBC presenter salaries are to be slashed. Interestingly, though, no one had ever said that either.

Sunday 14 June 2009

No, I won't wear a tiara, if it's all the same to you

Back in the 1980s, I seemed to spend half my life traipsing to Covent Garden to hire a dinner jacket and the other half mournfully explaining to the man on the returns desk that it was covered in sick when I rented it. And that, no, despite the strong smell of chlorine and the fact it was only 6 in long, it had most definitely not been in a swimming pool. What's more, every wedding, and there was one every weekend from what I remember, required the idiotic combination of a stovepipe hat and a morning suit. Which would then be ruined because I'd have to leave the reception and dash off to throw some food at the chap who was getting hitched the following Saturday. Inevitably, that led to more mournfulness at Moss Bros.

Back in those days, you couldn't go anywhere without going home first to get changed. Restaurants would turn you away if you weren't wearing a tie. Gentlemen were required to wear jackets. Shorts were for the playing field, and I was once turned away from Rotters Nitespot in Doncaster because, despite my claims that the jacket was actually velvet, the bouncer was most insistent it was made of corduroy. Corduroy was a big no-no in Donny back then. Because it was deemed cheap, publicans and club owners felt that you wouldn't care too much if it were torn in half in a fight. You had to be smart because that way, it was felt, you'd be less likely to stick a pint pot into the face of someone who was looking at you funnily.

Happily, these days things are very different. Last weekend

I went to a posh wedding and nobody's jacket went down to the backs of their knees. I wore a £40 suit I'd had made in Vietnam. One chap was in a pair of Levi's.

Then, last week, I was at a fundraising event for Palestinian children in London's glittering West End. Time was, I'd have had to dash into an Indian restaurant on the way to 'borrow' a waiter's bow tie. Not any more. People appeared to be wearing what they'd had on when they finished work. Lily Allen wasn't even sporting a bra. The hussy.

At the Royal Opera House not that long ago it was all veils and tails. Now they will let you in in your underpants. And why not? Who says that to see a woman on tiptoe you need to be mummified in starch? I think this casualization is excellent because, if you are staging a get-together, whether it be a fundraising event for the people of Gaza or a wedding, it is absurd to tell your guests what they must wear. That would be like forcing them not to smoke, or insisting that all the vegetablists eat meat. If you are a host, then it is your duty to make sure that your guests have as nice a time as possible. That means letting them wear and do and eat whatever takes their fancy. If I invite you round to my house, it's because I want to spend an evening in your company. And I don't care about what box you come in. Army boots and a jockstrap? Fine. Naked? That's fine too. Especially if you are Lily Allen.

However, even today, with liberalism running amok, the dress code has survived. And often you need Colossus to decipher it. 'Country casual'; 'purple and fun'; '1963'. Or, worst of all, 'fancy dress'. I was invited last week to a 'white tie and tiara' do and I'm afraid it went the way of all invitations where the host tells the guests what to wear. Into the bin. White tie and tiara? Do me a favour.

The worst offender, however, is Royal Ascot, which trundled into the summer last week with all the welcoming warmth of a bed of rusty nails. Gentlemen are required to wear a black or a grey morning coat and a top hat that may be removed only in restaurants or in enclosed seating areas. That's stupid enough but things are so much worse for women, who must wear a hat or a 'substantial fascinator'. Nope, I have no idea either. But then things get really idiotic. You may not bare your midriff, you may not wear a miniskirt, you may not wear anything with a halter neck, and dress straps must be at least 1 in across. Anyone whose dress has straps narrower than this will have their royal enclosure pass removed and may or may not be slapped lightly by the Queen.

Amazingly, women are allowed to wear trouser suits, the national costume of the terminally dull, but the trousers must match the jacket. Who dreams this stuff up? It's not taken from the pages of tradition because women did not wear trouser suits until the glass ceiling was removed in about 1993. It's recent. And that means somewhere out there, walking around, with a vote and a driving licence, is a person who actually sat down one day and decided women who wished to see a horse running past them very quickly with a small Irishman on its back would be allowed to wear trousers, but only if they were made from the same material as the jacket.

How empty must your life be to think of such a rule? How pointless and stupid? It genuinely baffles me because if you reach a point in your existence where you start to worry about whether men should be allowed to wear a hat while eating lunch, then you must have considered and done everything else that life has to offer. Up to and including what it would feel like to put a shotgun in your mouth and pull the trigger.

All a dress code such as this does is encourage the orange and the dim to come along and pretend that they are posh for the day. Meanwhile, the wicked and the interesting are doing something else. In a pair of jeans.

Sunday 21 June 2009

I'm not superstitious, Officer, but it's bad karma to harry a druid

I have only ever given my children one piece of advice. Other parents I know talk solemnly about drugs, sex, pregnancy, work, manners and the importance of good A-level grades. But all I've ever told my kids is this: 'No matter what, never salute a magpie.'

I don't know when I got into the habit. Or even why. Maybe it was peer pressure. Maybe it was boredom. But one day, while driving along, I saw a lone magpie hopping about on the grass verge and I saluted it. And that was that. I was hooked. And now, I know for sure that if I fail to salute even a single one of them I will catch cancer within the hour.

This is a huge problem in Milton Keynes, where, for reasons known only to Bill Oddie, there are one trillion magpies, all of which hang around by themselves on the endless sponsored roundabouts. I'd love to know how many people die on the town's roads each year because the driver was warding off bad luck. I bet it's millions.

All superstition is mumbo jumbo. I know that. As a result, I will happily walk under a ladder, and I know that if some bees come to my house it will not burn down. I realize too that a black cat will give me just as much asthma as a brown one and that if my left ear feels warm it's because it's a sunny day. And yet I have this magpie thing going on. It makes me very angry as there is no methadone. There is no clinic. There is no cure.

Still, it could be worse. I could believe in the power of ley lines, the magic of dance and that I have the ability, through deep concentration, to become a dog or a cow, so that I may experience life from its point of view. In short, I'm awfully glad I'm not a druid.

Last week they were at Stonehenge to mark the summer solstice. Apparently, 36,500 poor souls got up in the middle of the night and were dragged by their beliefs and their little Citroëns to a field in Wiltshire, where they were forced by custom to mark the disappointingly cloudy dawn by chanting and pretending to be King Arthur.

As a saluter of magpies, I have every sympathy with these people and I wish them well. I like having hippies in the world. They bring a richness and a calm, and while they like to wear hoods, they do not beat up old ladies.

And that brings me on to the point of this morning's column. What in the name of whatever god you hold dear were the police doing using an unmanned spy drone to fly around, taking pictures of these people as they swayed gently in the stillness of morning? Can you imagine the hullabaloo if Dixon of Dock Green used similar tactics during a Catholic church service? If the smells and bells were drowned out by the relentless buzz of a spy plane? And let's be honest, shall we? On the crime-o-meter, Johnny Pope's merry little gang of bachelors is far more likely to be involved in serious wrongdoing than some dizzy druid bird with flowers in her hair. I can see why the army might need a spy drone in Afghanistan. But how on earth could the Wiltshire constabulary justify the purchase of such a thing? To catch crop circlists? It's the most absurd thing I've ever heard.

And why were revellers limited to taking just four cans of beer each on to the site? This means there must have been a meeting at which a busybody in a trouser suit will have said 'two' and then a fat man will have said 'five', and much discussion will have taken place, at our expense, before the figure of four was arrived at.

This is even more absurd, come to think of it, than the police spy plane. Certainly I feel sure that early man would not have embarked on the road to civilization if he had thought that, one day, humankind would arrive at a point where one man has the right to determine how much beer another man may take into a field in the middle of the night.

Then there's the drugs business. Now, I'm not going to come here and defend the use of narcotics. But we learnt last week that there are now 1m cocaine users in Britain. Statistically then we can be assured that marching powder is being used in the House of Commons, in village halls, in business meetings, at dinner parties and even, perhaps, by pop stars.

So why pick on the druids? Why send sniffer dogs to their annual summer get-together? We know there will have been some dope and we know, because they'd stayed up all night, that some of the morris men will have got some marching powder up their schnozzers. But if it's busts they're after, Plod would probably have had a higher success rate if they'd had a snout about in their own locker rooms.

The fact is that despite the massive, and extremely costly, operation the police made only thirty-seven arrests, mostly for minor public-order offences. That's thirty-seven from a crowd of 36,500. One in a thousand or thereabouts.

I'm not suggesting that the police ignore large gatherings of people. Whether it's a football match or a bunch of Tamils in Parliament Square, the forces of law and order need to be on hand to give people directions to the nearest bus stop and break up whatever fights may occur. But I simply cannot understand why such large numbers were used to monitor a group of people who, by their very nature, pose about as much threat to the world as a flock of budgerigars. They hum. They make love to one another. They speak in Welsh. And they go home.

Certainly I can assure you that driving along while under the influence of a silly scare story about magpies is much more of a threat to the nation's peace and tranquillity.

Sunday 28 June 2009

After three brushes with death in planes I want a parachute

Can you imagine what it must have been like on board that Air France aeroplane that crashed into the Atlantic Ocean last month? Rather dreadfully, I can.

Admittedly, my first plane crash was a rather minor affair. The Vietnamese pilot had had several attempts to land the country's only jet, and I sort of knew as we bumped towards the runway for the fourth that it wouldn't go well. And it didn't. We ended up in a field.

The second crash was in Libya. Or Chad. Or possibly Mali. The pilot wasn't really sure where we were and, as it turned out, nor did he have any idea how to land. Because he was a bit drunk. Weirdly, he managed to get the nose wheel down first, and because it's not really designed for that, it snapped off, meaning we skidded in a sparky, bouncy sort of way through the Sahara for a while.

The third was not actually a crash. But it was by far the most terrifying, because it really did look for several minutes like there could be no other outcome.

I had boarded a small, windowless twelve-seater on an island off Cuba for a short flight to Havana. The plane had been built by the Russians at some point in the 1950s and then used by the Angolan air force throughout the seventies and eighties before it eventually arrived in Cuba as a city hopper. Judging by the amount of oil that streaked along the wings and the smoke that belched from the Lada engines when they coughed into life, it had been built by people who couldn't care less and serviced by no one, ever.

Shortly after takeoff the entire cabin filled with steam, which meant the pilots were unable to see the large thunderstorm that lay ahead. So they flew right into it. And moments later we were upside down. I want you to think how that might feel for a moment . . . You didn't think about the lavatories did you? When the plane is the wrong way up, they are too, and that means they empty their entire contents, including some home-made tampons, on to the roof.

Happily, I didn't think about that because the other thing you might not have considered is the cooling system on a 1950s ex-Angolan air force aeroplane. What you get above each seat is a small Pifco fan, and because I was upside down, hanging by my seatbelt, the top of my head was actually in the blades. It was very uncomfy, having a haircut while the wrong way up, in a tropical thunderstorm and knowing that, if the pilot regained control, I'd be getting a brown shower.

I turned at one point to a colleague who was sitting in the next seat, having a lovely Oh Brother Nimmo monk cut, and asked, because he had a pilot's licence, if we were in trouble. The white knuckled 'yes' was enough.

How did it feel? Pretty awful, if I'm honest. Because I didn't know whether the impact was one minute or one second away, it was impossible to brace or get my breathing right. It's like knowing you're going to be punched but not when.

I do remember thinking, though, that it would be quite a cool way to go. Better, I thought, to scream through the pearly gates in a Russian plane over Cuba than with a tube up my nose and a grey face.

And then, obviously, the story has a boring ending because the pilot did regain control and we did land safely and I wasn't killed. Or covered in shit.

Which brings me back to those poor souls on board the

Air France jet that didn't land safely. Last week, experts managed to work out that it did not break up in mid-air, which would have killed everyone instantly – one minute you'd have been snuggling into Russell Crowe with a glass of red and the next, you'd have been dead. Instead, it remained intact until it hit the sea. Which meant that those passengers had to sit there, for several minutes, knowing they were on a high-speed one-way ticket into oblivion. And what makes it even more poignant for me than that is that one of them was a friend of mine.

I imagine that being told by a doctor you have three months to live is scary. I imagine, too, that being burnt at the stake is bad. Or beheaded on the internet. But surely, the worst is being on a plane, over the middle of an ocean, pointing downwards and doing about 750 mph.

I know that I lived and I know that last week a twelve-year-old girl escaped almost unharmed from another Airbus tragedy in the Indian Ocean. But really, when a plane falls out of the sky, your chances are not even slim. And worst of all, you are jammed in a seat, unable to do a damn thing about it. With cancer, you think that if you only eat nuts and read the Bible a lot, you might pull through. In a car, you can take avoiding action as the lamppost looms. But in a plane, you are impotent.

And that's what brings me on to this morning's bright idea. At present, all passengers are given a life jacket even though they know they may as well have been given a piece of birthday cake or a pack of playing cards. I think I'm right in saying that in all of civil aviation history, not one life has ever been saved by the whistle, the torch or the toggles.

So why not give everyone a parachute instead? Of course, most passengers would be too paralysed with fear in a real emergency to put it on properly. Even if they had been listening to the safety briefing. But here's the thing. As the plane screamed downwards, you would at least have something to do. Finding it, reading the instructions, making your way to the door, working out how it can be turned to manual and so on. This would give people hope. Which is so much better than the horrific alternative: despair.

Sunday 5 July 2009

Just one word and my T-shirt offends the whole of Japan

There comes a point in a man's life when he is no longer able to wear a T-shirt. You have only to see an overweight American tourist wobbling around looking like Winnie-the-Pooh to know that I'm right; to know that T-shirts are fine for schoolboys on sports day. But not fine thereafter. As soon as the merest hint of a belly begins to emerge, nothing looks quite so idiotic as a T-shirt. And if, like me, you have what amounts to an overinflated space hopper down there, you know that, in a T-shirt, you couldn't look more ridiculous even if you were going around in a scuba suit.

The only thing in the world worse than a middle-aged man in a T-shirt is a middle-aged man whose T-shirt is tucked into his trousers. And the only thing in the world worse than a middle-aged man whose T-shirt is tucked into his trousers is a middle-aged man whose T-shirt is black and tucked into his trousers. Black T-shirts are worn by roadies so that they cannot be seen as they move about the stage at concerts preparing the next guitar and sorting out the drummer who's taken so much cocaine he's fallen off his seat. This is fine. But there is another group of people who wear black T-shirts. They are known as 'German paedophiles', and that's not fine at all. Oh, and Simon Cowell, come to think of it.

Then you have the pink T-shirt, worn predominantly to say you are so confident about your sexuality that you can get away with anything. Unfortunately, the problem with wearing a pink T-shirt is that I'm afraid you don't look confident at all. You look like a cruising homosexual. Which is fine if you are. But annoying if you are just shopping.

I should also point out that T-shirts really, really don't work if they didn't cost very much money. Because after one wash they'll look like a council-house nightie. And they don't work on a biblical level if you walk around with a CND slogan on the front. Especially if your dad is president of the United States of America.

The worst thing you can have on your T-shirt, however, is a place name, particularly if it's the exotic-sounding place name of somewhere far, far away from where you are at the time. You must have noticed this. If you are in Barbados, you will note that absolutely nobody wears Barbados slogans on their chest. It's always somewhere else. Which is why, when I'm on holiday, I'm often to be found lying on the beach in a T-shirt bearing the legend 'Wakefield'.

And that brings me to a new development in the world of the T-shirt. The humorous slogan. I saw a big chap wobbling towards me in the street only last week. He was wearing a brown T-shirt, which, as we know, is usually reserved for fans of Formula One. If you know what I mean. So, naturally, I was tutting away, until I saw what the writing on it said: 'Fat men are harder to kidnap'. That made me laugh. And that made him smile, and for a moment the world was a lovelier place.

I mentioned this to my family and now they buy me lots of 'funny' T-shirts. I have one that blends the Sex Pistols' 'God Save the Queen' single cover with the Jilted John classic. So it says, 'Gordon is a moron'. And I have another that says, 'I love animals. They're delicious'. Though I have to be careful about that one because often it doesn't make the world a lovelier place. It makes thin-lipped women launch into a tirade about meat and animals, and after a while, inevitably, why the penis is fundamentally evil.

However, both of these pale into insignificance alongside the T-shirt my wife brought back as a present from her three-day and three-night lost weekend at Glastonbury. It's grey, which is an acceptable colour, and it says, in huge letters, '****'. Actually, it doesn't say that at all. But I can't say here what it does say because what it says is the worst word in the world.

I liked my new T-shirt very much. I liked it so much that last week I wore it to the rehearsals of a *Top Gear* show, where everyone else liked it very much as well. But after a while, as is the way with these things, everyone had seen it, everyone had had their giggle and everyone had asked where they might get one. So, soon, the joke has been lost in a desert of familiarity. And that's why, later in the day, when I was approached by a group of Japanese people, I never gave my slogan a second thought.

It turned out they were there from the company that makes the incredible Gran Turismo computer racing game, and they were in England to map out and chart the *Top Gear* test track for inclusion in the next, even more realistic version. Of course, it was very important that I met the boss.

Naturally, there was much bowing, and a lot of accepting and presenting business cards with two hands. Obviously, I didn't give him my business card because I don't actually have a business. Or a card. But I found one in my pocket – from David Linley, the furniture maker, strangely – and gave him that. It didn't matter. He couldn't speak English. None of them could. Which is why they weren't offended by my shirt.

But then, equally inevitably, out came the cameras. Many hand signals suggested they wanted me to pose with their head honcho and, of course, I obliged. It would have been rude to say no. But not, as it turns out, half as rude as appearing in the firm's promotional material in a T-shirt bearing the worst word in the world. Which is what's happened.

I would like, therefore, to take this opportunity to apologize to the man, the company he runs, all of the children in the world who've been offended and the people of Japan. I am so very, very solly.

Sunday 12 July 2009

Stop, you're digging an early grave with that garden trowel

The Department for Environment, Food and Rural Affairs is plainly a bit stuck for something to do now there's plenty to eat, the environment's knackered and the Labour party thinks a rural affair is something that happens in Jilly Cooper's head. So it's filled its time compiling a report that indicates by next year almost 2.2m homes in Britain will not have a private garden. This is because developers are building lots of flats and – I never would have guessed – 'the likelihood of having a garden is greater for larger detached dwellings than flats'.

There are, however, some interesting nuggets in the forest of truisms. Apparently, two-thirds of all London's front gardens are now largely covered with concrete, paving or gravel rather than vegetation. Many back gardens have been sold to developers, who find it much easier to get planning permission for these infill sites than they do out in the sticks.

Naturally, all sorts of busybodies will now be running around demanding that brownfield developments must stop and that everyone must replace their gravel drives with lavender or carrots.

I believe there is another way of looking at this. If people are paving over their front lawns and selling their back gardens to Messrs Bryant and Barratt, it must mean they value a car-parking space and an extra bit of dosh more than they value spending half their weekend huffing and puffing behind a lawnmower.

Did you know that 27 per cent of adult male heart-attack

victims are struck down while cutting the grass? You didn't? That's because it's not true. But I bet the real figure is huge.

Whatever, the fact is that huge numbers of people plainly don't like having a garden, and I can understand why. It's because once you start gardening, there is no end, no point at which you can say, 'It's finished.' Because it never is.

First of all, there's the bothersome business of choosing from a vast array of plants, all of which have Latin names so people in garden centres can laugh in your face when you get it wrong. Flustered, you will make a panic purchase of something that is pink and won't grow in your particular garden because it's not north-facing, or the soil is too acidic, or the wind's too strong. And even if it does grow, it will turn out to be either a twig or something so rapacious that within five months it will have eaten your lawn, your shed, your house and most of your children.

First, though, it will eat your satellite dish. All plants do this. No matter how hard you encourage them to grow in one direction, they will make a beeline for the dish, so that in the middle of your favourite show you suddenly get a notice saying no signal is being received. Which means you have to go outside, in the wind and the rain, with a pair of secateurs and some dynamite to try to get your clematis out of Bruce Forsyth's ear. I have a rose that, in its desperation to get at my satellite dish, actually murdered three trees that lay in its path. It used them as a launch pad, until the poor things couldn't cope with the weight and snapped. Gravel does not do this.

I'm sure it's possible to untangle a rose from a tree but it's even more difficult and time-consuming than untangling the cable for your iPod. It's more bloody as well. And anyway, once you embark on a project such as this, there is no end. Next thing you know, you'll be in a greenhouse, making potions with a pestle and mortar, and not sleeping at night because of greenfly. Nobody ever loses sleep over their decking.

The worst thing about gardening, though, is the pruning. We're told that for a plant to become strong and tall so it may hide the block of flats your neighbour built on his vegetable patch, you must cut it back every year. You only have to look at the Brazilian rainforest to know this is rubbish.

Here we have an area the size of Wales, or is it the Albert Hall? Either way, it's the most beautiful garden in the world. And every time someone comes along to prune it a bit, so they may grow some cows, nature lovers get all cross.

Gardening is like doing a jigsaw. A pointless way of passing the time until you die. Pruning is like putting the completed picture back in the box so that you can start again. And the net effect is that the tree you planted to shield the neighbours' new skyscraper is now only 2 in tall and looks stupid.

But I haven't finished yet. About twelve years ago a friend and I both planted yew hedges. Mine has been pruned vigorously every year and is now about 6 ft tall and extremely boring. Hers was never pruned and, consequently, is a mass of topiary giraffes and farmyard animals. The only thing I could sculpt mine into is a mouse.

Let's just say you do like a garden, that you don't mind dragging your lawnmower through the house every weekend, and that you like digging. Fine. But because you are an amateur and your garden is likely to be fairly small, and because you are British and you therefore think pansies are pretty, you will end up with something that looks like a sponsored roundabout in Milton Keynes.

There are some great gardens in this country. But yours isn't one of them. Yours looks like it was planted and maintained by Ardman's Double Glazing. And it's not somewhere you can ever sit and relax, because every time you try, you will notice a bit of moss that needs removing or a beetle that needs spraying or a flower that needs deadheading. So you'll be up and down like a pair of whore's drawers, until one day, while doing a bit of hedge trimming, you will cut through the cord and be killed. Or you will have a heart attack. You will not be there when your grandchildren get married. And you would have been if only you'd sold the damn garden to Bryant Homes and spent the money on a decent holiday every year instead.

Sunday 19 July 2009

The conquerors are coming, Pierre – we Brits need more land

Last week, we heard about two neighbours fighting over a bit of lawn with a bush on it. And, at a cost of God knows how much, the case has ended up in the High Court in London. A court case. Over a shrub. It beggars belief.

Except it doesn't any more. A friend told me yesterday about the dispute she's having. 'The deeds to my house say people can drive cattle down the lane past my house but now my neighbour's son has passed his driving test and he's driving his car down there. So I've rebuilt the wall, which means his car won't fit any more. Ha.'

Then we have Griff Rhys Jones, who, last Wednesday, urged the nation's canoeists – all four of them, I should imagine – to 'disturb as many anglers as possible'. He claims that many stretches of river have been bought by private fishing clubs and are therefore out of bounds to exponents of the eskimo roll.

I'm not immune either. All week, my wife has been at a public inquiry, started because some militant dog walkers in the Isle of Man wish to ramble through my kitchen and take YouTube footage of me on the lavatory.

And then there's my mother, who moved house last year because the builder doing up the house next door took down a tree, or planted one. I can't remember which, but I remember it being a big deal. And, worse, it makes me wonder: are we perhaps starting to run out of space? When you look at the figures, it's hard to see why everyone is at one another's throat. At present, only around 19 per cent of the United

Kingdom's 95,000 square miles is built up, which doesn't sound so bad. Certainly, if you look at the country on Google Earth, it appears to be a patchwork of nothing but fields with a smallish grey bit near the Thames estuary.

But plainly there is a problem. When you have Griff Rhys Jones and Jeremy Paxman actively wrestling with each other on the banks of the Kennet and Avon canal, and neighbours fighting in the High Court over a bloody bush, it's very obvious the country is not just full. It's actually starting to burst.

Plainly, the planning regulations are to blame. You aren't allowed to build anything on Farmer Giles's cabbages unless you join the freemasons. And since most people don't wish to have their tongues pulled out for blabbing about the stupid handshake, developers are being forced to erect new dwellings in urban back yards. Which causes even more friction with the neighbours whose view is about to be ruined.

So what's to be done? Well, obviously, it would be stupid to relax the green-belt rules, partly because this would ruin the point of Britain and partly because we need all the space we can get for Ed Miliband's plans to carpet-bomb every hillside in the land with his stupid and useless bird-mincing windmills. And anyway, as the global population grows and farmland is built on, there will come a time when we all have somewhere to live. But bugger all to eat.

The obvious solution is to spread out a bit. At present, the south-east of England has a greater population density than Puerto Rico. And it's getting worse. Recent figures suggest that even a town such as Guildford in Surrey will need an extra 18,000 houses by 2050 to help to accommodate the national increase of 350,000 people a year.

The trouble is: where do we spread out to? Scotland is the obvious answer, but it can't be a very nice place to live, or there wouldn't be so many Scottish people in London.

Lincolnshire is a better bet in some ways but, from what I understand, it's being eaten at an alarming rate by the North Sea, and Wales doesn't really work either because it's too mountainous.

My gut reaction is that we must at least consider the possibility of conquering France. There are good reasons for this. First of all, we can be assured the French will not put up much of a fight – they never do – so casualties would be small. And second, the fact is they don't need all that space. And we do. Certainly, I can't see any reason why they don't hand over Lesser Britain, or Brittany, as they insist on calling it. I realize, of course, the United Nations would have something to say on the matter and that Britain might be ostracized internationally for a while, but I feel this could well be a price worth paying if it were to prevent Griff and Chris Tarrant from having an unedifying punch-up at the Cotswold Water Park.

Of course, I'm sure a lot of you reading this will be harbouring dark and dangerous thoughts about perhaps limiting the number of people who want to live in Britain. I'm thinking of the i-word.

We were told a few years ago by the Labour government that Britain needed many millions of Somalians and Estonians to fuel Mr Brown's booming economy. But now what? The economy's gone tits-up and I'm sure there are many people quietly harbouring a notion that perhaps Mr Mbutu and Mr Borat might like to go home again. I do not have these thoughts. I'd far rather have Mr Mbutu round for tea than, say, John Prescott. But I can quite understand why some people do. And that worries me.

Because how long will it be before Griff Rhys Jones stops attacking Ian Botham and starts throwing bricks through the window of his local Indian restaurant? How long before the stockbrokers of Guildford decide they don't want any more homes and that Mr Ng's Chinese takeaway must be burnt to the ground? In short, how long before this pressure on space and the need to breathe out once in a while leads to all sorts of problems that are very ugly indeed? Maybe, then, the government should consider asking GlaxoSmithKline to perhaps slow down the development of its vaccine for swine flu. Just a thought.

Sunday 26 July 2009

Soaking up the raw emotion of the best beetroot contest

As I write, millions and millions of pounds are being spent[1] developing new stunts for this year's *Top Gear Live* events in London and Birmingham. The reasoning is simple. Audiences are no longer happy to see a car behind a rope on a stand. They want to see it barrel-roll and explode. They want to see fire. They want to see Richard Hammond's head come off.

We see much the same thing in the theatre. Gone are the days when people would be happy with *The Corn Is Green* and a bit of Colonel Mustard in the library. Now they want Chitty Chitty Bang Bang to fly over their heads and for a helicopter gunship to land on the stage. And of course, in film, the drive for more excitement knows no bounds. In *The Way to the Stars*, audiences were spellbound by some men talking. Whereas now, nobody's really happy unless Paris blows up.

Or are they? I only ask because I've just been to a village show where nothing exploded. No one was raked with machinegun fire. Will Smith was not there. All we got was a burger van, a cow in a tent and some bees. But 10,000 people turned up.

City dwellers would argue that village shows remain popular because country folk lead such dreary lives. But I am a city boy at heart. I love Hong Kong and San Francisco. And yet, last weekend, there I was in the Women's Institute, commiserating

1. Relax. It's not millions and millions of licence fees. It's private money we're spending.

with Deirdre because her amazing knitted Elvis had been pipped to first prize by Maureen's mother-of-pearl, hand-painted fan. I was then distracted by the sheep. I've always thought that a sheep was a sheep. But no. There was one that had been fitted with the head from a buffalo. There were vicious wolf sheep with spiky horns for stabbing ramblers. (I'm definitely getting some of those.) And then there was a sheep with quite the largest testicles I've ever seen. They would have looked ridiculous on even a brontosaurus. I swear each one was 2 ft in diameter. If the RSPCA wasn't looking, you could have used them as space hoppers. I have seen *Miss Saigon* and I enjoyed it very much. But here's the thing. I enjoyed looking at that sheep's testes even more.

Other highlights? There were millions. I bought a jar of honey. I sat in a tractor. I had a lovely chat with a chap whose Yorkshire terrier had come second in the best dog competition because, just as he sat down, he was distracted by a fly and stood up again. The poor chap was inconsolable. All year he had been preparing for his moment of glory and because of one damn fly, one pesky little insect, he'd been beaten, yet again, by Brian and his 'Newfoundland monster'.

This is what makes the village show so fantastic. It allows everyone a chance to shine. If, after years and years of blood and sweat, you win the best beetroot competition, you understand how Usain Bolt felt when he took gold in the Olympic 100 metres. And you in the audience get to see that raw emotion up close.

Seriously. What's the difference between winning the Formula One world championship and winning the best beehive competition at a local agricultural show? Emotionally, there is none at all.

But the best thing about a village show is that there's always a brass band. Brass bands make the best noise in the world.

I have seen the Who. I have seen Pink Floyd. I have seen opera, ballet, piano recitals and the Proms. I have even heard a Ferrari V12 at full chat. But for sheer heart-tugging joy, nothing has matched the brass band I saw performing one chilly day at the National Coal Mining Museum in Wakefield. It is the soundtrack of the community. The village. The mine. The youth centre. And that's why it works so well at a village show. Bending over to peer at something you would never imagine you could possibly find interesting while a group of spotty youths with some trumpets oils your ears with a rendition of 'Danny Boy' – it's bliss.

Or rather it would be bliss, if only the man with the public-address system would shut up. I understand, of course, why village shows need such things. Lost children must be reunited with their mobile phones and it's important to know when judging for the best hen contest is about to begin. You need to be there to see the unbearable sadness in Derek's eyes when he's beaten. Especially if the spotty youths are playing 'Autumn Leaves' at the time. Unfortunately, however, the people who volunteer to spend all day with the microphone do so because what they love most of all is the sound of their own voice. This means they are not capable of shutting up. For 364 days of the year, Ian is a forklift truck driver. But for one glorious afternoon, he's the bugler. He's the general. He can move 10,000 people from one side of the field to the other with a simple announcement. He can reunite families. He can sort out lost dogs. And by lunchtime the power has gone to his head. This is why I always take a pair of pliers to a village show. To dismantle Ian's communication system.

Sadly, it's illegal to use pliers on the other problem: the local lord who turns up in a crap suit with a walking stick to mooch about with a grumpy face, judging bonsai trees, cauliflowers and the face-painting competition. He looks like he's hating it.

He'll tell his friends he hates it. But the fact is this: every year, he organizes his holidays around the show so that he can go. He loves it because for one marvellous day it's 1850 again. He is not some moth-eaten old buffer in a leaky house. He's the lord. He's in charge. And he's a prat for pretending it doesn't make his heart soar.

I only intended going to the village show for an hour or so. But I stayed till I was so drunk I could barely stand up. I'd seen more emotion than I've seen in the past 100 Hollywood movies. I'd eaten horrible food, got a massively sunburnt face and laughed, really laughed, with my children at the sheep's enormous testicles. It was, quite simply, the perfect day.

Sunday 2 August 2009

Nurse! The OAP mods are bashing the wrinkly rockers

We learnt recently that despite the best efforts of Herr Pope and Jude Law, there are now more old age pensioners in Britain than children under the age of sixteen. Many people have many theories on why this is happening: better medical care, better crumple zones in your car, less plague, fewer man-eating tigers, the invention of the high-visibility jacket and, of course, the increasingly zealous Health and Safety Executive with its bold remit that no one should die, ever.

There is, however, another, rather more serious reason for the general wrinkling of the general public that no one is talking about. It's this. These days, few people have the time or the money to rear a child because they spend all their free time and all their spare cash buying hearing aids and mashing food for the toothless old crone that used to be their mum.

My mother has made it very plain that at the first sign of incontinence my sister and I are to wheel her over Beachy Head. Other mums – and dads, for that matter – are less considerate, and continue to sit about in their expensive inconti-panties, dribbling and insisting that *The Antiques Roadshow* is played at full volume, for probably twenty or thirty years.

I should imagine it's jolly hard to make a baby with your husband if you spent the first half of the evening looking for your mum's teeth and the second half trying to pluck them from the puddle of her wee.

And what for? At least, with a child, you are able to see the fruits of your labours grow into adulthood and become self-dependent. You lavish all that care and cash on a parent and all that happens is they get worse and worse until one day, when they are nothing but a bag of skin and methane, they keel over and you have to fork out for a funeral.

It's also a huge problem for the state because in Britain there are now more than 2.7m people over eighty, and all of them have to be kept alive and fed using taxes from a working population that is shrinking.

However, there is a business opportunity here. Some people say that, right now, property is a good investment. Others say it's zinc or farmland. But they're all wrong. The absolute best, most watertight investment is an old people's home. You need only look at the numbers to see this makes sense. Because now that there are more people over sixty-five than there are under sixteen, it stands to reason that there should be more care homes for the elderly than schools. And I bet there aren't. Not by a long way.

Demand, then, is bound to be strong, and what's more, running an old people's home must surely be the easiest thing in the world. It's not like a school, where you have to have teachers and all your guests are either lippy or armed with a knife, or both. And it's not like running a hotel, where people want food at all hours of the day and hot and cold running satellite television. All you need in an old people's home is a pack of cards, a telly with big speakers, some Gracie Fields records and a bit of cabbage for the old dears to eat. They won't mind. They like cabbage. They think it's exotic.

The other great thing about old people is they don't complain. If you accidentally forget to change their nappies for a few weeks, they will tell you cheerfully that things were much worse during the blitz. And you needn't worry about their families getting angry, because the selfish bastards only come round at Christmas. And they're usually too busy making up excuses for leaving to notice the sheets are a bit crusty.

It's strange, but if you run a farm, the government will send inspectors round every five minutes to ensure your goats have Bang & Olufsen stereos. Indeed, the courts are always jammed up with people who've been nasty to a horse. But when did you last read about someone being cruel to a pensioner? It never happens. So you can feel free to turn the central heating off to save a bit of cash.

The only trouble is that you need to get in on the act quickly because soon, I suspect, it's going to be a lot more difficult to get away with a cabbage-only diet and a handful of wipe-down inconti-wingbacks. Today's old people grew up before global warming. They lived up a chimney until they were eight, they had one bath, made from tin, in the whole street and they spent most of their early lives fighting the Hun. They still think nylon is a luxury good and chocolate is for special occasions. So they don't mind a bit of discomfort. And, mostly, they have manners and respect authority. It'll be a very different story twenty years from now. Think about it. Last week there were photos of Mick Jagger in the news-paper, and it struck me that soon those from his generation are going to be populating the nation's old people's homes. Which means many changes will be necessary.

They're going to want to zoom about on wheelchairs, in ripped pyjamas, listening to 'Anarchy in the UK'. And you can forget beetle drives. They will want spitting competitions, and fights will break out, often with those who were new romantics. It'll be a nightmare when Sid has smashed up Ethel's collection of Spandau Ballet hits and you can't reason with him because he's been in the medicine cupboard again and used up every-one's crystal meth. What's more, many of your inmates will be from other cultures, in which families pop round on an hourly basis and want the very best for their parents. Not a beetroot once a week and a Monopoly set with Park Lane missing.

And then, before you know it, you'll be running a home full of people weeing while they Wii, demanding Call of Duty 4 on PlayStation 3 and complaining noisily every time the internet connection goes down. This, then, is the real problem we're facing today. Not how many old people there are. But what they are like.

Sunday 9 August 2009

Dr Useless, what's the Canadian word for 'lousy care'?

While I was away, there was a big debate about how Barack Obama might sort out America's healthcare system, which, say the critics, is chronically awful and fantastically unfair. It's also bonkers. I was once denied treatment at a Detroit hospital because the receptionist's computer refused to acknowledge that the United Kingdom existed. Even though I had a wad of cash, and a wallet full of credit cards, she was prepared to let me explode all over her desk because her stupid software only recognized addresses in the United States.

Some say America should follow Canada's lead, where private care is effectively banned. But having experienced their procedures while on holiday in Quebec, I really don't think that's a good idea at all. A friend's thirteen-year-old son tripped while climbing off a speedboat and ripped his leg open. Things started well. The ambulance arrived promptly, the wound was bandaged and off he went in a big, exciting van. Now, we are all used to a bit of a wait at the hospital. God knows, I've spent enough time in accident and emergency at Oxford's John Radcliffe over the years, sitting with my sobbing children in a room full of people with swords in their eyes and their feet on back to front. But nothing can prepare you for the yawning chasm of time that passes in Canada before the healthcare system actually does any healthcare. It didn't seem desperately busy. One woman had lost her face somehow – probably a bear attack – and one kid appeared to have taken rather too much ecstasy, but there were no more than a dozen people in the waiting room. And no one was gouting arterial blood all over the walls.

After a couple of hours, I asked the receptionist how long it might be before a doctor came. In a Wal-Mart, it's quite quaint to be served by a fat, gum-chewing teenager who claims not to understand what you're saying, but in a hospital it's annoying. Resisting the temptation to explain that the Marquis de Montcalm lost and that it's time to get over it, I went back to the boy's cubicle, which he was sharing with a young Muslim couple. A doctor came in and said to them: 'You've had a miscarriage,' and then turned to go. Understandably, the poor girl was very upset and asked if the doctor was sure. 'Look, we've done a scan and there's nothing in there,' she said, in perhaps the worst example of a bedside manner I've ever seen.

'Is anyone coming to look at my son?' asked my friend politely. '*Quoi?*' said the haughty doctor, who had suddenly forgotten how to speak English. '*Je ne comprends pas.*' And with that, she was gone.

At midnight, a young man who had been brought up on a diet of American music, American movies and very obviously American food, arrived to say, in French, that the doctors were changing shift and a new one would be along as soon as possible.

By then, it was one in the morning and my legs were becoming weary. This is because the hospital had no chairs for relatives and friends. It's not a lack of funds, plainly. Because they had enough money to paint a yellow line on the road nine yards from the front door, beyond which you were able to smoke. And they also had the cash to employ an army of people to slam the door in your face if you poked your head into the inner sanctum to ask how much longer the wait might be. Sixteen hours is apparently the norm. Unless you want a scan. Then it's twenty-two months.

At about 1.30 a.m. a doctor arrived. Boy, he was a piece of work. He couldn't have been more rude if I'd been General

Wolfe. He removed the bandages like they were the packaging on a disposable razor, looked at the wound, which was
horrific, and said to my friend: 'Is it cash or credit card?' This
seemed odd in a country with no private care, but it turns out
they charge non-Canadians precisely what they would charge
the government if the patient were Céline Dion. The bill was
C$300 (about £170).

The doctor vanished, but he hadn't bothered to reapply
the boy's bandages, which meant the little lad was left with
nothing to look at except his own thigh bone. An hour later,
the painkillers arrived.

What the doctor was doing in between was going to a desk
and sitting down. I watched him do it. He would go into a
cubicle, be rude, cause the patient a bit of pain and then sit
down again on the hospital's only chair.

Seven hours after the accident, in a country widely touted
to be the safest and best in the world, he applied sixteen
stitches that couldn't have been less neat if he'd done them
on a battlefield, with twigs. And then the anaesthetist arrived
to wake the boy up. In French. This didn't work, so she went
away to sit on the doctor's chair because he was in another
cubicle bring rude and causing pain to someone else.

Now, I appreciate that any doctor who ends up working
the night shift at a provincial hospital in Nowheresville is
unlikely to be at the top of his game, and you can't judge a
country's healthcare on his piss-poor performance. And nor
should all of Canada be judged on Quebec, which is full of
idealistic, language-Nazi lunatics. But I can say this. If private treatment had been allowed, my friend would have paid
for it. He would have received better service and, in doing so,
allowed Dr Useless to get to the woman with no face or
ecstasy boy more quickly. Though I suspect he would have
used our absence to spend more time sitting down.

The other thing I can say is that Britain's National Health Service is a monster that we can barely afford. But in all the times I've ever used the big, flawed giant, no one has ever pretended to be French, no one has spent more time swiping my credit card than ordering painkillers and there are many chairs.

Sunday 30 August 2009

It's just not fair – donkeys get all the breaks

Like most people, I can wire a plug and change a wheel. These are simple things. But I cannot reassemble the coffee machine that I took to pieces this morning, and I cannot drill a hole in a wall. Anything even remotely complicated and I'm stumped, which is why, when I came home yesterday to find one of my donkeys in the middle of the road, I knew the day would not end well.

Have you ever tried to move a donkey when it wants to remain stationary? It'd be easier to move France. So what do you do? If you break off from traffic control to fetch an enticing apple from the kitchen, you know that when you get back to the scene, Uma – for that is her name – will have entered a passing car via its windscreen. And quite apart from the sadness that such an accident would cause me and the relatives of the person in the car – whose death will have been neither comfortable nor dignified – there would be many forms to complete and many stern words from a policeman.

I was weighing all this up when the arrival of a noisy motorcycle galvanized Uma into action. Sadly, the action in question was a great deal of Elvis impersonations with the top lip and an industrial bout of heehawing. Eventually, other motorists arrived on the scene and, this being the country-side, where people have little else to do, everyone got out of their cars to help. When we had a thousand or so, we were able to push the poor animal, legs locked, back into the pad-dock from which she had escaped.

And then, two hours later, the police called round to say that she, along with her mate Eddie, was out again. This time, on what is called an A road but is actually a motorcycle race-track. With the help of most of the population of southern England, and tactical air support, they were heaved back into the field, and this time I set about finding the route they were using to get out. And it was the damnedest thing. I looked for holes in the fence. I looked under their stove. I looked under their vaulting horse. I even checked their beds for evidence of missing planks. But there was nothing, and so I concluded that they were getting airborne somehow. Maybe they'd built a glider.

This is the other part of my condition. Like many men, I can never find anything that I'm looking for, even when I'm actually looking at it. In a fridge, I think milk is actually invisible to the male eye. And so, it turns out, are dirty great holes in the fence.

I genuinely do not understand this. When an eighteenth-century carpenter tacked together two small pieces of mahogany, he could reasonably expect that they'd remain conjoined until the end of time. And yet fencing, which is held together by massive 6 in nails, falls to pieces, all on its own, every fifteen minutes.

Why does this happen? And what do you do when it happens on a bank holiday Sunday? There was no possibility of ringing for help, which meant I would have to fix the damn thing myself. This, I worked out, would require some nails and the tool of the gods – a hammer. But, astonishingly, the only hammer we have in the house is the sort of gaily painted little thing Jane Austen might have used to pin a picture of Little Lord Fauntleroy to her bedhead. So I decided to use the butt of my AK-47 instead.

Have you ever tried to nail two pieces of fence post

together? It is literally impossible. The nail goes in well to start with but then, as you up the tempo and the vigour of your strokes, it gets a kink in the middle and all is lost. Once a nail is bent, it can never be made to go straight. You need to start again.

I started again many thousands of times until, eventually, the nail went all the way through the first piece of wood and was ready to penetrate the upright. Which, I should explain, was a solid post, set in concrete. You'd imagine, then, that it would not flex at all. But it did. Each time I hit my nail with the AK, it simply boinged backwards, out of the way, until it fell over. So now the gap, which had been just about big enough for a desperate donkey to get through, had become wide enough for a main battle tank.

I'm not a man given to tears or tantrums, but as darkness began to envelop the scene, I felt close to both. And that brings me on to the thrust of this morning's missive. In the olden days, friends would have laughed at my hopelessness. They would have enjoyed my inability to knock a nail into a piece of wood. It would have been amusing. But these days we are no longer permitted to mock the afflicted.

If a child is dyslexic, it is no longer made to wear a dunce's cap. Indeed, it is allowed extra time in its exams. And there's more. I heard last week that if a child has hyperactivity problems, you don't smack its bottom. In fact, if it has hyperactivity problems at Thorpe Park it is allowed to jump the queues. We live in a time when the playing field is levelled out for everyone: when the rich and the privileged are rejected by the universities they've selected, while the weak and the ginger are given a leg-up at every opportunity. And yet nothing is being done to help people like me. People who are spanners.

You, reading this, can clear your drains. I cannot. You can

service your lawnmower. I cannot. You can knock nails into wood and mend your fence.

I ended up parking my car across the gap until I could find a professional. And now the horses have wiped their sweet-itch-ravaged backsides all over my Mercedes.

Don't you think, then, that if we are going to have a world where legislation erases all foibles and shortfalls, it should apply to everyone? In a society that's truly fair, I think I should get free plumbing and fence repairs. Or am I missing something?

Sunday 6 September 2009

Forget Antigua, 007 – all the real action is in Acacia Avenue

We've always known that in reality, not one of Britain's secret agents has ever successfully fought a shark or garrotted Robert Shaw on a speeding train. In fact, we are told, over and over again, that most of what our secret agents do is boring; that instead of trying to stop Spectre from stealing our nuclear bombers, they actually spend most of the day trying to stop their wives checking Max Mosley's hair for nits. To hammer the point home, they even advertise for new agents these days in the *Guardian*.

And to reinforce the view that it's all nasty coffee and budget meetings with flip charts, we should remember what happened in the run-up to the Iraq war. Instead of dispatching their best man to blow up some submarines and sleep with as many Iraqi women as possible, the security services simply asked Alastair Campbell what he wanted. And then went on the internet until they found it. 'Yes. Look. Saddam does have missiles with nerve-gas tips. It says so here in this student's essay.'

And yet, it became clear last week in the trial of some Muslims who wanted to blow up some airliners that the truth probably lies somewhere between the two points. Our agents are not shooting men with metal teeth in the face. But they are not getting all their intel from Wikipedia either. If you actually read the court reports, there is no doubt that what they did to catch those stupid weird-beards would make a better, more real and more gripping spy thriller than anything from the likes of Forsyth, Fleming or Ludlum.

Admittedly, the locations don't have the visual impact of Corfu or Bolivia. There are no deserts in Walthamstow and no glittering oceans in High Wycombe. And that's part of what makes the story so fantastic. These are ordinary British towns full of IT consultants and greengrocers. You expect to find arms dealing and bomb-making factories in Algiers and Marseilles. Not on a housing estate in Buckinghamshire.

So it begins. Bond is brought into M's office and told there is dirty work afoot. Pakistan's interrogators have pulled out some fingernails and it's emerged that some religious fanatics have hatched a plan to blow seven planes and thousands of people out of the sky, in a single day. The stakes are high and you're gripped already.

Bond heads off to the airport, where he's told there are no flights to Buckinghamshire. Instead he must catch the Heathrow Express back into London and then a commuter train from Marylebone to High Wycombe. For a bit of light relief, and in the name of reality, he might like to try using the lavatory on this service, to see if he can get the door to close.

On arrival, he has to wait until the fanatics are out before placing listening devices in their house. And presumably he must do this so that no one else in the Close notices. Maybe he could sleep with Mrs Needham at No 43 to keep her quiet. That bit's optional. I'm sure it didn't happen in real life.

But whatever, it transpires that there is a plot and several Muslims are in the process of building some advanced liquid bombs. And here's the really good bit. Bond can't simply take them to a field and leave them with nothing but a can of engine oil to drink. He must wait and collate evidence, because in the real world that's what is needed to secure a prosecution in the courts. Even when he knows, and M knows, and you and I know some of the men are guilty, he has to have enough hard facts to convince the looniest, stupidest jury. And juries can be very loony and very stupid indeed.

Then comes the twist. An idiotic American man called Dick Cheney decides he must make George Bush, another idiotic American man, look like he was winning the war on terror, so he ignores British pleas for patience and orders the arrest of a shadowy figure with links to Al-Qaeda and the bombers in Britain.

This is likely to derail the entire operation. With the shadow in jail in Pakistan, where people tend to talk eventually, some of the British bombers may feel their operation has been compromised and decide to go ahead sooner than antici-pated. So what do the intelligence people do? Arrest them, even though they know they probably don't have enough evidence for a conviction? Or continue to watch and wait with crossed fingers? Imagine what it must have been like at that meeting. The sheer rage at the American stupidity. The tension. And the certain knowledge that if a wrong decision is made, either the bombers walk free or thousands of people die. This is cinema gold. And it actually happened.

Eventually, some bombers were arrested and you'd imagine the film would be over. But no. Thanks to Britain's legal sys-tem, which allows tradition to trample all over common sense, the electronic intercept recordings of the men were inadmissible. And the jury could not agree on whether the plot to blow up aircraft actually existed.

So now you're in the cinema, shaking with impotent fury. How can this have happened? All that watching and listen-ing. All those late nights. Naturally, the film does have a happy ending because eventually they found a way around the rules on intercept evidence and at the retrial three men were found guilty of a plot.

Although, I do like the idea of a final scene in which Bond

is seen at a meeting with Colonel Gadaffi, arranging for BAE Systems to ship some missiles to Cuba in exchange for the release of the convicted men on compassionate grounds.

This, really, is what has emerged from the proceedings. That no matter how real and how gritty the Bond producers try to make their films, they will never be able to match the tension of what almost certainly is happening today, possibly just down your street, just outside the post office.

Sunday 13 September 2009

Mad Johnny Baa Lamb is here to save the pit bulls

Last week the ringleaders of a Lincolnshire-based international dog-fighting gang were found guilty of various offences and warned that they faced lengthy jail terms. Needless to say, the whole country is now in a state of shock, completely at a loss to understand why on earth someone would get pleasure from watching their much-loved dog being ripped in half in someone's front room.

This raises a question. Why are we so shocked? The pit bulls used in dog fighting are not like the doe-eyed mounds of fur and slobber that come to your breakfast table in a morning, hoping that a piece of bacon will fall on the floor. They are Millwall dogs. They are born to fight one another and when they are not fighting they fill their time by eating babies. Trying to get a pit bull to lead a peaceful life, reading poetry and pressing the buttons on pelican crossings for blind people, is as impossible as getting Michael Palin to hose down a bus queue with machinegun fire. It can't be done and for this reason you aren't even allowed to own such a dog in this country.

But people do. They take the risks. They spend the money. They train their animals and they meet with other members of the Enormous Tattoo Owners' Club in garages and sitting rooms in Lincolnshire, where they get their outlawed dogs to fight.

They've been doing this for ages. Dog fighting was such a big problem in the early nineteenth century that in 1835 Britain became the first country in the world to make it illegal. Today, almost every other country in the civilized world, and America, has followed suit.

Of course, fans of the 'sport' would doubtless maintain that it's traditional, that war dogs were used for fighting in Roman times and that in fourteenth-century Japan fighting dogs could be used instead of money for paying taxes to the shogun. Doubtless this is true but it's also nonsense. I'm happy to shoot a partridge and eat a cow's front leg. I'm also happy to watch a lion being torn apart by a crocodile – and so are you, to judge by the popularity of warts-and-all nature documentaries. But in a civilized country you can't really have people running dog fights. Common sense dictates it's just wrong.

So, what's to be done? The government, believing that everything can be solved with more laws and more enforcement, would undoubtedly decide that a special taskforce should be set up, but this is impossible since the police are far too busy these days learning how to use ladders and bicycles. Women with frizzy hair and disappointing breasts would inevitably say that it could all be solved if violent video games were banned and more money were spent on education. Publicans, meanwhile, would suggest that it's because all the nation's pubs are closing down so there's nothing else to do.

Me? I believe the best course of action is to provide those who like dog fighting with an alternative. In short, we should look for another sort of fighting animal they can use. Cocks won't work because watching two roosters going at one another is even more traumatic than watching two dogs. Especially as they can keep on fighting even when their heads have fallen off. Bears are right out too. I was minded to suggest moose because they seem to spend most of their lives trying to poke one another's eyes out with their antlers but I fear keeping them would be impractical. Butterflies would be easier but the fights would, I suspect, be boring.

So, what about sheep? There are many advantages to this, chief among which is that sheep are unique in the animal kingdom for having no sense of worth and no particularly strong will to live. You may think humans are imaginative when it comes to committing suicide. We jump in front of trains and off cliffs. We drive into Saigon and set ourselves on fire. Some of us even go to Switzerland. But when it comes to the art of killing ourselves, we are rank amateurs compared with Johnny Baa Lamb. Wales is a billion acres of pastureland but you must have noticed all the sheep hang around by the side of the road, choosing to saunter across whenever a motorcycle is coming. Sheep are the only animals in the world that like to garrotte themselves on fences and that can develop non-specific illnesses unknown to veterinary science. Given half a chance, a sheep will excrete its own lungs. That's what those dangleberries are: internal organs they've managed to squeeze out of their own bottoms.

There's another reason sheep fighting is sensible. They like it. When there are no cars to run them over, or fences to impale themselves on, they will run at one another and try to fracture their own skulls. You may have seen this on YouTube. It is very funny because, of course, it doesn't work. They just end up a bit dizzy, and that's funny too – watching a sheep walking round in circles and falling over because it's just headbutted its best mate.

Quite rightly, televised dog fighting would be condemned, but televised sheep fighting would be the comedy smash of the decade. And with the viewers would come the high-rollers. Pretty soon, everyone would forget all about their pit bulls because the rewards from sheep would be so much greater.

There's more good news too. Unlike dogs, sheeps don't use their teeth and have no claws, so a death is unlikely. But if there were to be a tragic accident, the body would not go to waste. Unlike a dead dog, which is useless, a dead sheep can be garnished with mint sauce and eaten.

This is what's missing from the legislature today. A bit of lateral thinking. Our leaders need to understand that we will never stop dog fighting with laws. But we will stop this heinous crime by offering its fans something better.

Sunday 20 September 2009

Up to the waist in Brown's slurry on my new farm

Last week I bought a farm. Though financially speaking, it's entirely possible I've bought the farm. But let's look on the bright side. I can't possibly make as much of a hash with the investment as the bankers made when they had the money.

Or can I? You might imagine it's very easy to buy a farm. Unlike a house, you don't need a surveyor to check on dry rot because a field cannot fall over, and rising damp is a good thing because it means free water. It turns out, however, that it's actually very difficult, mostly because of the Georgians. Let me give you one example so you can see the scale of the problem.

There are a number of springs on the farm I've bought, one of which provides water to several properties in a nearby village. This arrangement was made when the land belonged to a fat man who had tea interests in India, and sealed in a document written with a quill, on bark. Fine. But what if the water supply dries up, or the pipe breaks, or everyone in the village gets lead poisoning and grows two heads? Common sense dictates this would not be my problem, but under New Labour's legal guidelines, all landowners are in the wrong at all times. Especially when a little old lady with two heads is in court, sobbing and waving around a piece of bark from 1742. The legal fees for sorting this out have amounted to about £4.5 billion, and that's before we get to the cost of trying to understand what I may and may not do with the land I've bought.

I thought some sheep would be nice but it turns out

Gordon Brown has an opinion on this. He reckons the number of animals I have per acre should be determined by how much nitrogen is in their excrement. I am consequently allowed only 0.6 of a sheep per acre, which means I may have only seventy-five of the damn things.

Standard sheep are good lawnmowers but unless I buy a hitherto undiscovered breed that has blades instead of teeth, I'm going to need a tractor to keep the grass down, and this worries me. I don't trust tractors. It seems to me that every single component is designed specifically to remove the operator's left arm.

Then there are the woods. They seem perfectly nice to me, but according to experts, they need thinning. The cost of doing this, I'm told, is around £5 billion and none of the chopped-down trees can be sold because there is no demand for wood at all. I find that hard to believe, but there we are. I also find it hard to believe that a wood needs maintenance. When McDonald's does that sort of thing in Brazil, it gets into all sorts of trouble, but it seems it's my duty as the owner to execute the weaker trees so that the stronger ones may survive. I must also keep the woods warm. I have no idea how this might be achieved but I should imagine the cost will be about £2 billion.

One of the things I have accidentally bought is a Neolithic fort. It is, of course, no such thing. It is a slight ripple in an otherwise flat field, useful only as an exciting launch pad for the children's quad bikes. But I feel fairly sure that if we use it for this purpose, Brown will make me apologize, in public, to the Piltdown man.

Certainly I know he is using satellites to make sure that I plant the right crop in the right field. Also, he is employing men called Colin to come round regularly to make sure I don't have too many sheep. Can you believe that? That your tax money is being spent to pay a man whose job is to count sheep. How the hell does he stay awake? Then we get on to the thorny question of boundaries. I can see why they matter on a housing estate but trying to determine where they are when they're in the middle of a blackberry bush and half an acre of nettles seems a bit pointless. And expensive.

And it turns out I'm going to need some buildings in which I can dry my rape, tup my sheep and keep a telephone to use when the tractor has severed my arm. I'm also going to need a topper, and that's fine, except I don't know what one is and therefore I have no clue whether to try to get one at the local garage or Toys 'Я' Us.

Last week I had a long conversation with another local sheep farmer. And I promise you this. While I nodded sagely from time to time and gave the impression I agreed with his countryside ways, I did not understand a single word he said. Apparently, my soil is brashy, my herbage is low and I'll have to dog and stick my ewes.

What I want to do most of all is plant some game crop so that I can rear a few pheasants. But guess what? It turns out that Brown has an opinion on this as well, and it's not allowed. He has an opinion on everything, it seems. There's one field I thought would look nice if I grew some poppies and corn-flowers. But that's not allowed either. Strangely, however, he will give me cash money if I promise to make a trout lake, and even more cash money if I don't grow anything that could be turned into food. Quite how he squares this in his head when half the world is starving, I have no idea.

And nor do I understand why the forms I have to fill in to get this cash money are longer and more complicated than the instruction manual for a nuclear power station.

I thought that farming would be easy. You plant seeds, weather happens and food grows. But I fear that as the seasons slide by, I will discover that I'm working my nuts off for less return than I got from those useless bastards at AIG.

Perhaps that's why the people round these parts assume I'm going to turn it into a racetrack. They couldn't be more wrong. I'm going to grow buddleia for the butterflies and build boxes for the barn owls. I'm going to love it. Especially the cheap diesel that Brown says I mustn't put in my Range Rover. But I will.

Sunday 27 September 2009

Help, quick – I've unscrewed the top on a ticking bomb

Like any responsible parent, I would not leave a loaded gun in the children's playroom or keep my painkillers in their sweetie tin. But it turns out that for two years there has been a nuclear bomb in one of my kitchen cupboards, between the tomato ketchup and the Rice Krispies.

It's an American chilli sauce that was bought by my wife as a jokey Christmas present. And, like all jokey Christmas presents, it was put in a drawer and forgotten about. It's called limited-edition Insanity private reserve and it came in a little wooden box, along with various warning notices. 'Use this product one drop at a time,' it said. 'Keep away from eyes, pets and children. Not for people with heart or respiratory problems. Use extreme caution.'

Unfortunately, we live in a world where everything comes with a warning notice. Railings. Vacuum cleaners. Energy drinks. My quad bike has so many stickers warning me of decapitation, death and impalement that they become a nonsensical blur. The result is simple. We know these labels are drawn up to protect the manufacturer legally, should you decide one day to insert a vacuum-cleaner pipe up your bottom, or to try to remove your eye with a teaspoon. So we ignore them. They are meaningless. One drop at a time! Use extreme caution! On a sauce. Pah. Plainly it was just American lawyer twaddle.

I like a hot sauce. My Bloody Marys are known to cure squints. And at an Indian restaurant I will often order a vindaloo, sometimes without the involvement of a wager. So when I accidentally found that bottle of Insanity, I poured maybe half a teaspoonful on to my paella. And tucked in.

Burns victims often say that when they are actually on fire, there is no pain. It has something to do with the body pumping out adrenaline in such vast quantities that the nerve endings stop working. Well, it wasn't like that for me. The pain started out mildly, but I knew from past experience that this would build to a delightful fiery sensation. I was even looking forward to it. But the moment soon passed. In a matter of seconds I was in agony. After maybe a minute I was frightened that I might die. After five I was frightened that I might not. The searing fire had surged throughout my head. My eyes were streaming. Molten lava was flooding out of my nose. My mouth was a shattered ruin. Even my hair hurt.

And all the time, I was thinking: 'If it's doing this to my head, what in the name of all that's holy is it doing to my innards?' I felt certain that at any moment my stomach would open and everything – my intestines, my liver, my heart, even – would simply splosh on to the floor. This is not an exaggeration. I really did think I was dissolving from the inside out.

Trying to keep calm, I raced, screaming, for the fridge and ate handfuls of crushed ice. This made everything worse. So, dimly remembering that Indians use bread when they've overdone the chillies, I cut a slice, threw it away and ate what remained of the very expensive Daylesford loaf, like a dog.

Nothing was working. And such was my desperation, I downed two litres of skimmed milk – something I would never normally touch with a barge pole. I was sweating profusely as my body frenziedly sought to realign its internal thermostat. I felt sick but didn't dare regurgitate the poison for fear of the damage it would cause on the way out.

Even now, the following morning, I feel weak, shell-shocked, like I may die at any moment. And all I'd ingested was a drop.

Limited-edition Insanity sauce is ridiculous. It's made in Costa Rica, from hot pepper extract, crushed red savina peppers, red tabasco pepper pulp, green tabasco pepper pulp, crushed red habanero peppers, crushed green habanero peppers, red habanero pepper powder and fruit juice. Well, that's what it says on the tin. But I don't believe it. I think it's made from uranium, plutonium, fertilizer, sulphuric acid, nitric acid, hydrochloric acid and ammonia, with a splash of mace. I do not believe it's a foodstuff. It's a weapon. And I may have a point, since on the Scoville scale, which measures the intensity of chilli peppers, the habanero sits just below the 'daisy cutter', that American bomb designed to wipe out nations.

At present you are allowed to take 100 ml of liquid on to a plane because the authorities believe such a small amount could not possibly bring down an airliner. They are wrong. If I painted just 1 ml of Insanity sauce on the window of a 747, it would melt. And this is stuff you can buy on the internet. Stuff that has been sitting in my kitchen for two years.

So, what's to be done? As you know, I am not Gordon Brown. I do not think problems can be solved with a ban, even though I really believe that a bottle of Insanity sauce is more deadly than a machinegun. The obvious course of action is to remove warning notices from household goods that are not dangerous – cakes, for instance, and staplers. This way, we would pay more attention when something is supplied with labels advising us of great peril ahead.

Sadly, however, since we are now one of the most litigious countries in the world, this will never happen. Nor can Insanity be uninvented. It exists. A bottle of the damn stuff is sitting on my desk now and I have no idea what I should do with it.

I can't pour it down the sink because it would get into the water table. I can't put it in the bin because it would end up as landfill. And that's no good for something which has a half-life of several thousand years. I can't even take it – as I would with a grenade I'd found – to the police because they'd be tempted to use it as a legal device for getting information out of criminals. And that wouldn't work at all. Last night, when the bread had failed and the milk was finished, I would happily have confessed to forty-three counts of homosexual rape. Plus there is a side effect – certain death.

Sunday 4 October 2009

Cleverness is no more. It has ceased to be. This is a dumb Britain

Forty years ago, my dad came into my bedroom and made me get up. I was nine and sleepy. I was snuggly and warm. I wanted to stay under the covers. But he was insistent. 'There is something on television you need to see,' he said. And I remember the next bit vividly: 'It's going to be important.' So downstairs I went and there, in black and white, were some men talking, while nearby, various sheep fell out of trees. I laughed so much, my teddy bear's arm came off. And so it was that, at the age of nine, I became *Monty Python*'s first and youngest fan.

Aged thirteen, I was taken to the Grand in Leeds to see the Pythons perform in what they called their 'first farewell tour', and afterwards we all went out for supper together. John Cleese, whom my father had befriended, Eric Idle, Graham Chapman, Michael Palin, Terry Jones and me. They all signed a copy of my *Big Red Book* and it remains the one possession I would save should my house choose to explode.

I would spend hours listening to their records, and reliving their television programmes in my head. And eventually – my dad said it would be important – this fanaticism caused me to pass my English O-level. I was sitting there, in my study at school, listening to *Snow Goose*, with the dreary *Merchant of Venice* swimming around on the page, none of it making any sense at all. And then I thought: 'Hang on a minute, if it is possible to learn off by heart Eric Idle's travel agent sketch, then how hard can it be to memorize this twaddle?' So that's what I did. Learnt it.

I knew all the Python sketches off by heart. And the books.

And the films. I still do. And I still fly off the handle when someone misquotes. It was Norwegian Jarlsberger, you imbecile. I know it's really called Jarlsberg but that's not what Cleese said. How can you not know that??!!? Only last week, I was asked by a keen young reporter to recite my favourite Python sketch into her camera for a feature she was making. I did Novel Writing.

Novel Writing is another reason Python turned out to be important. It's the reason I'm married. My wife is a huge fan of Thomas Hardy and was deeply impressed that I knew the opening page of *The Return of the Native*. She never realized that I was simply reciting a Python sketch. In the same way that she never knew when I hummed 'Nessun Dorma' that I was singing what I thought was the music from a commercial for Pirelli. Novel Writing is at the very heart of what makes Monty Python so brilliant. The notion of Thomas Hardy writing his books, in front of a good-natured bank holiday crowd in Dorset while cricket-style commentators and pundits assess every word he commits to paper is a juxtaposition you don't find in comedy very much any more.

To get the point you need to know that, while Hardy may be seen as a literary colossus, there's no escaping the fact his novels are dirge. We see these attacks on intellectualism throughout Python. To understand the joke, you need to know that René Descartes did not say, I 'drink' therefore I am. You need to know that, if you cure a man of leprosy, you are taking away his trade. And that really Archimedes did not invent football.

Today my encyclopedic knowledge of everything Python is seen as a bit sad. Former fans point out that Cleese has lost it, that Jones is married to an eight-year-old and that Spamalot was a travesty. Worse. Liking Python apparently marks me out as a 'public-school toff'.

There's a very good reason for this. Nowadays people wear their stupidity like a badge of honour. Knowing how to play chess will get your head kicked off. Reading a book with no pictures in it will cause there to be no friend requests on your Facebook page. *Little Britain* is funny because people vomit a lot. *Monty Python* is not because they delight in all manifestations of the terpsichorean muse.

When you go on a chat show, it is important you tell the audience straight away that you were brought up in a cardboard box and that your dad would thrash you to sleep every night. If you want to get on and to be popular you have to demonstrate that you know nothing. It's why Stephen Fry makes so many bottom jokes.

And then you have my colleague James May, who says that, occasionally on *Top Gear*, he would like to present a germane and thought-provoking piece on engineering, but I won't let him unless his trousers fall down at some point. I'm ashamed to say that's true.

It's also true that today no one ever gets rich by overestimating the intelligence of their audience. Today you make a show assuming the viewers know how to breathe and that's about it. It's therefore an inescapable fact that in 2009 *Monty Python* would not be commissioned.

The only example of intelligent sketch-show comedy in Britain today is *Harry & Paul*. And what's happened to that? Well, it's been shunted from BBC1 to BBC2. And you get the impression it'll be gone completely unless they stop using Jonathan Miller as a butt for their wit. Today you are not allowed to know about Jonathan Miller because if you do, you are a snob.

That's why my *Monty Python* appreciation society is so small and secret. Members speak every morning, each giving one another a word or phrase that has to be placed in context by six that evening. Last month I was given one word: 'because'. And I got it. It's from the Four Yorkshiremen. 'We were happy . . . Because we were poor.'

The Pythons were laughing at that idea then. We're not laughing any more.

Sunday 11 October 2009

I've got a solution for the rainforest: napalm the lot

I've spent the past couple of weeks in Bolivia, and I didn't shoot a baboon. This is because there aren't any. In fact, there is no evidence of intelligent life at all. Let me give you a small example. I was lying in my hotel room one morning when, without so much as a knock, a cleaner walked in. With a mumbled, '*Buenos dias*', he went into my lavatory, closed the door and took a dump.

Let me give you another example. The electrical shower head in another hotel I stayed in was connected to the wall of the cubicle by several bare wires. There was even a fuse box in there as well. This, then, was a bathroom that could get you clean and give you an amazing new hairdo all at the same time.

If you ask a Bolivian to do something, he either won't do it at all or he will do it wrongly. This is because most Bolivians live at extremely high altitude, where there simply isn't enough oxygen to power your limbs and your brain at the same time. You either sit in a chair all day and think or you move about and don't. At one stage I spent several moments trying to light a cigarette with a battery.

You may wonder, then, why the Bolivians don't simply move out of the mountains and down to lower ground. Well, that's because all the country's low-lying area is covered with a massive and hideous wood. We call it the rainforest and say it is the 'lungs of the world' but plainly it isn't. Or there'd be some air in La Paz, and there isn't.

The rainforest is portrayed by rock stars and schoolteachers as a magical and mystical place full of wonder and majesty. This is nonsense. It is the worst place in the world, and the sooner a burger company chops it all down, the better. Everything in the rainforest is specifically designed to make your life either a little bit worse or completely over. At one point my left arm brushed against a leaf, and even now, many days later, it is a mass of weeping sores and pain. And that was just a leaf. One of my friends was bitten by a brown recluse spider. Another was chomped by a 12 ft anaconda. Twice, I climbed into my tent to find a bloody tarantula in there.

Strangely, however, it wasn't the deadly wildlife that caused the most annoyance. It was the stuff that buzzes about and tries to make a nest in your ears. We have flies and beetles and spiders in England, but nothing prepares you for the sheer size of the flies and beetles and spiders in the rainforest. They were big enough to have recognizable faces and character traits. One beetle I found, with Denis Healey eyebrows and a bit of a harelip, spent his night walking around my tent snipping the hind legs off grasshoppers. Well, I say grasshoppers, but of course they were no such thing. These things were 4 inches long and actually bled when their legs came off. I swear to God I heard one calling for its mummy.

Sleep was impossible. You would spend an hour in your tent, bashing everything you could find over the head with a shoe until you were convinced all was well, and then you'd lie down and close your eyes and, within a minute, you'd sense that a JCB was driving up your leg. This is extremely frightening.

Bashing rainforest insects over the head with a shoe is pointless. It just makes them sad. Setting them alight doesn't work either. At one point I ignited the spray from a can of deodorant and used the whole lot on a particularly stubborn cockroach that looked a bit like Sean Connery. Only with curly hair. Net result: he survived intact, I smelt nasty the next day and my tent caught fire.

You might imagine that it's worth putting up with the insect misery for the breathtaking array of flora and fauna. You're wrong. There are no flowers at all, and apart from some absolutely beautiful butterflies that are the colour of an LSD trip and the size of Boeings, it's all either dreary or deadly. One tree in particular caught my eye, quite literally, since it was made entirely from cocktail sticks. Others hide their roots under a thin veneer of moss so that you trip over them. And it goes on like this for ever. We're told that an area of rainforest the size of Wales, or the Albert Hall, is cut down every day, and that may be true. But this pointless and unpleasant wood still goes on for thousands of miles in every direction. Frankly, I'd napalm the lot.

Occasionally you do reach a clearing, but this doesn't necessarily mean you are out of the woods, so to speak. Because often it is full of armed men with mad eyes and sniffly noses who will shoot you in the head. Or, if you are unlucky, it will be a tumbledown and filthy village full of gap-year Brits with dreadlocked hair who have told their parents they wish to follow in Gordon Sting's footsteps but are actually spending six months gradually giving their trust fund to Pablo Escobar.

Tribes? Elders? Chaps with saucers sewn into their lips? They may well be in there somewhere but the only locals I saw were crowded round a television set getting agitated about Carlo Ancelotti's new diamond formation at Stamford Bridge.

If there are any people in the middle of the forest, it is not because they want to be there. Otherwise why, when they do get out, do they choose to live in La Paz, where all you can buy is cement and motor oil, and there is no air, and strangers take a dump in your lavatory every morning? It is our duty to help these poor people. Someone, then, must start a charity as soon as possible with the sole aim of turning that insect-filled forest of death, rain and misery into something a bit more like Hong Kong.

Sunday 1 November 2009

Get me a rope before Mandelson wipes us all out

I've given the matter a great deal of thought all week, and I'm afraid I've decided that it's no good putting Peter Mandelson in a prison. I'm afraid he will have to be tied to the front of a van and driven round the country until he isn't alive any more. He announced last week that middle-class children will simply not be allowed into the country's top universities even if they have 4,000 A-levels, because all the places will be taken by Albanians and guillemots and whatever other stupid bandwagon the conniving idiot has leapt on to in the meantime.

I hate Peter Mandelson. I hate his fondness for extremely pale blue jeans and I hate that preposterous moustache he used to sport in the days when he didn't bother trying to cover up his left-wing fanaticism. I hate the way he quite literally lords it over us even though he's resigned in disgrace twice, and now holds an important decision-making job for which he was not elected. Mostly, though, I hate him because his one-man war on the bright and the witty and the successful means that half my friends now seem to be taking leave of their senses.

There's talk of emigration in the air. It's everywhere I go. Parties. Work. In the supermarket. My daughter is working herself half to death to get good grades at GCSE and can't see the point because she won't be going to university, because she doesn't have a beak or flippers or a qualification in washing windscreens at the lights. She wonders, often, why we don't live in America.

Then you have the chaps and chapesses who can't stand
the constant raids on their wallets and their privacy. They
can't understand why they are taxed at 50 per cent on their
income and then taxed again for driving into the nation's
capital. They can't understand what happened to the hunt
for the weapons of mass destruction. They can't understand
anything. They see the Highway Wombles in those brand new
4x4s that they paid for, and they see the M4 bus lane and they
see the speed cameras and the community support officers
and they see the Albanians stealing their wheelbarrows and
nothing can be done because it's racist. And they see Alistair
Darling handing over £4,350 of their money to not sort out
the banking crisis that he doesn't understand because he's a
small-town solicitor, and they see the stupid war on drugs
and the war on drink and the war on smoking and the war on
hunting and the war on fun and the war on scientists and the
obsession with the climate and the price of train fares soaring past £1,000 and the *Guardian* power-brokers getting
uppity about one shot baboon and not uppity at all about all
the dead soldiers in Afghanistan, and how they got rid of
Blair only to find the lying twerp is now going to come back
even more powerful than ever, and they think, 'I've had enough
of this. I'm off.'

It's a lovely idea, to get out of this stupid, Fairtrade,
Brown-stained, Mandelson-skewed, equal-opportunities, multicultural, carbon-neutral, trendily left, regionally assembled,
big-government, trilingual, mosque-drenched, all-the-pigs-
are-equal, property-is-theft hellhole and set up shop somewhere
else. But where? You can't go to France because you need to
complete seventeen forms in triplicate every time you want to
build a greenhouse, and you can't go to Switzerland because
you will be reported to your neighbours by the police and
subsequently shot in the head if you don't sweep your lawn

properly, and you can't go to Italy because you'll soon tire of waking up in the morning to find a horse's head in your bed because you forgot to give a man called Don a bundle of used notes for 'organizing' a plumber.

You can't go to Australia because it's full of things that will eat you, you can't go to New Zealand because they don't accept anyone who is more than forty and you can't go to Monte Carlo because they don't accept anyone who has less than 40 mill. And you can't go to Spain because you're not called Del and you weren't involved in the Walthamstow blag. And you can't go to Germany . . . because you just can't.

The Caribbean sounds tempting, but there is no work, which means that one day, whether you like it or not, you'll end up like all the other expats, with a nose like a burst beetroot, wondering if it's okay to have a small sharpener at ten in the morning. And, as I keep explaining to my daughter, we can't go to America because if you catch a cold over there, the health system is designed in such a way that you end up without a house. Or dead.

Canada's full of people pretending to be French, South Africa's too risky, Russia's worse and everywhere else is too full of snow, too full of flies or too full of people who want to cut your head off on the internet. So you can dream all you like about upping sticks and moving to a country that doesn't help itself to half of everything you earn and then spend the money it gets on bus lanes and advertisements about the dangers of salt. But wherever you go you'll wind up an alcoholic or dead or bored or in a cellar, in an orange jumpsuit, gently wetting yourself on the web. All of these things are worse than being persecuted for eating a sandwich at the wheel.

I see no reason to be miserable. Yes, Britain now is worse than it's been for decades, but the lunatics who've made it so ghastly are on their way out. Soon, they will be back in

Hackney with their South African nuclear-free peace polenta. And instead the show will be run by a bloke whose dad has a wallpaper shop and possibly, terrifyingly, a twerp in Belgium whose fruitless game of hunt-the-WMD has netted him £15m on the lecture circuit.

So actually I do see a reason to be miserable. Which is why I think it's a good idea to tie Peter Mandelson to a van. Such an act would be cruel and barbaric and inhuman. But it would at least cheer everyone up a bit.

Sunday 8 November 2009

Stop the game, ref. We're all too cross to play by the rules

Last weekend a man in a blue shirt fell over while playing a game of football. And a free-kick was awarded by the referee against the team playing in red shirts. This made the man who manages the team in red shirts very furious. 'Och aye the noo,' He told waiting reporters, angrily. The man in question, Sir Alex Chewing-Gum, is always very angry about referees. Not that long ago he said one man was too unfit to monitor a football game, and on Sunday he said the chap in black was in an 'absolutely ridiculous' position.

I'm with him on this. Referees are a very strange bunch of people that no one ever sees outside the confines of a footballing ground. Seriously. I once met a man who sexes the queen's ducks for a living. I really do know a pox doctor's clerk. I also know a butcher and a lorry driver and a man who puts food in his mouth and then earns a living from telling people what it tastes like. But I don't know a single football ref. I've never even met anyone who knows one. This is because they must, by nature, be a bit weird. I mean, whatever they do at work, they can be assured that half the people watching will want to pull out their lungs and make them into comedy bellows. The only upside of the job is that you get to boss about a lot of very rich young men, and if they fight back you can make them stand in a corner. Football reffing is like being a policeman, only without the mace.

But, and I've given this a great deal of thought, there is no alternative. In rugby the official on the pitch may call on the assistance of a video recorder, and that is fine. It means the important decisions will be correct. But if a football official were to call for a slow-motion replay every time Didier Drogba fell over, each match would last about six weeks. One expert called last week for players to be asked if they have committed a foul. If they lie, and are subsequently found guilty in a video review, they face a five-match ban. That might work for handball, but what about the tackle that's only a bit iffy? That's where you need the little Hitler.

Yes, he will sometimes get it wrong, but that's okay because football is supposed to be a sport. And in a sport it is nice to win but it doesn't really matter if you don't. And therein lies the problem, because of course football is no longer a sport. It is a global business, a sponsorship opportunity, a massive television event, and you can't really have one little bloke with hairy knees deciding whether Samsung's multi-million-pound contribution to Chelsea is rewarded to a greater extent than AIG's multi-million contribution to the northernists.

We see the same sort of problem these days in all events that used to be sporting fixtures. In rugby big men cover themselves in fake blood so they can be substituted for a player who's more adept at whatever sequence of play is required next, and in motor racing we have people letting people past while under a 'go slow' yellow flag and then claiming they have been overtaken unfairly, resulting in the other driver's disqualification. We even have people crashing deliberately so that the safety car is deployed. In athletics, people with scrotums are pretending to be women; in cricket, people pick at the stitching on the ball – for something to do, I suppose; and in Scrabble, my wife claims 'jo' is a word in common usage when, plainly, it bloody well isn't.

Only tennis seems to have escaped the slow, inexorable slide into shadiness, greed and deceit. But even here we find players drifting around the court on crystal meth, in wigs.

Some say the easiest way of ensuring that this ugliness stops is to remove such massive prize funds from the events in question. They reckon that if Wayne Rooney were playing for the love of the game, he'd be less inclined to argue when a decision didn't go his way. Really? Ever seen a Sunday league pub game? Honestly, pop into your local accident and emergency centre on a Sunday afternoon and you'll find half the people in there are amateur refs who've been beaten up by amateur players for awarding free-kicks and penalties. I have spent most of my life watching children play rugby and you wouldn't believe how they behave towards the refs and one another. It's often nothing more than an eighty-minute brawl with a ball. I've even seen parents put down their BlackBerry, stride on to the pitch and punch the ref in the middle of his face for not spotting something no one else spotted either. So don't tell me it's money that's ruining sport these days because it isn't.

No. The real culprit is us, twenty-first-century man. We are simply not suited to playing games with one another any more, and there's a very good reason for this. In the past, people were allowed to abuse post office staff without fear of prosecution. We were allowed to shout at our children without being followed home and persecuted by social services and we were allowed to hate whatever country we were at war with. No one ever said in 1940, 'But you know, most Germans are decent, law-abiding souls.' Today, of course, none of this is possible. We must welcome foes into our midst and big signs insist that we remain calm when presented with gross stupidity at the post office. And if our children misbehave we must give them money and a few sweets.

It all sounds like utopia but of course the human being has a temper. It has an aggressive streak. It likes to take on an opponent and win, massively; not to have the game stopped halfway through so we don't hurt the other team's feelings.

The upshot is simple. Because we can't act normally any more, we vent our anger and bile on the sports pitch. We won't accept rules and we will cheat our way to victory. Banning big prize money won't stop this. Banning sport, I'm afraid, is the only way.

Sunday 15 November 2009

Call me a spoilsport but I'm glad my dad wasn't a lesbian

When it comes to sweeping generalizations, I am the daddy. All Germans have no sense of humour, all instruction manuals are pointless, all cruise ships are ghastly, every single American is fat, all golfers are boring, and all Peugeots are driven by people you wouldn't have round for dinner.

Of course, I'm well aware that most generalizations are nonsense. I know several very funny Germans, and Obama Barrack is actually quite skinny. But without generalizations, anecdotes would take two years, points would never get made, comedy would suffer and everyone would sound like James May: 'Actually, 42.7 per cent of instruction manuals are quite useful; but first let me quantify "useful" . . .' Life would be a terribly dreary assault course if every fact had to be precise, but, that said, generalizations have no place in serious scientific research, which is why I was a bit startled to read last week that a government adviser from the National Academy for Parenting Practitioners said lesbians made better parents than what we can no longer call 'normal couples'.

I'm not sure this is quite right because, so far as I can remember, a woman is not able to have a child after having sexual relations with another woman. Unless that woman is from an athletics squad. In order for a lesbian couple to have had a child, either a turkey baster must have been involved – which is not how most people would like to imagine they came into the world – or they must have visited the state-sponsored British Association for Adoption and Fostering, which thinks that anyone who objects to same-sex parents is a 'retarded homophobe'.

Happily, I'm a bit more sensible than this. I do not think that someone who objects to homosexual parents is a retarded homophobe. I believe they have an opinion. But, that said, I emphatically don't agree that lesbians necessarily make better parents than me. It is impossible to say that someone will make a better parent because she fancies other girls. There will be some lesbians who'll go out all night and take drugs and there will be some who'll read a child a bedtime story and be excellent.

I have done some checking on this, and the only evidence I can find comes from research endorsed by the national academy itself. The study examined children raised by just twenty-seven single mothers, twenty lesbian couples and thirty-six, er, differently genitalled parents and concluded that those raised by women grew up with a better psychological well-being. You can't possibly draw any conclusions after testing twenty lesbians. Test twenty Italians and you could well end up concluding the whole nation was full of calm, incorruptible dullards with no interest in sex. Test temperatures over just twenty years and you'd end up concluding the world's climate was changing.

I like lesbians, especially proper ones in stockings that you find on the internet. Certainly, I think more women should try lesbianism. It'd be great. But on a personal note, and please don't call me a retarded homophobe, I'm not sure I'd have been very happy if my mum had been one. I like to imagine that Angelina Jolie and Charlize Theron sometimes get it on under the covers, but my mother and Peggy from the tennis club? No. And the idea that Peggy from the tennis club would have been a better dad than my actual dad is laughable. Nearly as laughable, in fact, as the alarming news that the country has a parenting academy looking into this sort of thing.

All of us think that the way we bring up our children is correct and that the way everyone else brings up their children is completely wrong. They're too strict. Too lax. Too open. Too closed. Too heterosexual. No one gets it as right as you do. And that's the thing. Bringing up a child is personal, and there is really no space in the nature and nurture debate for a bunch of frizzy-haired lunatics running around making political points at our expense about lesbians. If the government is looking for savings, it should think very hard about disbanding an organization that tells people what to tell parents.

There are many things I need to know that I do not. How to contact someone at Facebook. How to get to Bournemouth when the main road is closed for a worm-removal programme. If the government provided advice on these things, that would be wonderful. But instead it tells me what time my daughter should go to bed at night and what she should have for breakfast. And how she would grow up to be a more rounded human being if only my wife would invite a girlfriend round for the night and slip into something see-through.

Yes, there are fat women in the north who need to be told their kids may not skip school and experiment with crystal meth until they are at least eight. But we already have an organization in place to deal with this sort of thing: it's called the police. And if the police are unable to help, we have another. It's called social services. Social workers go in, see the child is off its head on heroin and all covered in sick, and put it in a home. You don't need a national academy telling them what sort of home it should be because it's blindingly obvious to anyone with half a brain.

This is the problem we face here. I don't like the idea that lesbians, even the weird, big sort in dungarees, should be excluded from adopting a baby. They grew up with a predilection for members of the same genital group but that doesn't stop them being good parents. Banning a lesbian from parenting would be as cruel as banning someone because they had an interest in golf, which is what I'd do if I were in charge. Or because they had ginger hair. However, I'm afraid we must think about the children. Having two mums, whether you like it or not, is going to cause a spot of bother in the playground. But that's just my view and I'm only a parent. What do I know?

Sunday 22 November 2009

I'm so dead – shot by both sides in the website war

As you may know, Rupert Murdoch and his son James are engaged in a bitter dispute with the BBC over all sorts of things. This puts me in a tricky spot. Obviously, Rupert and James Murdoch are my bosses, not just here at the *Sunday Times* but also at the *Sun*, for which I write a column on Saturdays. I am therefore inclined to nod vigorously when they suggest the licence fee should be scrapped and all BBC web activities halted forthwith. But I am also employed by the BBC, which means I am inclined to nod vigorously whenever the director-general says the BBC is a fantastic institution and the envy of every nation in the world. This means I've been doing an awful lot of vigorous nodding in the past few months.

It's not just sycophancy either. I really do believe that both sides have a point. If you are paying your licence fee, you should be entitled to view the programmes you funded on whatever platform happens to suit your mood and lifestyle. If you wish to watch the news on your mobile phone and *Autumnwatch* on your computer, then it is the BBC's duty to make that possible. But that puts all newspapers, not just this one, in a difficult position. Running a website is ferociously expensive. I see the bills for the *Top Gear* site and it makes my eyes explode. And, of course, while it is possible to meet some of that cost with advertising, it should be remembered that every penny earned by the website is a penny in lost revenue for the printed newspaper.

The only realistic solution is to make people pay to see the site. But who's going to do that when the BBC is providing a news service for nothing? We therefore face the real possibility of various newspapers going out of business, which, combined with the problems at ITV and Channel 4, could mean the BBC becomes the only newsgathering organization in the country. This would be an extremely bad thing.

Of course, the two main political parties have massively oversimplified the debate. You have Jeremy Hunt for the Tories saying he's going to execute everyone at the BBC and put their heads on spikes. And Ben Bradshaw for Labour saying he's going to execute everyone at News International. Either way, I'm going to be killed. Which is why I have been examining the argument carefully and I've decided that the biggest issue in all of this is the internet. It's a monster. An invisible machine over which mankind has absolutely no control. We can't even turn it off.

Let us start by listing the good things it has achieved. Well, er, it is now possible to find out where James Garner was born without going to the library and order your Sunday lunch without going to the shops. And there are some jolly funny things on YouTube.

But now let's look at some of the bad things. Well, your children are being bullied mercilessly on Facebook and there is no one you can contact to have the bullying stopped; your husband is spending most of his evenings baring his private parts to some Ukrainian girl; your wife has rekindled a childhood romance; the twin towers have been knocked down; Stephen Fry has been driven to the edge of another breakdown; you have to spend half your day answering pointless e-mails; there is unimaginable cruelty in almost every blog, where the rules of defamation seem not to apply; and James Garner was not born, as suggested on one site, in Chicago.

It gets worse. Only a few weeks ago my colleague James May scuttled off into a Romanian wood to have a pee; the event was captured on a phone and now it's on the internet. And there is absolutely nothing he can do to have it taken off. These are just the minor issues, the annoyances. The big problem is just round the corner: the bankrupting of everyone in the world of film, art, literature, news and music. The fact is this. If something can be digitized, it can be stolen. You record a song, you sell one copy, it goes on the internet and it will be nicked. If you write a book, the same thing can happen. Newspapers, magazines, films, jokes, music: all of it can be, and is being, circulated for nothing, which means the person who wrote and prepared and slaved over the original product is not being paid. That's not so bad if you are ten and you've posted some mobile phone footage of your friend pulling funny faces on YouTube. But if you are running Paramount Pictures, it is very bad indeed.

I do not know how much it cost to make this year's surprising hit comedy *The Hangover*, but it will have been several million dollars. None of that will have been recouped at the box office because the film stars no one you've ever heard of. But word of mouth means that some of the cash could be clawed back in DVD sales. 'Fraid not. Because this film is extremely popular with internet-savvy teenagers, it is being downloaded for nothing at an alarming rate. And, speaking as the host of the most illegally downloaded TV show in the world, I know how annoying this can be. It's why I've explained to my kids that they can smoke, drink and push old ladies into boating lakes. But if they steal a song or a film, I will make them live in the chicken run for a year.

Sadly, I'm alone. Your kids are nicking things on an industrial scale. They have been brought up to expect everything for nothing on the web and they simply cannot understand why they should use money they need for mobile phone calls to pay for something that is available free.

I do not think there is a solution to this. Companies can build in as many electronic safeguards as they like but the fact is this: somewhere out there in cyberland there is a geek who can pick his way through the electronic locks and steal the booty.

The debate, then, is not whether the BBC should be allowed to peddle its warnings of global doom on the internet. It's how you control a monster that seemingly cannot be controlled at all.

Sunday 29 November 2009

Sing about the fat man again and I'll shoot Tiny Tim

In the olden days, before the Christmas No 1 slot was invariably bagged by the winner of Simon Cowell's annual karaoke competition, there was always a mad scramble among record companies and artistes to bang a big one in the yuletide goal. This brings me directly to Bob Dylan's first seasonal album – *Christmas in the Heart*. Well, it had to be in the heart, didn't it, because it wasn't very likely to happen in his synagogue.

I suppose I ought to mention before we begin that Dylan is not my favourite recording artist. Or my second-favourite. In fact, he is my 2,507th favourite recording artist, just after Pinky and Perky. Some say he is the heart of modern music. But I don't think he's even the stomach lining. He's just an annoying wart on the gall bladder of rock'n'roll. Certainly, I'd never tire of flushing everything he's written or recorded down the lavatory. Even when he's doing a happy song, he always manages to sound so bloody miserable, like a widower trying to be cheerful at his wife's funeral. And when he's being down in the dumps, which is usually, I can't understand why he would want to inflict his bad mood on everyone else. If I want to feel sad, I'll poison my donkeys. It'd be better than listening to Bob droning on.

But that's enough about Bob, because while listening to the chief miserablist's awful collection of Christmas songs, one of which seems to suggest that one of Santa's reindeers is called Clinton, I began to wonder what had been the worst Christmas song of all time.

Bob, we must remember, is by no means the first big-name

star to take the yuletide shilling and bash something out for the world's Xmas stockings. Who, for instance, can forget Bruce Springsteen's 'Santa Claus Is Coming to Town' or Madonna's 'Santa Baby' or John Denver's 'Please, Daddy (Don't Get Drunk This Christmas)'. Quite something from a man who had two drink-driving arrests to his name.

But the winner of the Surely You Don't Need the Money award must be Ringo Starr for his 1999 collection of Christmas songs, one of which, I seem to recall, contained the lyric: 'It's been around since you know when.' Er, didn't 'the year dot' rhyme? The worst? Well, obviously, you have to consider Boney M's syrupy 'Mary's Boy Child' and 'When a Child Is Born' by Johnny Mathis. But for me, it will always be Bing's dreadful 'White Christmas'.

I accept of course that we need a constant supply of new Christmas records because the old ones become turgid and dull. 'Silent Night', for instance, is a monstrously dreary hit from yesteryear, and if I hear 'Away in a Manger', I'm filled with a sometimes uncontrollable need to kill myself. I will also accept that some of the more recent offerings have been very fine. Slade's 'Merry Christmas Everybody' is nearly boisterous enough to get me dancing and is, with hindsight, just good enough to have kept Wizzard's 'I Wish It Could Be Christmas Everyday' off the top spot in 1973. I also admit to a fondness for Greg Lake's 'I Believe in Father Christmas', although I know that owning up to that is like owning up to a fondness for child molestation. And I still like to hear Chris Rea's 'Driving Home for Christmas'. Then we have the Pogues and Kirsty MacColl, whose 'Fairytale of New York' I ought to hate as heartily as I hated Bryan Adams's stupid 'Reggae Christmas'. But I don't.

Mostly, though, Christmas songs are dreadful for a very good reason. The story on which they are all based only really works if you have the mental age of a four-year-old. It is possible to write songs about love, breaking up, getting back together and – in country music, anyway – breaking up again. Just after your dog dies. And your pick-up truck breaks down. You can write songs about a bohemian rhapsody and the dark side of the moon, but you cannot really write a song about what most people think is a bit of a fairy tale. Not if you want to emerge from the release with any dignity.

The notion that Springsteen, that hard, blue-collar chap who normally sings about broken heroes on a last-chance power drive, can be even remotely convincing while singing about a fat man on an airborne sledge is utterly nonsensical.

It's the same story with the nativity. The virgin birth. The wise men. This is where Boney M went wrong. One minute, they were singing about an extraordinary figure from the Russian revolution. And the next, about a bunch of shepherds who came down from the hills to find a bloke in a stable explaining that his wife had just given birth to the son of God. Basing songs on goblins and mystical figures in the woods is fine in prog rock and in the primary-school classroom. But in the mainstream? On the radio? Over your breakfast? No.

It's why I was glad when Bob Geldof and Midge Ure blasted their Band Aid hit into our consciousness. Because this was not a song about the baby Jesus or some fat bloke on a sleigh. It was about how we should feel towards others over the Christmas period. Which is somehow a bit more relevant.

Weirdly, and I'm not admitting to liking it, Cliff Richard achieved the same sort of thing with his hit 'Mistletoe and Wine'.

The trouble is that if we'd continued down this route, Christmas songs would have stopped being happy and bouncy. They'd have become hectoring. Pretty soon, we'd have ended up with Muse urging us to buy the *Big Issue* and Kasabian asking us to share our turkey with a tramp. Nobody wants that sort of nonsense when we're cruising the streets looking for a Go Go Hamster.

And that's why we should all be grateful to Cowell's karaoke competition. Because the winner's guaranteed Christmas No 1 is also guaranteed not to be about Christmas.

Sunday 13 December 2009

The BA strike is off – so that's many a Christmas ruined

I can't believe that British Airways' cabin crew thought it might be a good idea to go on strike. It seems so old-fashioned. Like banging the side of your television to stop the picture juddering, or getting a new penny in your Christmas stocking.

I remember well my first day at work. I walked through the door, turned round and went on strike. I had no idea why. But it didn't seem unusual in the least. Back in 1978, no one ever actually went inside their office or factory. They stood outside, round a brazier, throwing stones at policemen for amusement.

I suppose we were all a lot stupider in those days, unwise in the ways of the world. We didn't realize that if the company that employed us to stand outside all day had lost £400m the previous year, it couldn't very well afford to give us all a 3,000 per cent pay rise and some scented logs for the brazier. That's why I was so amazed about the BA nonsense. I can't imagine for a minute that those pretty boys who point at doors for a living wanted to spend their Christmas break in donkey jackets, chanting: 'Willie, Willie, Willie. Out, out, out.' They might have thought it'd be nostalgic and fun to throw a stone at a policeman and call a pilot a scab. But if they'd all turned up for picket-line duty in their Audi TTs – the car of choice for cabin crew – I doubt they would have got many honks of support from passing motorists. They'd have just been rather cold and bored.

Of course, the courts decided on Thursday that you can't really go on strike in 2009, any more than you can beat your whippet to death with a burning effigy of Margaret Thatcher. And this, I'm sure, will be a great relief to the many thousands of people who were looking forward to a bit of sunshine over the yuletide break. Strangely, though, I don't see why . . . I once went away for Christmas and it was terrible, because not only do you have to pack all the usual assortment of holiday rubbish – shorts, sun cream and 8,500 battery chargers – but also you have to think about all the presents you'll be handing out on Christmas morning. Packing is already the worst thing in the world – after being executed, and trying on a pair of trousers in a shop – but when you also have to pack the chrysanthemums you bought as a present for your wife from the petrol station, and 8,500 more battery chargers for all the kids' new toys, it's a bloody nightmare. You have to go to the airport in a lorry.

And then, when you get to whatever godforsaken hellhole the travel agent has recommended, the weather is all wrong. Even in Australia they send seasonal cards with robins on them, and all of us know that Jesus was born in a blizzard. It's a fact. That's why the shepherds came down from the hills. Because they wanted to get warm.

Have you ever tried singing 'O Come, All Ye Faithful' when it's 90°F in the shade? It's as wrong as playing 'The Birdie Song' at a funeral. Or singing 'Swing Low, Sweet Chariot' while watching Manchester United.

Christmas abroad confuses the hell out of young children as well. The hotel I stayed at in the Caribbean laid on a special treat, with Santa coming down the drive in a horse and cart. But the lack of antlers and skis was not what baffled my five-year-old most of all. 'Daddy,' she squeaked, 'Santa's all brown.'

You try explaining your way out of that one. 'Yes, well, I know that Santa at home is a drunken white paedophile who hangs around in shopping centres with a tent pole in his trousers but here he's called Winston and he's er . . . er . . .' There's a much bigger problem, though, with the other people you encounter while on a Christmas break. In short, they are almost all very nasty, and there's a good reason for this.

Think about it. At this time of year, there are many parties. People are in a convivial mood and everyone's welcome. The roads are full of happy, cheery people whizzing from drinks do to lunch at the pub with mates. And then: 'Sorry, we've got to go; we're at the Fotheringtons' tonight . . .' The only reason you might choose to go away and miss all this is that you haven't been invited to anything. And the only reason you haven't been invited is that no one likes you. Ipso facto every single person who goes away at Christmastime is either a dullard or extremely unpleasant. And that means the hotel bar will be a complete no-go area.

On my one and only Christmas holiday, while I waited for my silly drink with an umbrella in it, I was approached by a man who spent an hour reeling off Aston Martin chassis numbers. I thought for the first thirty minutes I might kill myself. And then for the next thirty that it'd be better for all concerned if I killed him. I didn't, which means this Christmas he's still out there, lurking behind a pot plant with his adenoids and sandals. And because the courts have said the BA staff must work, you might be meeting him. You will also be trying to stuff down six sheets of roast turkey and gravy shortly after a dust devil has left it coated with a veneer of sand.

And working out how on earth you will get the mini submarine your wife gave you on Christmas Day home in your suitcase.

You'll also have the usual, year-round travel problems. You'll have to queue for six hours so that someone can X-ray your shoes and confiscate your toothpaste. You'll get deep-vein thrombosis and sunburn and explosive diarrhoea and chlamydia.

Sure, it's nice to be warm when it's cold back at home. But Christmas is supposed to be cold. It's supposed to be a time of families and friends, and trees and log fires, and useless nutcrackers and horrid jumpers, and falling asleep in front of the Queen.

So trust me on this. If you are going away at Christmas, twang the hostesses' suspender belts when they walk by and call the stewards 'ducky'. That way, they will ignore the courts next year and strike anyway. Then you won't have to go away again.

Sunday 20 December 2009

So, Piggy, Buttocks and Rat – what shall we call Gordon?

As we know, there is an awful lot wrong with the education system in Britain. Nobody learns to read or write, most children are stabbed, no primary teachers have scrotums, there are too many managers, history is almost nonexistent and too much emphasis is placed on league tables – it's a school, for crying out loud, not the second division in football. But the thing that's wrongest of all is that, so far as I can tell, nobody at school has a nickname any more. My children regularly bring their friends round to the house and all of them are known by their Christian names. Even if they are enormous and ginger.

It was a different story when I was at school. The housemaster was Buttocks, James Smith – a white boy from Trinidad – was Chicken George, the man who taught English was Rat, the clumsiest boy in school was Spanner, my history teacher was Piggy and I was Ness. I like to think this is because I was long and thin but I suspect it's because I looked like a monster. There was one girl we called Butterface. This is because she was ravishingly beautiful in every single respect . . . but her face, which was that of an eroded gargoyle. Then there was a boy who, because he hadn't started shaving at the age of fourteen, was referred to always in the third person as 'she'.

There is absolutely no doubt in my mind that this simply wouldn't be allowed any more. Calling a boy 'she' would be an infringement of his human rights and the school would undoubtedly be demoted to the Gola League. The headmaster might even be branded a paedophile and banned from the sports pitches.

We still see nicknames in the army and I'm delighted to say we still have nicknames in the *Top Gear* office, where there is Jewish Brian and German Brian – which is a bit annoying for the poor soul because he's Danish. But he sounds German to us. Then there are two researchers who were once sent out to buy some clothes needed for a shoot. They are now called Dolce and Gabbana.

Elsewhere, though, nicknames are found only on blogs, and that's not right at all. You cannot give yourself a nickname, because it will be Pretty Face or Massive Cock, and that's completely wrong. You have a Christian name, which is bestowed on you by the baby Jesus, and you have a nickname bestowed on you by Old Nick, aka the Devil, aka Lucifer. It must therefore be unpleasant and insulting.

The best nicknames are born in a moment of excruciating embarrassment. That's why one chap I sometimes work with is called Adam – after the apple he found on the neck of the, er, girl he took to bed one night in Hong Kong. Then you have the fighter jocks who fly F-16s in America. They are all known as cross-dressers because one of their number was once found in a hotel room in Las Vegas in items of women's apparel.

I realize, of course, that nicknames are exclusively a male thing. This is because boys rejoice in the downfall of others. We like to watch our friends fall over and say the wrong thing at the wrong time. We love it when they come out of the loo having not shaken their old chap properly. The boy–boy bond is glued together with teasing, and nicknames are part of that. As a general rule, girls console one another when they fall over. They ring one another for uplifting chats. The girl–girl bond is glued together with something fluffy and pink and nice. That's why a girl who accidentally farted in a lift is not known by her mates for the rest of time as Windy.

And that brings me nicely on to the thrust of this morning's missive. How come we still all call Gordon Brown 'Gordon Brown'? Why is he not called Cyclops? Or, bearing in mind that funny thing he does with his lower jaw while talking, Concorde? It's the same story with Alistair Darling. How in the name of all that's holy has he not been tagged Badger? John Prescott once admitted that he had a Jaguar at home and a Jaguar for work and that was it. He was known for the rest of his professional career as Two Jags. But I'm stumped to think of any other politician who has a nickname. Even Margaret Thatcher escaped. And Tarzan never really caught on, any more than the Beast of Bolsover did.

Boris Johnson is an obvious candidate. His hair looks like seaweed, his suit has gravy on it, he likes to speak in ancient Greek and there have been revelations of a personal nature too, all of which are fertile hunting grounds for a nickname. But we all call him Boris. Then there's Charles Kennedy. He has ginger hair. He likes a dram. He's Scottish. But we call him Charles. And who's that other Lib Dem? That Limp Biscuit chappie? The one with the dislocated face? You know . . . the one who pulled a Cheeky Girl? How in God's name is he not called Bloody Hell, There's Hope For All Of Us? Then you've got Douglas Hogg, who charged the nation £2,000 to clean his moat. And David Heathcoat-Amory, who bought some manure with our taxes. I think we can be assured that if I used licence fee money to buy a duck house, you'd start calling me Viggers. So how come Viggers got away with it? Historically, I suspect politicians were spared the ignominy of a foisted moniker because they were respected by those who'd elected them to high office. Nobody ever called Winston Churchill Fatso, for instance. But these days, we don't respect them at all. And the other thing we don't do is like them very much.

That's presumably why Gordon Brown is called Gordon Brown. Because we all pretty much hate him and you don't give a nickname to someone you can't abide.

It's why I can't bring myself to call Peter Mandelson 'Mandy'. Mr Mandelson is so much more insulting.

Sunday December 27, 2009

JEREMY CLARKSON

THE WORLD ACCORDING TO CLARKSON

The world is an exciting and confusing place for Jeremy Clarkson – a man who can find the overgrown schoolboy in us all.

In *The World According to Clarkson*, one of the country's funniest comic writers has free reign to expose absurdity, celebrate eccentricity and entertain richly in the process.

And the net is cast wide: from the chronic unsuitablity of men to look after children for long periods or as operators of 'white goods', Nimbyism, cricket and PlayStations, to astronomy, David Beckham, 1970s rock, the demise of Concorde, the burden of an Eton education and the shocking failure of Tom Clancy to make it onto the Booker shortlist, *The World According to Clarkson* is a hilarious snapshot of the life in the 21st century that will have readers wincing with embarrassed recognition and crying with laughter.

It's not about the cars!

JEREMY CLARKSON

AND ANOTHER THING . . . :
THE WORLD ACCORDING TO CLARKSON VOLUME 2

Everyone knows that Jeremy Clarkson finds the world a perplexing place – after all, he wrote a bestselling book about it. Yet despite the appearance of *The World According to Clarkson*, things don't seem to have improved much. However, Jeremy is not someone to give up easily and he's decided to have another go.

In *And Another Thing . . .*, our exasperated hero discovers that:

He inadvertently dropped a bomb on North Carolina

We're all going to explode at the age of 62

Russians look bad in Speedos. But not as bad as we do

No one should have to worry about being Bill Oddie's long lost sister

He should probably be nicer about David Beckham

Thigh-slappingly funny and – as ever – in your face, Jeremy Clarkson bursts the pointless little bubbles of idiots, while celebrating the special, the unique and the sheer bloody brilliant . . .

JEREMY CLARKSON

DON'T STOP ME NOW

There's more to life than cars. Jeremy Clarkson knows this. There is, after all, a whole world out there just waiting to be discovered. So, before he gets on to torque steer and active suspension, he takes time to consider:

The madness of Galapagos tortoises

The similarities between Jeremy Paxman and AC/DC's bass guitarist

The problems and perils of being English

God's dumbest creation

Then there are the cars: whether it's the poxiest little runabout or an exotic, firebreathing supercar, no one does cars like Clarkson. Unmoved by mechanics' claims and unimpressed by press junkets, he approaches anything on four wheels without fear or favour. What emerges from the ashes is rarely pretty. But always very, very, very funny.

JEREMY CLARKSON

FOR CRYING OUT LOUD

Jeremy's one man war on crimes against common sense has not yet been won. And our hero's still scratching his head at the madness of it all. But it's not all bad. He's learnt a little along the way, including:

Why binge drinking is good for you

The worst word in the English language

The remarkable secret of eternal youth

The problem with America

And how to dispose of a seal

For anyone who has been driven to wonder just what is the matter with people these days *For Crying Out Loud* is the perfect riposte. Surprising, fearless and always laugh-out-loud funny, Clarkson's back. And he's got a point . . .

'Highly entertaining' *Daily Telegraph*

JEREMY CLARKSON

DRIVEN TO DISTRACTION

Brace yourself, Clarkson's back. And he'd like to tell you what he thinks about some of the most awe-inspiring, earth-shatteringly fast and jaw-droppingly gorgeous cars in the world (alongside a few irredeemable disasters ...). Or he would, if there weren't so many things competing for his attention first. And so much to get off his chest, because the world according to Clarkson is a perplexing place, filled with thorny subjects like:

The prospect of having Terry Wogan as president

Why you'll never see a woman driving a Lexus

The unforeseen consequences of inadequate birth control

Why everyone should spend a weekend with a digger

Fearless, independent, surprising and laugh-out-loud funny, *Driven to Distraction* is full-throttle Clarkson at his best, a unique look at the joys, absurdities and frustrations of modern life. With wheels. Buckle up, get comfortable, and hold on tight. There's no one who writes about cars like Jeremy ...